COOKING WITH NUTS

COOKING

OTHER BOOKS BY THE AUTHOR:

La Gourmette Violette
The Peanut Cookbook

WITH NUTS

DOROTHY C. FRANK

 Clarkson N. Potter, Inc./Publishers NEW YORK

DISTRIBUTED BY CROWN PUBLISHERS, INC.

*Inquiries should be addressed to Clarkson N. Potter, Inc.,
One Park Avenue, New York, N.Y. 10016*

PRINTED IN THE UNITED STATES OF AMERICA
Published simultaneously in Canada by General Publishing Company Limited
Designed by Betty Binns
Library of Congress Cataloging in Publication Data

Frank, Dorothy C
  Cooking with nuts.

  1. Cookery (Nuts)   I. Title.
TX814.F72 1979   641.6′4′5   78-26513
ISBN 0-517-53727-3
ISBN 0-517-53728-1 pbk.

In memory of my parents
Abraham and Henrietta Cohen,
who lovingly educated my palate as well as my whole being
and regularly exposed me at home and abroad
to the finest of cooking

Contents

ACKNOWLEDGMENTS

Unending appreciation to my family: Justin, who has endured wall-to-wall nutty recipes for an impossibly long time; Justin Jr. and Micheline, a great team who have created and tested innumerable culinary delights; and Ellen, who has given invaluable support and professional guidance. And in a class by themselves, my much-more-than-secretary Meryl Renee Davis, without whom I could not have survived; my indispensable friend Arlene Greendale, ready from dawn to midnight with creative ideas, evaluations, know-how, and comfort too; and of course infinite thanks to good friend Barbara Monahan for her indefatigable editing, designing, and meticulous supervision in the initial stages of the book, and to Kevin Burke, whose creative photography speaks for itself. Special gratitude, too, to my brother and sister-in-law, Dan and Elizabeth Cohn, for sharing family recipes and to my niece Joann Cazden for her enthusiasm and ideas.

Cooking With Nuts has been in progress and research for over three years so I have accumulated much help from many many people, and it is impossible always to do justice to each. But each and everyone, I shall always remember. A special message of appreciation to Genie Shapiro. Sincere thanks, that much overused word, to Lorayne Stein for her ability with words, to Edith Scheinman for testing and checking, to Nancy Sternberg and Martha Slimp for an infinite variety of help, to Marcella Meharg for really pushing me into this writing, to Mildred and Arnold Kahn, Doris Roth, Edna Shaw, and Pat McCollum and Rita Norton of the San Vicente County Library. Many friends, many names — some helped a lot, some a little, but all are important and appreciated. And of course over the long years, thanks to Rosie Miles and Lettie Black.

I shall always remember my former office associates who found time to test, adjust, and confer: Barbara Driggett, Christine Felix, Charlotte Johnson, Cle Walker, Irene Bogawa, Penny Steinberg, Barbara Wilson, Barbara Uchida, Anne Adler, and Frances Kaplan. Sincere thanks to public relations expert and friend Edith Weiss; to Doris Levinson and my husband for coming up with the same title; to Marilyn Gradeck Friend, Dorothy Goldman, and Ginny McKay, who years ago really started the research; to Beth Olch for specialized information; to Barbara Firoozye of Iran; and to Jean Jackson. Special acknowledgment to Gertrude Simon for her creative thinking and Mildred Harris for generously sharing her collection of antique nutcrackers.

And again, over the years, repeated thanks to Christine Larsen, Brazil Center; Mrs. Ruth Price, Photography Division of Office of Communication, U.S.D.A., Washington, D.C., whose generosity in helping will never be forgotten; Dr. Genevieve Ho of U.S.D.A.; Herman and Gretchen Schmid of Edelweiss Chocolates of Beverly Hills; Illiffili Gourmet Nuts; Michael Michaud; Joanne Purcell; and the very helpful and generous All American Nut Company. For other props: Anne Kupper, Williams and Sonoma of Beverly Hills; Diane Poste, The Brass Tree, Beverly Hills; Eddie Egan, Flooring; Friedman Bag Company, and The Pottery Barn of Westwood. For recipes and suggestions, much thanks and special appreciation to Oregon Filbert Commission of Tigard, Oregon, and to its Executive Secretary, D. J. Duncan, and repeated thanks to Royal Hawaiian Macadamia Nut Co.; the California Macadamia Society; Ms. Rowena M. Hubbard, Castle & Cooke Foods, San Francisco; De Doring of Diamond Walnut Kitchens of California; Almond Board and Keith Thomas of San Francisco; Harry and Jane Wilson, Sunnyland Farms, Albany, Georgia; Hammons Products Co., Stockton, Missouri; Steve Stiefvater, Continental Nut Company; Van Holland, Richardson & Holland; Mal Williamson, Kelley-Clarke Company; John C. Bohan, Theodore R. Sills, Inc.; Funsten Nut Division, Pet, Inc., St. Louis; Baker General Foods; and Homa Company, New Jersey.

And for the Peanut section, my affectionate appreciation to our First Lady Rosalynn Carter for the Cream of Peanut Pie and to her and Ms. Lillian Carter for sharing other Carter family favorites and Plains, Georgia, recipes.

The Peanut associations I have warmly acknowledged in *The Peanut Cookbook* have also been of inestimable help in this book: Peanut Growers of Georgia and Alabama; Peanut Butter Manufacturers & Nut Salters Association; Morton E. Nitzberg, Vice President, Phoebe Alvarado and Naomı Hacker of Peanut Associates, Inc., of New York; William Flanagan of Oklahoma Peanut Commission; Virginia Blair and Sheila Sandy of National Peanut Council of Chicago; Joe S. Sugg of North Carolina Peanut Growers Association, Inc., North Carolina; and Virginia Peanut Growers' Associations; Georgia Agricultural Commodity Commission for Peanuts; Betsy Owens, Director, Growers' Peanut Food Promotions; and all the other allied and participating "peanut people." Thanks one and all!

And last, and obviously not least, my appreciation, past as well as present to Betty Binns for her great artistry in design, my thanks to Nancy Novogrod for her final editing, helpfulness, and support, and special affectionate gratitude to Jane West for her discerning judgment, editorial skills, and esteemed friendship. They truly brought it all together!

A Little History
in the Proverbial Nutshell

THE NUT HAS a huge family tree with some branches dating back to prehistoric times. Forty thousand years ago, nuts and fruits were part of the dietary scene along with cannibalism. The Greeks and Romans used nuts as a symbol of fertility; instead of throwing rice at the bride and groom, they threw nuts. For the Indians they were a food staple, converted into flour for soups and fritters and added as an enrichment to many dishes. Marzipan, the world's oldest candy, considered of Arabic-Egyptian origin, has been made chiefly of pulverized almonds for four thousand years. Nuts such as almonds, pistachios, walnuts, hazelnuts, and pine nuts have been aristocrats for millennia; they appeared before royalty in ancient Persia and China and even found a place in the Bible.

However, some nuts are truly nouveau-nuts, accepted and popularized in the United States only since the American Civil War. The peanut, one of the newest to be recognized and appreciated worldwide, isn't even a nut in the true sense; it is a pea-nut, pod-nut, ground nut, or goober, starting its growth on a small bush and ending with its pod ripening underground.

Each branch of the nut family has its own characteristics—a special look and shape both in and out of the shell, a distinctive taste and aroma, and often a particular culinary usage. All nuts share special dietary values: they are great sources of protein, minerals, and vitamins; some have high carbohydrate content; some have their own special oils. Nuts do not contain cholesterol—most nuts actually include plant sterols, which have been shown to reduce blood cholesterol levels (U.S. Dept. of Agriculture; Agriculture Information Bulletin, No. 361, 1974).

Nuts relate well in both old and new culinary associations. They make particularly good friends with grains and fruits.

Some have even developed a "going-steady" relationship, such as "date and nut" and "olive and nut." Early in the history of India and Persia, they were part of the popular trio of fruit, nuts, and wine.

Some nuts are elegant and expensive, some are plentiful and inexpensive. The less costly ones are often used in large quantities in recipes, and are fine substitutes for meat because of their high protein and nutritional value. Others are used for their good looks, as decoration, and for the suggestion of a special taste. Nuts in their shells make handsome fall centerpieces for tables and gorgeous wreaths. Decorating with nuts became fashionable in the mid-nineteenth century.

The nut has played many ingenious and creative roles in history since it was first harvested from wild trees. When animal milk was meager or unavailable, "milk" was made by soaking ground or pulverized nutmeats in water to cover until a milky-looking liquid developed. This liquid was then strained and used as a milk substitute. Long before the advent of flour or cornstarch, pulverized nuts were a thickening agent for sauces and gravies. Several kinds of nut butters predated our contemporary favorite, peanut butter, and added nourishment, flavor, and color to foods. Once pounded out by mortar and pestle, now blenders and that new delight of the kitchen, the food processor, can miraculously whip up nut butters in minutes!

Nuts have been prized for their flavor, crunch, texture, and interesting appearance in simple primitive cooking and elegant sophisticated haute cuisine alike. In cooking, the heat releases the fat of the nut and permits its flavoring and tenderizing properties to go into action. Until the present interest in health foods and vegetarianism, particularly in the United States, the main use for nuts was in pastries, candies, and desserts. Now, however, they appear in practically any kind of dish. In addition, they are used extensively for nibbling to provide quick energy as well as enjoyment.

The health-food-conscious segment of our population, who prize natural foods and enjoy preparing from scratch, have become the principal users of raw nuts. They feel the raw nut performs best baked along with the rest of the ingredients, allowing for a fuller, more definite flavor. This new generation of cooks also believe in using nuts unblanched for extra food and taste value.

There are so many things you can do to and with nuts: blanch (remove the inner skin), chop, sliver, slice, dice, grind them . . . toast, salt, sweeten, pickle, spice, and even devil them. . . In markets and specialty shops, nuts are a- vailable raw and roasted with or without salt. For people on salt-free diets, nuts can be eaten right out of the shell, or roasted or toasted without salt.

In England, the immature walnut in its soft green shell is beloved for pickling and is also used in making marmalades and walnut catsup. In Germany and some of its neighboring countries, the green hazelnut is esteemed for eating, espe- cially in salads. The green almond is considered a delicacy too.

In *Cooking with Nuts,* we are concentrating on nuts as food; and our cookbook is as complete as a traditionally praised banquet that goes from soup to nuts, from nutty soups to nuts. The recipes are tried and true. I have used many of them for years—created and collected from family and friends who cook and from my extensive travels—I am always a culinary scout. In addition, some recipes are the quintessence of nut dishes, offered by associations and kitchens whose special concern is nuts and the exploration of their use in cooking.

There is a nut in every dish. In England, there is a famous nuttery, which is really a small garden of nut trees at the home of the late writer Miss Vita Sackville-West in Sissing- hurst Castle, Kent. This book, then, is my nuttery—a gar- den of recipes that should flourish in any kitchen.

ALMOND

Amygdalus communis

ALMOND

KNOWN LONG BEFORE biblical times, almonds are considered a first cousin to the peach, whose stone contains in its center a small, delicious, slightly bitter almond. There are bitter and sweet almond trees. Our interest is definitely in the sweet almond, delicate in its unadorned shelled state; when blanched and either plain, toasted, roasted, or salted, it is a food historically considered fit for a king. The sweet almond tree is reputed to have pink flowers, and the bitter tree, white; but many authorities claim the color is interchangeable. Both types of almond trees are breathtakingly beautiful in full bloom.

Considered a native of West Asia, the almond tree grows profusely in the Mediterranean area and has been successfully introduced into California where the almond industry is now burgeoning. In its ancient habitats, Palestine and Syria, the almond tree is not only prized for its beauty and delicious fruit but seen as a symbol of rebirth, blossoming in January. The sweet almond also does well in Australia and South Africa. The bitter almond grows mainly in North Africa. The bitter almond is used gingerly for flavor along with sweet almonds; its primary use is in the making of some almond extract.

According to Greek legend, Phyllis pined in constancy for her erring lover Demophon and was turned into a tree whose branches were beckoning always. When Demophon returned, guilty and aghast at learning of Phyllis's death and transformation, he fell at the base of the tree and watered it with his flowing tears; the tree broke into blossom. Phylla is the Greek word for almond.

A well-traveled nut from the time it was first tasted, the almond long ago made migrations from its native Asian-African origins. It bloomed in Greece and when it finally reached the Romans, they called it the Greek nut. Almonds were among the presents the sons of Jacob took to Egypt. Since the 14th century, almonds have been cultivated in the south of France. However, it was not until 1850 that they reached the state of California, which immediately seemed a natural habitat. In California, the almond generally ripens in August and September, but early in spring there is the green almond. Young, sweet, with soft green shells, these green almonds are considered a great delicacy but are usually eaten only in the areas in which they grow and are not distributed commercially. In European and Asiatic countries, these often are preserved in sugar and liqueurs.

The bitter almond is considered poisonous in any great quantity because it contains prussic acid; in small amounts, such as one or two bitter almonds in an almond dish using a cup or so of sweet almonds, it is perfectly safe and has been used for thousands of years. There are two kinds of almond extracts or almond essences, the sweet and the bitter. The bitter almond is used in many pastries, particularly in pastries containing almond paste or marzipan, to enhance the taste of the sweet almond.

In early days, the almond, ground and covered with water, produced what was then called almond milk. The almond has been a thickening agent and has been ground to make almond meal, paste, and butter. Almond oil long has been used for cooking and medicinal purposes. The ground almond is world-renowned as the basis of the candy, marzipan, dating back to 2000 B.C.

A little-known virtue of the almond is its relatively low sugar and carbohydrate content; it makes good nibbling for people who have to watch their sugar intake. Almond meal is an appropriate food for diabetic patients and can be bought in health food stores or made at home.

Almond butter is delicious, especially on fried or broiled fish. Since almonds do not have the oil content of several nuts, almond butter is made in the proportions of 1 pound nuts to ½ pound butter. It is quite subtle and elegant as a flavoring for vegetables too. It can also be converted into almond syrup and combined with orange flower water and sugar to make orgeat syrup. In early medieval times, almond flavoring was used almost daily; eaten as appetizers with wine, almonds were believed to promote thirst. The Arabs use almonds profusely in their rice dishes, for stuffing chickens, and in preparing fish pilaus. Some of the lavish Persian desserts feature almonds too.

While California is a leading producer of almonds, they also grow extensively in Italy, Spain, France, Portugal, Morocco, and Persia. There are two specially named almonds, Jordan and Valencia, which refers to type and shape, and not to be confused with the multicolored, crisp, sugar-coated almonds available commercially. These especially large and flavorful nuts come from southern Spain and Italy, where they play important culinary roles.

There are many classic almond dishes. By the 17th century, the city of Nancy in France was famous for almond macaroons, many made by an order of nuns later known as the Macaroon Sisters. The Chinese have used almonds since the 6th century, and they are a feature of all Oriental and Indian cooking. Almonds are becoming more widely recognized—the chocolate-almond candy bar is known even by toddlers. Almond rocco and almond nuggets are familiar foods. In addition, there are delicious almond liqueurs, crème de noya and amoretti that are wonderful endings to delicious almond-oriented meals.

PURCHASE

Almonds are available in the shell at most markets that have sizable produce departments. They should be unbroken and undented, and their straw-colored shells should be bright and fresh looking.

In a cool place or refrigerated, almonds in the shell will last 6 months.

Shelled almonds can be found in vacuum-packed tins or plastic bags and in bulk at specialty nut shops. They are available whole, either blanched or raw (with inner skins on), or split, chopped, sliced, slivered, or shredded.

Almond paste comes in 8-ounce to 5-pound cans and in bars or cakes in smaller amounts. It should be kept cold until just before using.

You can make almond paste at home. The best contains only almonds and sugar. Some fine cooks, however, do insist on the use of a whole egg; others, the whites; and still others, water. Almond paste purchased in cans is most adequate and far easier; it is also available in bars or bulk in specialty shops. This is the basis for many pastries, confections, and marzipan, which can then be formed into fruits and gorgeous culinary sculpture.

PREPARATION

It is relatively easy to shell the paper-shelled almonds, which can be eaten immediately or used for cooking. Some prefer eating them and cooking them with their inner skin on in an unblanched form. Others want to blanch them for all uses.

To blanch.   Put almonds a few at a time in boiling water 3–5 minutes; remove them with slotted spoon; cool to avoid finger burns; and slip nuts between your thumb and middle finger, quickly removing the red skin. Dry blanched nuts with absorbent paper towels and spread out on baking sheet to dry. They are now ready for cutting or chopping. When whole blanched, put into 350° oven on baking sheet only 5 minutes to warm and soften; then you can split in half for halved almonds or slice them more easily. If they are to be kept before using, refrigerate them in an airtight container; and if they are to be kept for any length of time, freeze them.

To fry.   French fry almonds in vegetable oil that is heated to 360° only 2–3 minutes until a light golden color. Remove by slotted spoon or small sieve, and drain on paper towel. Salt or keep plain, and use for eating out of hand, for cooking, or for culinary decoration. If you plan to keep these any length of time, place in airtight containers in the refrigerator.

To roast.   Put blanched or natural almonds in single layer on unbuttered baking sheet at 350° about 15 minutes, stirring to achieve the most even color. You can add 2 tablespoons butter and roast nuts at 300°, but the butter makes the burning possibilities greater; stir and watch. Drain on absorbent paper towel, and salt. The roasted buttered almonds are more perishable.

Special seasoning.   After french frying or roasting, you can use any favorite hot seasoning instead of plain salt: pepper, curry powder, garlic salt, onion salt, or both garlic salt and onion salt. Be quite creative and use even a dash of Tabasco sauce.

 ## AMOUNTS

1 pound unshelled almonds equals approximately 1 cup whole or 1½ cups chopped.

4 ounces shelled almonds equals 1 cup.

8 ounces shelled almonds equals 2 cups or ½ pound.

32 ounces shelled almonds in any form generally equals 2 pounds.

STORAGE

In the shell, almonds survive in a cool dry place for months. Shelled, eat them or use them for cooking without too much delay, or store them for later use in airtight containers in the refrigerator.

STUFFED MUSHROOMS

12 large mushrooms
½ cup diced roasted
almonds
¼ cup shredded Jack
cheese
½ cup tartar sauce
2 tablespoons chopped
green onions
dash of salt
⅓ cup vermouth
3 tablespoons butter

1. Preheat oven to 425°.
2. Wash mushrooms; cut off stems. Arrange cup-side up in shallow baking dish.
3. Chop mushroom stems. Mix with ¼ cup nuts, cheese, tartar sauce, green onions, and salt.
4. Spoon stem mixture into mushroom caps. Sprinkle with remaining nuts.
5. Pour vermouth and butter into baking dish. Bake 8–10 minutes.

Makes 1 dozen.

Hint: The vermouth and butter eliminate scorching of mushrooms.

 ## ALMOND SPREAD

1 package (3 ounce) cream
cheese
½ cup chopped roasted
almonds, blanched
¼ cup sweet pickle relish
⅛ teaspoon hot pepper
sauce
½ teaspoon salt
½ teaspoon horseradish
1 teaspoon mayonnaise
⅛ teaspoon paprika
1 bunch watercress or
parsley
16 favorite crackers

1. In small bowl, cream cheese.
2. Add nuts, relish, hot pepper sauce, salt, horseradish, mayonnaise, and paprika to cheese. Cream to blend thoroughly.
3. Chill.
4. Serve crowned with watercress and accompanied by crisp crackers.

Makes 16

MUSSELS WITH ALMONDS

60 mussels
1 cup white wine
1 garlic clove, crushed
2 tablespoons powdered
  almonds
3 tablespoons finely
  chopped parsley
3 tablespoons butter,
  melted
1 tablespoon lemon juice
salt to taste
pepper to taste
⅓ cup chopped toasted
  almonds
½ cup chopped onion

1. Wash and scrape mussels. Place them and wine in large pan over high heat to open rapidly. Cover and shake pan 5 minutes to make opened mussels come to the surface.

2. Remove 1 shell from each mussel. Put 10 mussels in the half shell in 6 individual baking dishes.

3. Preheat oven to 475°.

4. Mix together garlic, powdered nuts, parsley, butter, lemon juice, salt, and pepper.

5. Put 1 teaspoon mixture in each shell. Garnish with chopped nuts.

6. Just before serving, put 6 baking dishes in oven until contents bubble. Garnish with onion. Serve with toasted peasant bread.

Serves 6

Hint: Strain leftover wine to save for another use.

 ## MYSTERY HORS D'OEUVRE-RELISH

1 cup pitted dates
½ cup chili sauce
1 teaspoon grated orange
  rind
½ cup orange juice
2 tablespoons chopped
  onion
1 teaspoon canned green
  chilies, seeded, minced
1 square (1 ounce)
  unsweetened chocolate,
  grated
¼ cup coarsely chopped
  toasted almonds,
  unblanched

1. Cut dates in sixths.

2. In small saucepan, combine chili sauce, orange rind, orange juice, onion, green chilies, and chocolate.

3. Bring relish to rolling boil over medium heat, stirring often. Remove from heat.

4. Stir in nuts. Chill.

Makes 1¾ cups

Hint: One teaspoon green salsa sauce can substitute for green chilies.

This is good with crackers and drinks. It is also delicious as a relish with poultry.

SUPER ALMOND SOUP

¼ cup butter
2 finely chopped green
  onions
1 cup chopped almonds,
  blanched
1 tablespoon cornstarch
1 can chicken broth
¼ teaspoon salt
dash of freshly ground
  pepper
1 bay leaf
dash of garlic salt
1 tablespoon sherry
1 egg yolk
1 cup half-and-half
sliced toasted almonds to
  taste

1. In small skillet, melt butter. Sauté green onions in butter.
2. Grind half green onions with half chopped nuts in blender; repeat with remaining green onions and chopped nuts.
3. In medium saucepan, blend cornstarch with 3 tablespoons chicken broth; add remaining broth, salt, pepper, bay leaf, garlic salt, and sherry. Combine and simmer slowly, stirring carefully.
4. Beat egg yolk with half-and-half and slowly stir into soup mixture. At this point, transfer soup to a double boiler to heat thoroughly but avoid danger of boiling.
5. Serve hot or cold with sliced nuts sprinkled on top.

Serves 4–6

 ## SPANISH SPINACH BISQUE

½ cup sliced almonds,
  unblanched
1 can (10½ ounce) cream
  of potato soup,
  undiluted
½ soup can half-and-half
1 package (10½ ounce)
  frozen spinach, partially
  thawed
salt to taste
1 orange, unpeeled, very
  thinly sliced

1. In oiled skillet over medium-high heat, stir nuts until lightly roasted. Set aside 2 tablespoons for garnish.
2. In blender, combine remaining roasted nuts with soup, half-and-half, and spinach. Process until spinach is finely chopped.
3. Turn spinach bisque into saucepan and heat until piping hot, stirring often.
4. Add salt.
5. Serve in wide soup bowls. Garnish each serving with thin slice of unpeeled orange and a sprinkling of remaining nuts.

Serves 4-6

BEAN SPROUT-ALMOND SALAD

⅓ cup slivered toasted
  almonds
2 cups bean sprouts, fresh
  or canned, drained
½ cup sliced celery
2 tablespoons chopped
  green pepper
¼ cup mayonnaise
1 tablespoon lemon juice
⅛ teaspoon ginger
¼ teaspoon paprika
1 teaspoon sugar
1 head romaine lettuce,
  torn in bite-size pieces
1 head iceberg lettuce,
  torn in bite-size pieces

1. In medium bowl, toss nuts with bean sprouts, celery, and green pepper.
2. Blend mayonnaise, lemon juice, ginger, paprika, and sugar. Stir into nut mixture.
3. Spoon combination over platter of torn salad greens.

Serves 6

 ## CURRIED TURKEY SALAD

3 teaspoons curry powder
¼ teaspoon crushed
  coriander
¼ cup chicken broth
1 tablespoon lemon juice
¾ cup mayonnaise
½ cup chopped green
  onions
1 cup chopped red
  peppers
3 cups turkey, roasted,
  diced
1½ cups halved grapes
1 cup diced apples
1 cup diced celery
½ cup sliced almonds

1. In large saucepan, simmer curry powder and coriander with chicken broth 1 minute. When cool, blend in lemon juice and mayonnaise. Fold in green onions and red pepper.
2. Add turkey, grapes, apples, and celery to broth mixture.
3. Place salad in serving bowl. Just before serving, decorate with nuts.

Serves 4–6

AMANDINE SAUCE

½ cup butter
⅓ cup chopped almonds,
    blanched, or slivered
    almonds, blanched
½ teaspoon salt
3 tablespoons lemon juice

1. In small saucepan, melt butter. Add nuts to butter and cook over low heat until nuts are thoroughly heated, stirring frequently.
2. Blend in salt and lemon juice well.
3. Serve immediately over broiled or fried fish.

Makes ¾ cup

 ## CRANBERRY RELISH

1 package (1 pound) fresh
    cranberries, washed,
    picked over
1⅔ cups sugar
1 whole orange, with rind,
    finely diced
1 green apple, cored, with
    skin, finely diced
½ cup water
⅓ cup diced almonds

1. In deep saucepan with lid, combine cranberries, sugar, orange, apple, and water. Cook over fairly high heat until mixture pops, covered.
2. Uncover and cook 10 minutes or until relish is thick and apple and orange pieces are tender.
3. Stir in nuts. Serve cold with any poultry.

Serves 8

Hint: Total cooking time is approximately 30 minutes.

 ## GREEN BEAN BUNDLES

1. String beans; if they are slender and young, they do not need to be "Frenched" or sliced lengthwise.
2. Cut beans at each end, making them even-sized in length. (You can put ends in vegetable soup.)

2 pounds young green
    beans
3 cups boiling salted water
4 tablespoons butter
½ cup shaved almonds or
    sliced almonds
1 jar (2 ounce) pimientos,
    cut in long strips

3. Drop beans into boiling salted water and cook until just tender.
4. During or before cooking process of beans, melt butter and brown nuts in it.
5. Drain beans and arrange in small bundles or stacks on flat serving dish.
6. Pour browned butter and nuts over the stacks.
7. Arrange strip of pimiento on each stack to make beans appear as a package tied with a red ribbon.
8. Serve promptly with serving spatula and fork.

Serves 8

SWEET-AND-SOUR BEEF TONGUE

1 fresh beef tongue (4–5
  pound)
1 large onion, sliced
3 stalks celery, sliced
3 bay leaves
2 sprigs parsley
1 small garlic clove
  (optional)
½ teaspoon whole
  peppercorns
4 whole cloves
½ teaspoon seasoned salt
parsley to garnish

1. Wash tongue and place in heavy large Dutch oven with lid.

2. Pour in water to cover tongue. Add vegetables and seasonings. Stir to blend well.

3. Bring tongue to a boil. Cook just under rolling boil 3–3½ hours, covered, until tender when a fork is thrust into it.

4. Remove tongue; cool and peel, cutting root away too. Slice in medium-thick slices. Set aside.

5. Prepare sauce.

6. Place slices of tongue in sauce, spooning sauce to cover meat.

7. Place pot over hot water. Heat tongue thoroughly, allowing enough time for flavor to permeate meat.

8. Serve on heated platter. Garnish with parsley sprigs.

Sauce

3 tablespoons butter
2 tablespoons flour
1 teaspoon seasoned salt
1¾ cups hot, strained
  tongue broth
¼ cup apple cider vinegar
¾ cup brown sugar,
  tightly packed
⅓ cup golden raisins,
  plumped 10 minutes in 1
  tablespoon sherry
⅓ cup whole almonds,
  blanched, or split
  almonds, blanched

1. In top of a double boiler, melt butter. Blend in flour and seasoned salt, stirring with wire whisk. Cook gently 5 minutes to avoid raw-flour taste.

2. Gradually add hot tongue broth, stirring to keep sauce smooth.

3. Pour vinegar and brown sugar into mixture; continue whisking until sauce is smooth and thick.

4. Add raisins and nuts.

Serves 6

Hint: This is especially tasty served with whipped potatoes.

MEATBALLS SPECIAL

1½ pounds ground beef
1 cup toasted wheat germ
¾ cup diced toasted
  almonds
1 cup chicken bouillon or
  dry white wine
1 can (10½ ounce) onion
  soup, undiluted
1½ teaspoons salt
¼ teaspoon pepper
4 tablespoons butter
1 can (10½ ounce) cream
  of mushroom soup,
  undiluted
½ cup wine or bouillon

1. In large bowl, mix ground beef, wheat germ, ½ cup nuts, chicken bouillon, ½ can onion soup, salt, and pepper.
2. Shape beef mixture into 24 balls. In large skillet, melt 2 tablespoons butter. Brown balls in butter.
3. In large skillet, combine mushroom soup, remaining butter, remaining onion soup, and wine. Bring to a boil.
4. Add beef balls. Simmer 30 minutes, uncovered, turning occasionally.
5. Sprinkle remaining nuts over meatballs before serving.

Serves 6

Hint: Serve over hot cooked noodles or rice.

LAZY NUTTY CHICKEN 'N RICE

1 cup chicken broth,
  undiluted
1 cup raw long grain rice
4 chicken breasts, split
2–4 chicken thighs
1 envelope dry onion
  soup, without liquid
1 can (10¾ ounce) cream
  of chicken soup,
  undiluted, or cream of
  mushroom soup,
  undiluted
⅓ cup shaved almonds,
  blanched
parsley to garnish

1. Preheat oven to 350°.
2. Use an oblong casserole or pan at least 1¾–2 inches deep and approximately 12 x 8 inches or the equivalent. Pour chicken broth into casserole. Add rice. Arrange chicken pieces over this skin-side up.
3. In little bowl, blend dry onion soup without liquid to meld seasonings. Sprinkle over chicken.
4. Paint top of chicken with cream of chicken soup, covering it well.
5. Cover casserole with heavy foil and tuck foil in to induce steaming. Bake 1 hour.
6. Remove foil top and bake 30–45 minutes; during last 15–20 minutes, sprinkle nuts on top.
7. Decorate with parsley and serve in casserole directly from oven.

Serves 6

Hint: The amount of chicken is flexible. This particular amount serves 6 well.

ALMOND CHICKEN CONTINENTAL

2 frying chickens, cut up
salt or seasoned salt to
 taste
pepper to taste
¾ cup butter
minced parsley to taste
¼ teaspoon powdered bay
 leaf
4 tablespoons finely
 minced shallots or finely
 minced green onions
4 tablespoons flour
2 cups chicken broth
½ cup sliced, lightly
 toasted almonds,
 blanched
⅓ cup dry white wine

1. Season chicken with salt and pepper.
2. In large skillet, melt ½ cup butter. Over low heat, brown chicken in butter 30 minutes, turning.
3. Mix parsley, bay leaf, and shallots with chicken.
4. In small saucepan, melt remaining butter. Blend flour into butter for roux. Gradually add chicken broth, stirring constantly. Sauce will be fairly thick.
5. Add sauce to chicken mixture. Cook 30 minutes or until chicken is completely tender. Stir in nuts and wine. Serve accompanied by large bowl of white rice or noodles.

Serves 8

 # ALMOND CHICKEN ORIENTAL

1 pound boned chicken,
 sliced, cut in small strips
1 tablespoon vegetable oil
15 water chestnuts, sliced
2 large bamboo shoots,
 sliced
3 large mushrooms,
 slivered
½ cup slivered toasted
 almonds
4 stalks celery, sliced
½ cup chicken stock
½ cup water
1 teaspoon cornstarch
1 teaspoon salt
½ cup Chinese peas,
 blanched

1. In large skillet, stir-fry chicken in oil 1 minute.
2. Add water chestnuts, bamboo shoots, mushrooms, ⅓ cup nuts, and celery to chicken. Stir-fry 2 minutes.
3. In small saucepan, combine stock, water, cornstarch, and salt. Add to chicken mixture and cook until gravy thickens.
4. Garnish chicken with remaining nuts and Chinese peas.

Serves 6

CHICKEN FROM COLUMBIA

2 tablespoons butter
1 tablespoon minced onion
½ cup dry white wine
1 cup chicken stock,
    homemade or canned,
    undiluted
1 whole clove
1 bay leaf
3 egg yolks, well beaten
½ cup heavy cream
¼ cup sherry
¼ cup raisins
2–3 cups chicken, cooked,
    diced
½ cup minced almonds

1. Prepare white sauce.
2. In large skillet, melt butter. Sauté onion in butter.
3. Add white wine, white sauce, chicken stock, clove, and bay leaf to onion. Cook 5 minutes.
4. In small bowl, beat egg yolks with heavy cream and sherry. When white wine sauce is hot and thickened, add egg yolk mixture.
5. Stir in raisins, chicken, and nuts. Cook 1 minute; do not allow to boil. Serve hot.

White Sauce

3 tablespoons butter
3 tablespoons flour
1 cup milk

1. In small saucepan, melt butter. Blend flour into butter for roux.
2. When roux is bubbling, gradually add milk, stirring until thick and smooth.

Serves 8

CHICKEN CURRY

½–¾ pound onions,
    finely chopped
2 tablespoons olive oil
2 large frying chickens (6½
    pounds total), cut in
    pieces
2 containers (8 ounce)
    yogurt
2 tablespoons madras
    curry powder
pinch of saffron
1 pound tomatoes,
    skinned, seeded
2 garlic cloves, crushed
20 coriander seeds
salt to taste
pepper to taste
cayenne to taste (optional)
1 cup sliced almonds

1. In large casserole with lid over moderate heat, sauté onions carefully in olive oil until they become soft, but not brown.
2. Add chicken to onions, browning slowly.
3. In separate bowl, beat together yogurt, curry powder, and saffron. Pour this into casserole in which chicken has been browning. Stir in tomatoes, garlic, coriander seeds, salt, pepper, and cayenne.
4. Remove casserole from heat. Let stand to marinate 1 hour.
5. After sufficient marinating, add just enough water to marinade to cover chicken. Bring to a boil, cover, and reduce heat to simmer chicken in sauce. Simmer 1 hour.
6. Add nuts to casserole. Cook until chicken is tender.
7. Correct seasoning, adding a little more curry powder or cayenne if necessary. If there is not enough sauce, add a little water or coconut milk.
8. Serve with white rice, grated coconut, and a dish of yogurt beaten with a handful of chopped fresh mint leaves.

Serves 8

FISH WITH LEMON SAUCE

1 Eastern whitefish (3
   pound or more),
   cleaned, not boned, cut
   in 5 serving pieces
3 cups water
½ teaspoon salt
2 teaspoons seasoned salt
1 medium Spanish onion,
   finely chopped
½ cup chopped celery
2 tablespoons chopped
   parsley
½ cup fresh lemon juice
4 thin slices fresh lemon
2 tablespoons butter
1 tablespoon flour
4 egg yolks
3 tablespoons sugar
⅓ cup whole almonds,
   blanched, or split
   almonds, blanched
⅓ cup golden raisins,
   plumped in 1 tablespoon
   sherry

1. Have fish at room temperature.

2. Season water with salt, seasoned salt, onion, celery, parsley, lemon juice, and lemon slices in white enamel pot, if available, which prevents discoloration and, as per old wives' tale, is especially kind to fish cookery. Cook 5–10 minutes to mellow seasonings.

3. Gently lower fish into pot. Avoid crowding; if necessary, cook in installments. Cook 10–15 minutes until fish flakes.

4. With slotted spatula, carefully transfer fish slices to rimmed dish that preferably can go in refrigerator and, later, to table. Set fish aside in this dish while completing sauce.

5. In top of a double boiler, melt butter. Add flour and cook 2–3 minutes to avoid raw-flour taste.

6. Reduce liquid that fish was cooked in by rapidly boiling 10 minutes. Strain 1½ cups of this liquid into measuring cup for use in sauce.

7. Gradually add 1¼ cups of this hot liquid to flour mixture, stirring until thick and smooth.

8. Beat remaining ¼ cup liquid with egg yolks. Gradually stir this into thickened sauce.

9. Place sauce over boiling water to avoid curdling, and cook until thick and custardlike, stirring constantly. Blend in sugar.

10. Stir in nuts and raisins. Taste and correct seasonings if necessary.

11. Pour sauce over fish. Cool.

12. Cover fish and sauce with plastic wrap or foil; refrigerate until sauce is thick and cold.

13. Serve cold, garnished with parsley and grapes. Hot buttered potato balls are excellent accompaniment.

Serves 4–5

Hint: This is delicious warm too, served right after assembling. The sauce is not quite as thick and custardy as when it is chilled, but it is still creamy. Cold or warm, this is elegant enough to serve as a company dish.

18

 SAFFRON BREAD

¼ teaspoon powdered
  saffron
1 tablespoon brandy
1 cup milk
½ cup butter
1 cup sugar
⅛ teaspoon salt
1 cake yeast
¼ cup warm water
4 cups sifted flour
1 egg
½ cup raisins
1 egg yolk, beaten with 1
  tablespoon water
1 cup coarsely chopped
  almonds
sugar to sprinkle

1. Soak saffron in brandy.
2. In small saucepan, scald milk with butter. Dissolve sugar and salt in milk. Cool to lukewarm.
3. Dissolve yeast in warm water. In large bowl, blend 1 cup flour and dissolved yeast into milk mixture. Stir.
4. Mix in saffron, egg, and raisins.
5. Add about 3 cups flour to form soft dough. Knead well, and brush with melted butter. Let rise to double.
6. Knead dough. Divide in half. Shape into 2 long braided breads on baking sheet.
7. Paint loaves with beaten egg yolk. Sprinkle with nuts and sugar. Let rise to almost double.
8. Preheat oven to 350°.
9. Bake 30–35 minutes until golden brown.

Makes 2 loaves

 CHOCOLATE-ALMOND ZUCCHINI BREAD

3 eggs
2 cups sugar
1 cup vegetable oil
2 squares (1 ounce)
  unsweetened chocolate
1 teaspoon vanilla
2 cups finely grated
  zucchini
3 cups flour
1 teaspoon salt
1 teaspoon cinnamon
¼ teaspoon baking
  powder
1 teaspoon baking soda
1 cup coarsely chopped
  almonds

1. Preheat oven to 350°.
2. In small bowl, beat eggs until lemon colored. Beat in sugar and oil.
3. Melt chocolate over hot water.
4. In large bowl, add egg mixture, vanilla, and zucchini to chocolate.
5. Sift flour with salt, cinnamon, baking powder, and baking soda.
6. Stir sifted dry ingredients into zucchini mixture.
7. Mix in nuts.
8. Pour batter into 2 well-buttered 9 x 5 x 3–inch loaf pans. Bake 1 hour and 20 minutes or until done.
9. Cool in pans 15–20 minutes. Turn out on a rack. Cool thoroughly before serving.

Makes 2 large loaves

ALMOND GRANOLA

1½ cups slivered almonds
4 cups old-fashioned oats,
  not instant
½ cup shredded coconut
1 cup toasted wheat germ
½ cup vegetable oil
½ cup honey

1. In large bowl, mix nuts, oats, coconut, and wheat germ.
2. Preheat oven to 350°.
3. Combine oil and honey; work into oat mixture, using fingers to remove lumps.
4. Turn mixture into 18 x 12–inch pan. Bake 30 minutes, stirring every 10 minutes for even browning.
5. Cool, stirring occasionally to break up any lumps.

Makes 2 quarts (2 pounds)

Hint: Store in airtight containers in freezer.

 OMELET WITH ALMOND GREEN SAUCE

¼ cup parsley sprigs,
  packed
1 green chili, seeded
1 small green onion,
  chopped
¼ teaspoon salt
½ cup sour cream
⅓ cup slivered toasted
  almonds
3 eggs
2 tablespoons water
¼ teaspoon thyme
1 package (3 ounce) cream
  cheese, finely cubed
2 tablespoons butter

1. In blender, puree parsley sprigs, green chili, green onion, salt, and sour cream. Turn into small saucepan.
2. Stir in nuts. Heat thoroughly, but do not boil.
3. Beat eggs with water and thyme. Add cream cheese.
4. In medium skillet, heat butter until bubbly; pour in egg mixture.
5. As egg mixture sets, gently lift edges and tilt pan so uncooked portion flows to bottom and cooks. Slide omelet onto warm platter and fold to fan shape.
6. Pour almond sauce over omelet and serve.

Serves 2

MOCHA ALMOND CAKE

1 cup butter
2 cups sugar
4 eggs, separated
1 cup grated unsweetened
    chocolate, melted
2 cups flour
2 teaspoons baking
    powder
1 cup strong coffee
¾ cup chopped almonds
favorite chocolate frosting

1. Preheat oven to 350°.
2. In large bowl, cream butter and sugar together until light and fluffy. Beat in egg yolks until light. Blend in chocolate.
3. Sift together flour and baking powder. To creamed mixture, add sifted dry ingredients alternately with coffee.
4. In small bowl, beat egg whites until stiff enough to hold a peak; fold into batter with nuts.
5. Turn batter into buttered waxed-paper-lined tube pan. Bake 1 hour or until cake tests done.
6. Frost cake with favorite chocolate frosting before serving.

Serves 10

 FRENCH CHOCOLATE TORTE

6 squares (1 ounce)
    semisweet chocolate
¾ cup butter, softened
⅔ cup sugar
3 eggs
1 cup finely ground
    almonds
1 tablespoon freshly grated
    orange rind
¼ cup bread crumbs
2 squares (1 ounce) bitter
    chocolate
2 tablespoons honey
⅓ cup shaved almonds

1. Preheat oven to 375°.
2. Butter bottom and sides of 8-inch springform pan. Line bottom with buttered waxed paper.
3. Melt 4 squares semisweet chocolate.
4. In large bowl, cream ½ cup butter until light and soft. Gradually add sugar, beating constantly.
5. When all sugar is in, add eggs 1 at a time, beating hard after each addition.
6. Stir in melted chocolate, ground nuts, orange rind, and bread crumbs. With rubber spatula, mix ingredients thoroughly.
7. Pour batter into prepared pan. Bake 25 minutes.
8. Allow cake to cool on a rack 30 minutes.
9. Turn cake out on a rack and ease off paper. Cool completely before glazing. Center of cake will not seem thoroughly cooked: this contributes to its soft texture and exceptional flavor.
10. In small saucepan, combine remaining chocolates, butter, and honey; melt. Remove from heat and beat until cool, but not too thick for pouring.
11. Pour glaze over cake on rack, spreading evenly over top and sides. Decorate rim of cake with shaved nuts.

Serves 8–10

ORIENTAL ALMOND COOKIES

3 cups flour
1 cup almond powder
  (optional)
1 teaspoon baking soda
½ teaspoon salt
1 large egg
1 teaspoon almond extract
1 cup sugar
1⅓ cups butter
½ cup split almonds,
  blanched

1. Preheat oven to 350°.
2. Sift together flour, almond powder, baking soda, and salt.
3. Beat egg with a fork until lemon colored. Add almond extract.
4. In large bowl, cream sugar and butter well. Mix in flavored egg thoroughly.
5. Gradually stir sifted dry ingredients into creamed mixture.
6. Roll dough into balls about 1 inch in diameter. Place on buttered baking sheet.
7. Press thumb gently in center of top of each ball. Fill each depression with nut half.
8. Bake 20 minutes.

Makes 4 dozen

 ## FRENCH ALMOND MACAROONS

½ pound almond paste,
  canned or homemade
1 cup sugar
2–3 egg whites
¼ teaspoon almond
  extract or vanilla
  (optional)
¼ cup powdered sugar

1. Preheat oven to 325°. Line baking sheet with unbuttered brown paper. Set aside.
2. In medium bowl, mash almond paste until it is pliable. Gradually add sugar.
3. Blend in 2 egg whites; if mixture is too stiff, gradually add third egg white, using only what is needed.
4. Blend well. Add almond extract. Drop macaroons by small teaspoonsful on paper-lined baking sheet 2 inches apart. Sprinkle powdered sugar on top of each mound. You can press mixture out with pastry bag, using star tube.
5. Bake 20–30 minutes. Cool on a rack. For ease in removing macaroons from paper, moisten back of paper with sponge or cloth.

Makes 30

Hint: Mixture should be soft but not runny.
   You may decorate macaroons with halves of green or red glacé cherries.

FAVORITE ENGLISH TOFFEE

1 cup white sugar
1 cup butter
1 cup slivered almonds
6 chocolate bars (1.2 ounce)
½ cup finely chopped walnuts

1. In medium saucepan, heat sugar and butter until light brown.
2. Mix almonds into sugar mixture.
3. Butter 12 x 7 x 2-inch pan and line it with buttered waxed paper. Pour sugar mixture into pan.
4. Press chocolate bars on top of sugar mixture. Sprinkle walnuts on top.
5. Refrigerate 2 hours.

 MARZIPAN

1 cup almond paste
½ teaspoon almond extract
½ cup light corn syrup
¼ teaspoon salt
1 pound powdered sugar
food coloring of choice

1. In small bowl, beat almond paste, almond extract, corn syrup, and salt until smooth.
2. Gradually beat in powdered sugar, working in last of it with hands if it is too stiff for beater.
3. Knead food colors into portions of mixture as desired.
4. Wrap well in airtight plastic wrap or foil. Store in refrigerator until ready to use.

Makes 1⅓ cups

 HOMEMADE ALMOND PASTE

1½ cups almonds, blanched
1½ cups sifted powdered sugar
1 egg white
1 teaspoon almond extract
¼ teaspoon salt

1. Grind nuts a portion at a time in blender or food chopper with fine blade, making about 1¾ cups ground nuts.
2. Combine ground nuts with powdered sugar, egg white, almond extract, and salt; work to a stiff paste.

Makes 1⅓ cups

Hint: Store almond paste in refrigerator tightly wrapped in plastic wrap or disposable plastic bag. With airtight refrigerator storage, almond paste will keep for months.

BRAZIL NUT

Bertholletia excelsa

BRAZIL NUTS

THE FRUIT OF the *Bertholletia excelsa*, a huge tree native to the Amazon forests, is called the Brazil nut only in the United States. Elsewhere, particularly in Brazil and all of the other nut-bearing, tropical South American countries, it is known as the Para nut after the Brazilian state of Para. It is also known as cream nut and, in France, American chestnut. By whatever name, South Americans regard the Brazil nut as the king of nuts.

Brazil, Bolivia, and Peru produce large crops. The *Bertholletia excelsa* tree is huge. Even its lowest branches are usually at least 100 feet above the ground. Clusters of nuts are within a hard casing about ½ inch thick. Depending on the size of the container, which can be as large as 6 inches in diameter, these pods have 12–30 nuts nestled inside similar to segments of an orange.

When the nuts ripen, the pod falls crashing to the ground and sometimes breaks open. Usually, though, a sledgehammer must be used to open the pods.

The nuts have bright blackish-brown, rough, hard shells. Their triangular shape gives them a modern geometric look. A hardy nutcracker or hammer is necessary to open them. Recommendations vary about easy ways of shelling them; you may boil them in the shell for 2–3 minutes or soak them in cold water overnight to make the shells more tractable.

A thin, slightly wrinkled brown skin covers the shelled nuts. Blanch shelled Brazil nuts by simmering them in water, draining, and rubbing the skin off in a towel. The solid, creamy white nut is crisp at the first bite and has a rich creamy taste; it slightly resembles the macadamia in crunch and taste.

As with most of the nuts featured in this book, you can pound or grind Brazil nuts into a nut paste or nut butter and make Brazil nuts into nut flour. In South America, Brazil nuts are available in all these forms, and Brazil nut oil is also used as a table oil. In the Amazon valley, a special fish is cooked in Brazil nut milk. Throughout South America, the nut is prized for its high caloric value and low cost compared to almonds.

In the United States, we usually eat Brazil nuts raw, seldom roasting them. We enjoy them mostly in the fall and during the Thanksgiving–Christmas holiday season. However, growing acquaintanceship with the Brazil nut has made us realize that it is delicious roasted and salted, as an accompaniment to drinks, and as an addition to many foods for both its taste and texture. In fact, we are learning that the Brazil nut easily substitutes for other nuts. We are finally beginning to appreciate our neighboring South American nut, the only popular nut not yet grown in the United States.

PURCHASE

Brazil nuts are available both in the shell and shelled whole.

The shells should be bright blackish-brown, not dull and dingy. They should be unbroken and uncracked.

The whole shelled Brazil nuts are usually unblanched; they should look fresh, not dried and frumpy. Airtight or cellophane bags are the usual packaging.

PREPARATION

Relatively hard-shelled Brazil nuts require a hardy nutcracker or hammer. Two methods facilitate cracking: boil the nuts in their shells 2–3 minutes or soak them in cold water overnight.

You can shave, cut in slightly thicker chips, and coarsely or finely chop Brazil nuts. A chef's knife and a chopping bowl and chopper constitute good tools. For ease in shaving or chipping, use unblanched nuts. Warm them slightly in a 300° oven 5 minutes to soften.

To toast. Toast them in a single layer in an unbuttered pan 15 minutes in a 350° oven, stirring twice, or place them in a frying pan over low heat with a bit of butter, again stirring until toasted. If you use butter with the oven method, reduce heat to 300°.

 **STORAGE**

Brazil nuts in the shell keep fairly well in a cool room. Shelled, they are best relatively fresh or refrigerated in sealed jars.

Freeze Brazil nuts if you plan to keep them long, processing them in the form you desire before freezing so that they will be available for quick use.

BACON 'N' BRAZIL

16 whole Brazil nut.
salt to taste
paprika to taste
8 slices thin-cut bacon, cut
   in half

1. Blanch nuts.
2. Sprinkle nuts with salt and paprika.
3. Roll each nut in half slice of bacon and secure with a toothpick.
4. Broil appetizer until bacon is crisp. Place on paper to absorb grease.
5. Serve hot.

Serves 8

 ## CRUNCHY STUFFED MUSHROOMS À LA BRAZIL

6 large fresh mushrooms
5 tablespoons butter
1 tablespoon minced
   chives or finely minced
   green onions
¼ teaspoon garlic salt
1 teaspoon seasoned salt
¼ teaspoon basil
¼ cup seasoned bread
   crumbs
1 egg, hard-boiled, finely
   chopped
½ cup finely chopped
   salted Brazil nuts or
   finely chopped unsalted
   Brazil nuts
3 tablespoons mayonnaise
3 tablespoons vermouth or
   sherry

1. Preheat oven to 350°.
2. Wash, peel, and remove stems from mushrooms; dry them well.
3. Chop or grind mushroom stems. In small saucepan, melt 2 tablespoons butter. Sauté mushroom stems in butter with chives, garlic salt, seasoned salt, basil, and bread crumbs 10–15 minutes.
4. Remove from heat and stir in egg, nuts, and mayonnaise.
5. Mound nut mixture high in mushroom caps.
6. Place stuffed mushrooms in shallow 9 x 5 x 2-inch pan with remaining butter and vermouth.
7. Bake, uncovered, 20 minutes—or 30 minutes if mushrooms are very large.

Serves 6

Hint: These are delicious as a first course or a vegetable.

BRAZIL NUT SOUP

1 cup Brazil nuts
½ cup golden mushroom
  canned soup, undiluted
1 cup chicken broth
¼ cup garlic-flavored
  bread croutons or
  garlic-flavored toasted
  bread crumbs
½ cup half-and-half or
  extra chicken broth or
  cream of chicken soup
½ cup sour cream
chopped parsley
4 whole Brazil nuts

1. In blender, blend nuts and mushroom soup until smooth and thick.
2. Add chicken broth and bread croutons; blend. The soup can be served thick, as is, hot or cold, or thinned with half-and-half.
3. Garnish each serving with dab of sour cream. Sprinkle with parsley and place 1 whole nut in center.

Serves 4

INDIAN SUMMER SALAD

1 small fresh pineapple,
  shredded, or 1 can (20
  ounce) crushed
  pineapple
¾ cup sliced Brazil nuts
1 pimiento, minced
2 cups heavy cream
¼ teaspoon salt
dash of curry powder
3 tablespoons lemon juice
1 head butter lettuce
2 eggs, hard-boiled, sliced
8 whole Brazil nuts

1. Mix pineapple, sliced nuts, and pimiento.
2. Combine cream with salt, curry powder, and lemon juice.
3. Arrange pineapple mixture on bed of lettuce.
4. Pour cream combination over salad. Garnish with eggs and whole nuts.

Serves 6

BRAZILIAN POTATO SALAD

6 boiled potatoes, cubed
1 beet, cooked, cubed
3 small pickles, finely cut
1 stalk celery, finely
  chopped
salt to taste
pepper to taste
½ tablespoon grated onion
salad dressing
1 cup sliced Brazil nuts
1 egg, hard-boiled, sliced

1. Prepare salad dressing.
2. Mix potatoes, beet, pickles, and celery; season with salt and pepper.
3. Stir in onion, salad dressing, and ½ cup nuts.
4. Chill. Serve on lettuce with remaining nuts and egg.

Salad Dressing

⅓ cup olive oil
⅓ cup vegetable oil
2 tablespoons lemon juice
½ teaspoon sugar
2 teaspoons salt
½ teaspoon freshly
  ground pepper

1. Combine ingredients.

Serves 6

 ## SUPER WALDORF SALAD

1½ cups diced, cored,
  unpared apples
1½ cups finely cut celery
½ cup sliced Brazil nuts
¾–1 cup mayonnaise or
  cooked salad dressing
4 lettuce cups

1. Combine apples, celery, and nuts.
2. Moisten mixture with mayonnaise.
3. Serve on chilled salad plates, heaping salad in individual lettuce cups.

Serves 4

Hint: If 1 lettuce cup is too fragile or insufficient, use 2 or 3 inside each other. They hold their shape well.

SWEET-AND-SOUR GREEN BEANS

1 can (16 ounce vertical
  pack) whole green
  beans, liquid reserved
2 tablespoons butter
1 tablespoon cornstarch
½ teaspoon seasoned salt
2 tablespoons apple cider
  vinegar
½ cup brown sugar,
  tightly packed
¼ cup golden raisins
¼ cup shaved Brazil nuts

1. Pour reserved bean liquid into measuring cup, adding water or chicken broth if necessary to end up with 1 full cup. Leave beans in can while preparing sauce.
2. In top of a double boiler, melt butter.
3. Add cornstarch and seasoned salt to butter and stir with wire whisk until well blended and bubbly.
4. Gradually add bean liquid, stirring until thick and smooth.
5. Pour in vinegar and brown sugar, continuing to stir with whisk. Sauce should be thick and smooth.
6. Stir in raisins and nuts well.
7. Drain beans again to avoid diluting sauce. Place beans in sauce. Put pot over hot water, and heat thoroughly, allowing enough time for beans to absorb flavor.

Serves 4–6

 ## SPINACH-STUFFED ONIONS

8 large onions, peeled
1 cup mayonnaise
¼ cup lemon juice
⅓ cup milk
1 package (12 ounce)
  frozen chopped spinach
1 teaspoon salt
1 cup chopped Brazil nuts
2 pimientos, cut in strips

1. Cook onions in boiling salted water 20 minutes or until tender; do not overcook. Drain immediately.
2. Combine mayonnaise, lemon juice, and milk.
3. Cook spinach and drain well.
4. Remove centers from onions. Chop onion centers and mix with spinach, salt, and 2 tablespoons mayonnaise mixture. Stir in ½ cup nuts.
5. Preheat oven to 350°.
6. Stuff onions with spinach mixture.
7. Place onions in 12 x 9 x 2-inch pan, and cover each onion top with remaining mayonnaise mixture.
8. Sprinkle remaining nuts on top of each onion and garnish with pimiento strips.
9. Bake 20 minutes.

Serves 8

SAVORY MEAT LOAF

1½ pounds ground beef
1 cup ground Brazil nuts
2 cups tomatoes, canned
  or fresh, heated to
  boiling
½ cup tapioca
2 teaspoons salt
¼ teaspoon pepper
1 small onion, finely
  chopped

1. Preheat oven to 350°.
2. Mix all ingredients together.
3. Pour mixture into buttered 9 x 5 x 3-inch loaf pan. Bake 1 hour. Serve hot or cold.

Serves 6

 MOLDED HAM LOAF

1 package (3 ounce) lime
  gelatin
4 tablespoons vinegar
1 teaspoon salt
2 cups ham, cooked,
  chopped
¾ cup sliced Brazil nuts
¾ cup finely chopped
  celery
1 tablespoon minced onion
3 pimiento-stuffed olives,
  finely chopped

1. Place gelatin in large bowl, and stir in boiling water according to package directions.
2. Add vinegar and salt.
3. Chill. When slightly thickened, stir remaining ingredients into mixture.
4. Place in oiled 7 x 3 x 3-inch loaf mold. Chill until firm.

Serves 6–8

Hint: A mustard-mayonnaise sauce is excellent with this.

 HAM PATTIES

1 cup ground cooked ham
1 cup ground Brazil nuts
½ cup bread, soaked in
  water, squeezed dry
1 egg
½ onion, finely cut
salt to taste
pepper to taste
bread crumbs to coat
4 tablespoons butter

1. Mix together ham, nuts, bread, egg, onion, salt, and pepper thoroughly.
2. Shape mixture into 4 large or 6 small patties. Roll patties in bread crumbs.
3. In large skillet, melt butter. Fry coated patties in butter until they are golden.

Serves 4

CHICKEN-BRAZIL NUT CASSEROLE

6 tablespoons butter
3 tablespoons flour
2 cups hot milk
2 cups chicken, cooked,
　　cubed
salt to taste
pepper to taste
dash of chili sauce or
　　Tabasco sauce
½ teaspoon brown sugar
8 ounces noodles, cooked
2 cups chopped Brazil nuts
½ cup chopped green
　　olives
bread crumbs
⅛ cup sliced Brazil nuts

1. Preheat oven to 350°.
2. In large saucepan, melt 4 tablespoons butter. Stir flour into butter. Cook 3 minutes.
3. Gradually add hot milk and cook until thick and creamy.
4. Fold in chicken.
5. Season with salt, pepper, chili sauce, and brown sugar. Keep warm.
6. Butter oven-to-table 2-quart casserole and put in layer of noodles. Add a few dots of butter, a layer of chopped nuts, and a layer of olives. Repeat layers, ending with layer of noodles on top.
7. Pour sauce over noodles and sprinkle thickly with bread crumbs.
8. Scatter sliced nuts over bread crumbs and dot liberally with butter.
9. Bake 30 minutes.

Serves 6

ESCALLOPED CRAB

4 tablespoons butter
2 tablespoons flour
1 cup milk
1 tablespoon lemon juice
½ teaspoon salt
½ teaspoon paprika
2 tablespoons chopped
　　parsley
2 cups crab meat
¾ cup ground Brazil nuts

1. Preheat oven to 350°.
2. In medium skillet, melt butter. Add flour. Cook 3 minutes. Slowly stir in milk. Carefully cook mixture until smooth and thick.
3. Add lemon juice, salt, paprika, and parsley.
4. Stir in crab meat thoroughly.
5. Fill 6 baking shells with ½ cup mixture each. Sprinkle liberally with nuts.
6. Bake 15–20 minutes, being careful nuts do not become too dark.

Serves 6

BAKED STUFFED LOBSTER

4 live lobsters
2 cups cracker crumbs
2 cups ground Brazil nuts,
  blanched
2 tablespoons paprika
1½ cups butter, melted
½ cup extra butter, melted
lemon wedges

1. Preheat oven to 375°.
2. Split lobsters, and remove sac and black vein.
3. Scoop out liver and mix it with cracker crumbs, nuts, paprika, and ½ cup butter.
4. Stuff lobster cavity and brush meat and stuffing heavily with remaining 1 cup butter.
5. Bake 20 minutes, basting with additional butter as necessary.
6. Serve with extra ½ cup melted butter and lemon wedges.

Serves 4–8

 TUNA BAKE

4 tablespoons butter
4 tablespoons flour
¾ teaspoon salt
¼ teaspoon pepper
½ teaspoon
  Worcestershire sauce
2 cups milk
2 pimientos
1 cup ground Brazil nuts
1 can (7 ounce) tuna
6 whole Brazil nuts

1. Preheat oven to 350°.
2. In medium saucepan, melt butter. Stir in flour, salt, pepper, and Worcestershire sauce. Cook gently 3 minutes to avoid raw-flour taste.
3. Blend in milk. Cook until thick and smooth.
4. Cut 1 pimiento in small pieces. Stir this pimiento and ground nuts into cream sauce.
5. Flake tuna and add to white sauce.
6. Pour mixture into buttered 9 x 6-inch baking dish.
7. Cut remaining pimiento in strips, and garnish top of dish with pimiento strips and whole nuts.
8. Bake 15 minutes.

Serves 4–6

NUT-POTATO CROQUETTES

2 cups hot mashed
  potatoes
¼ cup cream or milk
½ teaspoon baking
  powder
½ teaspoon salt
pepper
1 cup crushed Brazil nuts
4 tablespoons butter

1. To potatoes, add cream, baking powder, salt, and pepper; blend.
2. Mix in ½ cup nuts. Cool.
3. Shape mixture into balls and roll in remaining nuts.
4. In large skillet, melt butter. Brown balls in butter.

Serves 6

 ## BRAZILIAN SWEET POTATOES

2 pounds sweet potatoes
3 egg yolks, beaten
2 tablespoons milk
salt to taste
pepper to taste
1 can (1 pound) pineapple
  chunks
flour
2 egg whites
½ cup finely chopped
  Brazil nuts
1 quart vegetable oil for
  frying

1. Scrub sweet potatoes and cook in boiling salted water 30 minutes or until quite tender.
2. Peel sweet potatoes and mash with egg yolks, milk, salt, and pepper.
3. Let mixture cool before proceeding.
4. When potato mixture has cooled, form it into balls around each pineapple cube, making sure there are no cracks.
5. Roll balls in flour. Refrigerate 30 minutes.
6. Beat egg whites until stiff but not dry. Roll floured balls in stiff egg whites and then in nuts.
7. Fry sweet potato balls in deep hot oil until golden.

Serves 6–8

 ## CANDIED SWEET POTATOES

6 sweet potatoes
3 tart apples
20 Brazil nuts, sliced
½ pound bacon

1. Boil potatoes until soft. Peel, slice, and set aside.
2. Preheat oven to 375°.
3. Core and slice unpeeled apples.
4. Cover bottom of 9 x 6-inch baking dish with a layer of potatoes.
5. Cover potatoes with half of apples.
6. Sprinkle half of nuts over apples.
7. Repeat layers of potatoes, apples, and nuts.
8. Place bacon on top.
9. Bake 20 minutes or until bacon is crisp, basting potatoes with bacon fat once during cooking.

Serves 6

APRICOT-NUT BREAD

½ cup dried apricots
1 egg
1 cup sugar
2 tablespoons butter,
    melted
2 cups sifted flour
1 tablespoon baking
    powder
¼ teaspoon baking soda
¾ teaspoon salt
½ cup strained orange
    juice
1¼ cups water
1 cup sliced Brazil nuts

1. Soak apricots in water 30 minutes; drain and dice.
2. Preheat oven to 350°.
3. In large bowl, beat egg until light. Add sugar and blend well. Stir in butter.
4. Sift together flour, baking powder, baking soda, and salt. To batter, add sifted dry ingredients alternately with orange juice and water.
5. Blend in nuts and apricots well.
6. Place batter in buttered 9 x 5 x 3-inch loaf pan. Bake 90 minutes.

Serves 8

 ## WHOLE WHEAT-NUT BREAD

3 cups whole wheat flour
1½ cups bread flour
5 teaspoons baking
    powder
2 teaspoons baking soda
1½ teaspoons salt
1½ cups brown sugar
1½ cups sliced Brazil nuts
3 cups sour milk or
    buttermilk

1. Preheat oven to 325°.
2. In large bowl, mix together flours, baking powder, baking soda, salt, and sugar.
3. Mix in nuts well.
4. Stir in milk thoroughly.
5. Place mixture in 2 buttered 9 x 5 x 3-inch loaf pans. Bake 1 hour.

Serves 16

 ## GINGER GEMS

3 tablespoons butter
½ cup sugar
1 egg, well beaten
1½ cups flour
½ teaspoon salt
1 teaspoon baking powder
¼ teaspoon baking soda
1 teaspoon cinnamon
1 teaspoon ginger
¾ cup milk
½ cup molasses
1 cup chopped Brazil nuts

1. Preheat oven to 350°.
2. In large bowl, cream butter. Gradually add sugar, creaming well. Blend in egg thoroughly.
3. Sift together flour, salt, baking powder, baking soda, cinnamon, and ginger.
4. To butter mixture, add flour mixture alternately with milk and molasses.
5. Stir in nuts well.
6. Place batter in well-buttered muffin pans. Bake 25 minutes.

Makes 8 large or 12 small

BANANA-BRAZIL CAKE

½ cup butter
1½ cups sugar
2 eggs
¾ cup mashed banana
2 cups sifted flour
¼ teaspoon baking
  powder
¾ teaspoon baking soda
½ teaspoon salt
¼ cup buttermilk
2 teaspoons vanilla
¾ cup chopped Brazil nuts
2 teaspoons powdered
  sugar
2 cups heavy cream,
  whipped

1. Preheat oven to 350°.
2. In large bowl, cream butter. Gradually add sugar, creaming well.
3. Add eggs to butter mixture 1 at a time, beating thoroughly after each addition.
4. Stir in banana.
5. Sift together flour, baking powder, baking soda, and salt.
6. To banana mixture, add sifted dry ingredients alternately with buttermilk.
7. Stir in 1 teaspoon vanilla and nuts.
8. Pour batter into 2 buttered 9-inch round layer pans. Bake 30–35 minutes.
9. Remove from pans and cool.
10. Blend powdered sugar and remaining vanilla into whipped cream. Spread sweetened and flavored whipped cream between layers and on top and sides of cake.

Serves 8

 ## TORTE FROM BRAZIL

6 eggs, separated
¼ teaspoon salt
1 cup sugar
2 cups ground Brazil nuts
2 teaspoons powdered
  sugar
2 teaspoons vanilla
1 cup heavy cream,
  whipped

1. Preheat oven to 350°.
2. Butter and line with waxed paper three 8-inch round layer pans.
3. In large bowl, beat egg yolks with salt and ½ cup sugar until thick and creamy. Stir nuts into egg yolk mixture.
4. In small bowl, beat egg whites until stiff but not dry, gradually adding remaining sugar. Quickly fold into nut mixture.
5. Pour batter into 3 prepared layer pans. Bake 35 minutes. Cool in pans on a rack.
6. Blend powdered sugar and vanilla into whipped cream. Put torte together with sweetened, flavored whipped cream, and cover tops and sides with either more whipped cream or favorite chocolate frosting.

Serves 8

DEVIL'S FOOD CAKE

½ cup butter
½ cup white sugar
½ cup brown sugar
4 egg yolks
1½ cups cake flour
¾ teaspoon baking
  powder
¾ teaspoon baking soda
¾ cup sour milk or
  buttermilk
1½ cups ground Brazil
  nuts
4 squares (1 ounce)
  unsweetened chocolate,
  melted
2 egg whites, stiffly beaten
fudge frosting

1. Preheat oven to 350°.
2. In large bowl, cream butter. Gradually add sugars, creaming well.
3. Beat in egg yolks thoroughly.
4. Sift together flour, baking powder, and baking soda.
5. Add sifted dry ingredients alternately with milk, mixing well.
6. Stir in nuts and chocolate.
7. Gently fold in egg whites.
8. Pour batter into 3 buttered 8-inch round layer pans. Bake 30–40 minutes. Cool on a rack before removing from pans.
9. Put together and frost with favorite frosting.

Serves 10

FUDGE CAKE

⅓ cup butter
1 cup sugar
1 egg, well beaten
2 squares (1 ounce)
  unsweetened chocolate,
  melted
1¾ cups cake flour
2 teaspoons baking
  powder
½ teaspoon salt
¾ cup milk
1 cup ground Brazil nuts
1 teaspoon vanilla

1. In large bowl, cream butter. Add sugar and beat well. Stir in egg and chocolate.
2. Preheat oven to 350°.
3. Sift cake flour with baking powder and salt.
4. To butter mixture, add flour mixture alternately with milk.
5. Stir in nuts and vanilla.
6. Place batter in 2 buttered 8-inch round layer pans. Bake 30–35 minutes.
7. Cool on a rack before removing from pans.
8. Prepare fudge frosting.
9. Put layers together with frosting. Cover cake with remaining frosting.

Fudge Frosting

3 squares (1 ounce)
  unsweetened chocolate
2½ tablespoons hot
  half-and-half
1½ cups sifted powdered
  sugar
3 egg yolks
4 tablespoons butter,
  softened

1. In top of a double boiler over hot water, melt chocolate.
2. Stir in hot half-and-half and powdered sugar to blend.
3. Put mixture in electric-mixer bowl. Beat in egg yolks 1 at a time.
4. Add butter and continue beating until thick and smooth.

Serves 8

SPICE CAKE

½ cup butter
1 cup sugar
2 eggs, well beaten
⅔ cup finely chopped
   Brazil nuts
1½ cups cake flour
2½ teaspoons baking
   powder
½ teaspoon salt
½ teaspoon cinnamon
¼ teaspoon ground cloves
¼ teaspoon ginger
½ cup strong coffee
favorite frosting
⅛ cup sliced Brazil nuts

1. Preheat oven to 350°.
2. In large bowl, cream butter and sugar. Add eggs and beat together until thick and puffy.
3. Stir in finely chopped nuts.
4. Sift together flour, baking powder, salt, cinnamon, cloves, and ginger.
5. To butter combination, add flour mixture alternately with coffee.
6. Line 2 buttered 8-inch round layer pans with waxed paper. Pour batter into prepared pans. Bake 35 minutes. Cool.
7. Use favorite frosting to put layers together and cover cake. Arrange sliced nuts on top.

Serves 8

Hint: Mocha or lemon-flavored frostings are especially good on this cake.

 ## HAVE-A-DATE-WITH-A-BRAZIL-NUT SQUARES

¼ cup butter
¾ cup flour
2 tablespoons sugar
2 tablespoons cold
   half-and-half
2 eggs
¾ cup chopped pitted
   dates
¼ teaspoon baking
   powder
1 cup brown sugar
1 teaspoon vanilla
¾ cup chopped Brazil nuts
1 cup powdered sugar
1 teaspoon grated lemon
   rind
2–3 tablespoons lemon
   juice

1. Preheat oven to 350°, and keep oven at this temperature for whole baking process.
2. Blend butter, flour, sugar, and cold half-and-half until smooth. Line bottom of buttered 8-inch square pan with this mixture. Bake 10 minutes. Cool on a rack.
3. In medium bowl, beat eggs well. Stir in dates. Sprinkle with baking powder and mix well.
4. Add brown sugar, vanilla, and nuts, stirring vigorously.
5. Pour over pastry base, spreading with a knife or a spatula.
6. Bake 20 minutes. Cool.
7. Mix powdered sugar, lemon rind, and lemon juice; spread over cooled sweet.
8. Cut in 1-inch squares.

Makes 64

DARK FRUIT CAKE

1 pound seeded raisins
1 pound currants
½ pound pitted dates, sliced
½ pound candied citron, sliced
¼ pound candied lemon peel, sliced
¼ pound candied pineapple, sliced, or candied cherries, sliced
½ pound Brazil nuts
2 cups flour
¾ teaspoon salt
1½ teaspoons cinnamon
1 teaspoon nutmeg
1 teaspoon allspice
½ teaspoon mace
1 cup butter
1 cup sugar
6 eggs, well beaten
scant ⅓ cup lemon juice
¼ cup grape juice, wine, or brandy
¼ cup orange juice

1. Preheat oven to 275°.
2. Wash raisins and currants; drain. Coarsely chop raisins.
3. Mix dates, citron, lemon peel, pineapple, and nuts.
4. Sift together flour, salt, cinnamon, nutmeg, allspice, and mace. Add to fruit mixture.
5. In large bowl, cream butter. Gradually add sugar, creaming well. Stir in eggs.
6. Combine liquids.
7. To butter mixture, add flour mixture alternately with combined liquids, mixing well.
8. Place batter in 2 well-buttered 9 x 5 x 3-inch loaf pans that have been lined with heavy, brown wrapping paper. Bake 2–3 hours. Do not remove paper lining from cake until ready to cut.

Makes 2 loaves

Hint: It is advisable to store fruit cakes 1–2 months in airtight container before cutting.

 ## CINCHY GRAHAM CRACKER BARS

¼ cup butter, softened
1 cup sugar
3 cups fine graham cracker crumbs
1 cup evaporated milk
1 package (6 ounce) semisweet chocolate bits
½ cup chopped Brazil nuts
1 teaspoon vanilla

1. Preheat oven to 350°.
2. In large bowl, cream butter and sugar.
3. Add graham cracker crumbs alternately with milk.
4. Stir in chocolate bits, nuts, and vanilla, mixing batter well.
5. Pour batter into buttered 9-inch square baking pan. Bake 30–35 minutes.
6. Cool on a rack. Cut in bars.

Serves 6

CASHEW

Anacardium occidentale

CASHEW

THE CASHEW NUT has zoomed to first
place in the esteem of Americans, rivaling the peanut in popularity. A kidney-shaped nut, it grows on the large tropical
evergreen cashew tree. There are two well-documented conflicting theories concerning the origin of the cashew. The dominant
theory is that the cashew is a native of Brazil and was distributed by early Portuguese and Spanish explorers. They carried it
to their own countries and to India, where the Portuguese took
pride in having planted the first cashew tree in Goa. Now the
world's leading producer of cashews is India. This legend traces
the name cashew to caju, which in turn was only slightly altered
from the original Brazilian name, acaju. The competing theory
is that the Portuguese found the cashew in Asia and brought it
to Brazil, referring to it by the word acajoba or acaju.

The cashew tree is highly prized for its nut, fruit, and wood;
thrives well in dry areas; and is found extensively in the South
American tropics. The problems and pattern of preparation of
the cashew nut account for its relatively high cost.

The tree grows 20–40 feet in height and bears a pear-shaped
fruit that is red, yellow, or sometimes almost completely white,
known as the cashew pear or cashew apple. From the flower end
of this fruit, the kidney-shaped cashew nuts hang pendant-
fashion. The cashews are olive colored, that is, a greenish-tan.
They are housed in a double shell and cushioned with membranes containing an acrid caustic acid which irritates and
burns if touched before the nuts-in-shell are treated. A manda-
tory step in preparing cashews for eating is roasting them right
in their shell immediately upon harvesting. The roasting pro-

cess dissipates the thick caustic liquid and makes the nuts safe for handling, shelling, and eating. That caustic acid protected the nuts from insects while they still hung from the cashew apple; later the acid is sometimes used in the industrial manufacture of varnishes and insecticides. After the roasting, another shell is discarded. Because cashews do not have an inner skin, they do not need blanching. The nut itself is about 1 inch long; has a sweet, creamy, mealy taste; and has a mild almond flavor. It is always exported shelled because of the safeguard treatment needed and is available raw (perfectly safe), roasted, with or without salt, and pickled. It makes marvelous nut butter.

The cashew apple is eaten by the natives where the cashew trees grow as a fruit and is also fermented to produce liqueurs. In India, cashew liqueur and a nut vinegar known as Anacard are popular. Brazil produces a very famous wine from the cashew fruit. Cashews yield a light-colored oil popular in the West Indies and Haiti, where it is used to flavor wine, especially Madeira. The English import it for that purpose too.

Today cashews are available in their raw state, particularly in health food stores, and are increasingly popular in vegetarian cooking. They are used extensively in Oriental cuisine because of their mealiness, which is enhanced by cooking. Accordingly, the cashew has limited use in pastries and cakes since it lacks two of the main attributes of most nuts, crispness and crunchiness. Nonetheless, it is a desirable nut, particularly for eating out of hand, salted or unsalted.

 PURCHASE

Since cashews are available only out of the shell, without an inner skin that requires blanching, be sure, by sampling if possible, that in bulk they are fresh, whether raw or roasted.

Cashews are available whole or mixed whole and pieces; the latter are more economical for cooking.

Cashews sold in airtight tins or jars have their freshness ensured. For cooking purposes, it is less costly to buy them in pieces.

STORAGE

Cashews are somewhat perishable, particularly because of their high fat content. Roasted and salted, they have the shortest shelf life. For short periods, refrigerate in tight-topped containers; for longer storage, freeze.

CREAM OF CASHEW SOUP

1 tablespoon butter
2 tablespoons finely
  chopped celery
2 tablespoons finely
  chopped onion
2 tablespoons flour
1 cup milk
2 cups chicken broth or
  chicken bouillon
⅛ teaspoon salt
pepper to taste
¼ teaspoon hickory salt or
  Worcestershire sauce
1 cup finely chopped
  salted cashews
paprika or minced parsley
  to taste

1. In large heavy saucepan, melt butter. Cook celery and onion in butter until tender, stirring frequently. Blend in flour.

2. Gradually stir in milk, broth, salt, pepper, hickory salt, and nuts. Bring soup to a boil, stirring as necessary. Cook 1 minute longer.

3. Garnish with paprika. Serve soup hot or cold.

Serves 4

CHINESE CHICKEN SALAD

1 chicken (3 pound),
  roasted or boiled,
  shredded
1 head iceberg lettuce,
  shredded
2 tablespoons sesame
  seeds
2 teaspoons salt
1 teaspoon pepper
6 tablespoons vinegar
4 tablespoons sugar
½ cup vegetable oil with
  optional dash of sesame
  seed oil
1 package (6¾ ounce) rice
  sticks (bean thread-Mai
  fun), deep fried until
  light brown
½ cup slivered cashews
Chinese parsley (cilantro)
  to garnish

1. In large bowl, combine chicken, lettuce, and sesame seeds.

2. In small bowl, mix together dressing of salt, pepper, vinegar, sugar, and vegetable oil.

3. Deep fry rice sticks in 2 to 3 batches for 1 minute only.

4. Toss chicken salad with dressing, adding rice sticks and nuts at last minute. Garnish with Chinese parsley and serve immediately.

Serves 8

Hint: It is important to have rice sticks keep their crispness.

BROCCOLI WITH CASHEWS

2 packages (10 ounce)
   frozen broccoli
2 tablespoons butter
2 tablespoons minced
   onion
1 cup sour cream
2 teaspoons sugar
1 teaspoon white vinegar
½ teaspoon poppy seeds
½ teaspoon paprika
dash of salt
1 cup chopped cashews

1. Cook broccoli according to directions on package.
2. In small saucepan, melt butter. Sauté onion in butter.
3. Remove pan from heat and stir in sour cream, sugar, vinegar, poppy seeds, paprika, and salt.
4. Pour sauce over cooked, drained broccoli. Sprinkle nuts on top to serve.

Serves 6

 ## BRUSSELS SPROUTS

2 pounds Brussels sprouts
¼ cup butter, melted, hot
2 tablespoons lemon juice
dash of salt
dash of pepper
½ teaspoon summer
   savory
¼–½ cup chopped
   toasted cashews

1. In small amount of boiling salted water, boil Brussels sprouts about 15 minutes until tender, covered. Drain.
2. Combine hot butter with lemon juice, salt, pepper, and summer savory. Pour hot sauce over Brussels sprouts.
3. Sprinkle nuts on vegetable and serve immediately.

Serves 8

 ## CABBAGE WITH NUTS

3 pounds white cabbage
4 tablespoons butter
1 tablespoon lemon juice
1 tablespoon sugar
salt to taste
pepper to taste
½ cup chopped cashews

1. Wash cabbage and cut in quarters, taking out hard stem. Discard any coarse outer leaves, and then finely shred cabbage.
2. In heavy-bottomed saucepan, melt butter. Sauté cabbage in butter until cabbage begins to color slightly.
3. Mix in lemon juice, sugar, salt, and pepper well. When hot again, cover and turn down heat to low.
4. Cook cabbage in its own steam 20 minutes, and then check to make sure there is a little liquid in bottom of pan. If not, add another tablespoon butter.
5. Cook 20 minutes more. Stir in nuts and serve.

Serves 8

Hint: For a more pronounced sweet-and-sour taste, use more lemon juice and sugar.

ONIONS WITH RICE STUFFING

6 medium onions
½ cup butter
1½ cups cooked rice
dash of salt
dash of pepper
dash of celery seed
½ cup finely chopped
  cashews
4 tablespoons grated
  Parmesan cheese
1 can (12 ounce) tomato
  sauce, thinned with ¼
  cup chicken broth or
  sherry

1. Preheat oven to 375°.
2. Peel onions, keeping root end intact so onion case can be stuffed. Cut off thick slice from top.
3. In boiling salted water or chicken broth, cook onion cases and slices 15 minutes or until barely tender. Drain. Scoop out center and turn cases upside down.
4. In large skillet, melt 2 tablespoons butter. Chop onion centers and slices cut from top. Sauté them in butter until tender and hot.
5. Combine rice with salt, pepper, remaining butter, celery seed, about 1 cup onion centers, and nuts. Fill onion shells with combination. Sprinkle cheese and 1 tablespoon prepared tomato sauce on each.
6. Place remaining sauce in 12 x 9-inch baking dish which is at least 2 inches deep. Put stuffed onions on top of sauce. Bake 15 minutes or until hot. Serve with sauce.

Serves 6

 ## BAKED STUFFED TOMATOES

6 large tomatoes
5½ tablespoons butter
½ cup finely chopped
  onion
1 small garlic clove,
  pressed
1½ cups chopped cooked
  spinach
½ teaspoon thyme
1 scant teaspoon salt
½ cup seasoned bread
  crumbs
1 cup coarsely chopped
  cashews
2 eggs, slightly beaten
½ cup grated Parmesan
  cheese

1. Preheat oven to 350°.
2. Remove stem end of tomatoes and scoop out seeds; turn upside down to drain.
3. In large saucepan, melt 4 tablespoons butter. Sauté onion and garlic in butter until clear and tender.
4. Add spinach, thyme, salt, bread crumbs, and nuts to onion mixture, reserving a few nuts to mix with cheese for topping. Mix well.
5. Add eggs. Cook until eggs are firm, stirring constantly.
6. Stuff tomatoes with spinach mixture. Sprinkle cheese and remaining nuts over top, and dot with remaining butter.
7. Bake 10 minutes.

Serves 6

NUTTED SWEET-AND-SOUR PORK

2 tablespoons peanut oil
2 pounds boned pork loin,
    cut in strips
2 medium green peppers,
    cut in 1-inch squares
½ cup sliced green onions
1 can apricot halves,
    drained, juice reserved
½ cup whole roasted
    cashews
⅓ cup vinegar
¼ cup soy sauce
1 large garlic clove, minced
¼ teaspoon ginger
2 tablespoons cornstarch
¼ cup water
4 cups hot cooked rice
½ cup chopped roasted
    cashews

1. In large skillet, heat peanut oil. Brown pork in oil.
2. Add green pepper and green onions to pork. Cook several minutes.
3. Add reserved apricot juice to pork with whole nuts, vinegar, soy sauce, garlic, and ginger. Cook over low heat 45 minutes or until pork is tender, covered, stirring occasionally.
4. Blend together cornstarch and water. Stir into pork mixture. Cook, stirring until thickened.
5. Add apricots to pork mixture; heat.
6. Combine rice and chopped nuts.
7. Serve pork over rice.

Serves 6–8

 MEDITERRANEAN CHICKEN

1 tablespoon butter
1 tablespoon finely
    chopped onion
½ cup chopped celery
1 package (10 ounce)
    frozen green beans,
    French style
1 tablespoon chopped
    pimiento
2 cups chicken, cooked,
    diced
2 cans (10½ ounce) cream
    of mushroom soup,
    undiluted
½ teaspoon oregano
white pepper to taste
⅔ cup cashews
1 tablespoon minced
    parsley (optional)

1. In 2- or 3-quart saucepan, melt butter. Add onion, celery, and beans. Simmer over low heat about 15 minutes until beans are tender, covered, stirring occasionally.
2. Add pimiento, chicken, soup, oregano, and white pepper. Cook 10 minutes to blend flavors, stirring as needed to prevent sticking.
3. Stir nuts into chicken dish. Sprinkle with parsley before serving.

Serves 4

GOLDEN CASHEW CHICKEN

1 frying chicken, cut up
½ cup finely chopped
  cashews
1½ cups cereal flakes
1 teaspoon celery seed
½ teaspoon garlic salt
¼ teaspoon salt
dash of pepper
4 tablespoons minced
  parsley
1 egg
2 tablespoons milk
½ cup pancake mix
4 tablespoons butter

1. Steam chicken 30 minutes.
2. Preheat oven to 375°.
3. Mix together nuts, cereal, celery seed, garlic salt, salt, pepper, and parsley.
4. Mix together egg and milk.
5. Coat chicken pieces with pancake mix; dip into egg mixture; and dip into nut mixture.
6. In shallow baking dish with lid, melt butter. Arrange chicken in single layer. Bake 45 minutes, covered.

Serves 4

 ## CREAMED SWEETBREADS WITH SHERRY

2 pairs sweetbreads
1 teaspoon lemon juice
salt to taste
pepper to taste
4 tablespoons butter
½ cup small mushroom
  buttons
1 teaspoon finely chopped
  green onions, with tops
4 tablespoons sherry
2 egg yolks
1 cup heavy cream
salt to taste
paprika to taste
dash of curry powder
1 cup chopped toasted
  cashews

1. Parboil sweetbreads. Cover sweetbreads with ice-cold water and soak 30 minutes; remove loose membranes. Just ¾ teaspoon lemon juice in cold water will keep sweetbreads snowy white.
2. Cut sweetbreads in medium slices. Season with salt and pepper.
3. In large skillet, melt butter. Sauté sweetbreads in butter 3 minutes. Add drained mushrooms. Sauté 5 minutes.
4. Add green onions and sherry. Simmer 15 minutes.
5. Blend together egg yolks, remaining ¼ teaspoon lemon juice, and 2 tablespoons cream.
6. Remove sweetbreads from heat and slowly stir in egg yolk mixture, stirring gently from bottom of pan. Place in oven-proof dish.
7. Whip remaining cream and flavor with salt, paprika, and curry powder. Spread over sweetbreads.
8. Set dish under flame of broiler 1 minute to glaze. Make border of nuts. Serve.

Serves 6

STUFFED ROCK CORNISH HENS

6 rock Cornish hens
4 teaspoons salt
1 teaspoon pepper
2 cups raw wild rice
1 can (10½ ounce) chicken broth
1 cup water
½ cup butter
¾ cup chopped onion
10 chicken livers
1 cup chopped cashews
½ cup Dubonnet

1. Season hens with 2½ teaspoons salt and ¾ teaspoon pepper.
2. Wash rice in several changes of water. In large saucepan with lid, combine rice with broth and water; bring to a boil, covered. Cook over low heat 25 minutes or until tender but firm.
3. In small skillet, melt 3 tablespoons butter. Sauté onion in butter 10 minutes. Remove.
4. Meanwhile, in small skillet, melt 2 tablespoons butter. Sauté livers in butter 7 minutes. Chop livers coarsely.
5. Into rice, mix onion, livers, nuts, ¼ cup Dubonnet, remaining salt, and remaining pepper. Correct seasoning. Cool.
6. Preheat oven to 350°.
7. Stuff hens with rice mixture; close openings with skewers or thread.
8. In baking pan, melt remaining butter. Arrange hens in this pan and baste them with this butter. Roast 1 hour, adding remaining Dubonnet after 30 minutes and basting frequently thereafter.

Serves 6

 TURKEY WITH SOUR CREAM

6 thick slices cooked turkey breast
1½ cups turkey broth
4 tablespoons butter
1 garlic clove, minced
2 tablespoons chopped green onions
2 tablespoons flour
3 tablespoons sherry
½ cup chopped cashews
1 teaspoon seasoned salt
1 teaspoon marjoram
¾ cup sour cream
3 tablespoons grated mild cheddar cheese
¼ cup whole cashews
parsley sprigs to garnish

1. Warm turkey slices in broth. Remove turkey and set aside on warm platter.
2. In large skillet with lid, melt butter. Sauté garlic and green onions in butter 3 minutes. Stir in flour until well blended.
3. Add broth and sherry. Over low heat, cook until mixture is hot enough to boil, stirring constantly.
4. To skillet, add turkey, chopped nuts, seasoned salt, and marjoram. Simmer 10 minutes, covered.
5. Return turkey to platter.
6. Stir sour cream into sauce in skillet and blend, stirring rapidly over low heat. Keep heat as low as possible at this point; sauce must not boil after sour cream is added.
7. Pour sauce over turkey, sprinkle cheese on top, and garnish with whole nuts and parsley sprigs.

Serves 6

NUTTY TURKEY MOLÉ

¼ pound large, dark red, dried chilies (mulato)
¼ pound long, thin, red, dried chilies (pasillo)
½ pound wide, light red, dried chilies (ancho)
5 cups boiling water
½ cup finely chopped almonds, blanched
1 cup finely chopped toasted cashews
5 tablespoons butter
½ cup sesame oil
¼ teaspoon ground cloves
1 tablespoon cinnamon
1 tablespoon sugar
2 tablespoons unsweetened chocolate, melted
1 small turkey (about 8 pounds)
½ pound pork loin, diced
7 cups cold water

1. Soak chilies in boiling water 30 minutes; drain. Cut open chilies and discard seeds.
2. Finely chop pods. In large skillet, melt 3 tablespoons butter. Fry pods, almonds, and cashews in butter 5 minutes.
3. Add sesame oil, cloves, cinnamon, sugar, and chocolate. Fry a few minutes. Add half of boiling water, stirring until blended.
4. Cut turkey in pieces for serving. In another large skillet, melt remaining butter. Fry turkey with pork in butter until browned.
5. In large pot with lid, combine turkey and pork with nut mixture and add remaining boiling water.
6. Simmer 1 hour, covered, adding cold water whenever it begins to boil and stirring occasionally.

Serves 12

Hint: Mexican and South American cooks prefer lard to butter.

SHRIMP CURRY

4 tablespoons butter
1 large onion, finely chopped
½ cup finely chopped apple
½ cup finely chopped celery
1½ cups water
2 tablespoons curry powder
salt to taste
pepper to taste
2 cups cream
3 pounds shrimp, boiled, peeled, deveined
¾ cup chopped cashews, browned in butter

1. In large skillet, melt butter. Sauté onion, apple, and celery in butter.
2. Add water. Let mixture simmer gently until apple and celery are tender and most liquid has evaporated.
3. Stir curry powder, salt, and pepper into mixture. Add cream and shrimp.
4. Cook gently until cream sauce has thickened. Stir in nuts.
5. Serve with plenty of well-cooked rice. Have small bowls of grated coconut, chutney, chopped cashews, and pickle relish for your guests.

Serves 6–8

LASAGNE

8 ounces wide lasagne
  noodles
6 ounces cream cheese
2 cups sour cream
½ cup chopped onion
1 pound ground beef
½ pound ground pork
1 can (6 ounce) tomato
  paste
6 tablespoons red wine
½ cup sliced fresh
  mushrooms
½ teaspoon oregano
½ teaspoon sweet basil
⅛ teaspoon cayenne
1 teaspoon salt
¼ teaspoon pepper
1 cup chopped cashews
½ cup grated Romano
  cheese

1. Preheat oven to 350°.
2. Cook noodles according to package directions; set aside.
3. Blend cream cheese, sour cream, and onion; set aside.
4. In large skillet, brown ground beef and ground pork, crumbling with a fork. Drain excess fat.
5. Stir tomato paste, wine, mushrooms, oregano, basil, cayenne, salt, and pepper into meat. Cook 5 minutes.
6. In buttered casserole, layer cheese mixture, noodles, nuts, and meat mixture. Repeat layers and sprinkle top with Romano cheese. Bake 1 hour.

Serves 6

 ## TURKISH RICE

⅓ cup butter
1 cup raw rice
½ cup chopped cashews
1 can (10½ ounce) beef
  consommé

1. Preheat oven to 250°.
2. In small saucepan, melt butter. Brown rice in butter.
3. Mix nuts and consommé into rice well. Put in baking dish. Cook 1 hour.

Serves 4

Hint: You may add diced chicken.

SPICED APPLE-CASHEW MUFFINS

2 cups flour
3 teaspoons baking
  powder
⅓ teaspoon sugar
½ teaspoon salt
½ teaspoon nutmeg
½ teaspoon cinnamon
1 egg
¾ cup milk
4 tablespoons butter,
  melted
1 cup diced apples
½ cup coarsely ground
  salted cashews

1. Preheat oven to 425°.
2. Sift together flour, baking powder, sugar, salt, nutmeg, and cinnamon.
3. In large bowl, beat egg. Stir in milk. Mix in sifted dry ingredients.
4. Stir butter into batter. Fold in apples and nuts.
5. Fill buttered muffin pans ⅔ full. Bake 20–30 minutes.

Makes 1 dozen

 ## BRAN MUFFINS

2 tablespoons butter
3 tablespoons sugar
1 egg
¾ cup milk
1 cup bran
1 cup flour
½ teaspoon salt
2 teaspoons baking
  powder
1 cup chopped cashews

1. Preheat oven to 425°.
2. In large bowl, cream butter and sugar. Beat in egg well.
3. Stir milk into butter mixture, then stir in bran.
4. Sift flour with salt and baking powder; stir sifted dry ingredients into butter mixture until just moistened. Quickly fold in nuts.
5. Fill buttered muffin pans ⅔ full. Bake 20–30 minutes.

Makes 1 dozen

Hint: For Fruit-Bran Muffins, add ½–¾ cup raisins or chopped pitted dates.

CASHEW CAKE À L'ORANGE

½ cup butter

1 cup sugar

3 egg yolks

4 tablespoons freshly
grated orange rind

2 cups sifted cake flour

½ teaspoon salt

3 teaspoons baking
powder

½ cup orange juice

3 egg whites, stiffly beaten

1 cup chopped cashews

favorite filling and frosting

1. Preheat oven to 350°.

2. In large bowl, cream butter and sugar. Beat in egg yolks and orange rind well.

3. Sift together flour, salt, and baking powder.

4. To creamed mixture, add sifted dry ingredients alternately with orange juice, beating well after each addition. Fold in egg whites.

5. Pour batter into 2 well-buttered 9-inch round layer pans. Sprinkle nuts over top of each layer. Bake 35 minutes. Cool on a rack. Put cake together with favorite filling and frosting.

Serves 8

Hint: This cake is delicious with orange-flavored custard filling between layers and frosted with orange-flavored frosting.

CHESTNUT

Castanea sativa

CHESTNUT

ONCE THE FOOD OF royalty, known as early as Greek and Roman times, chestnuts have spurred two contrasting theories of their origin. Some historians claim that they are from Castanea, a city of Thessaly, Greece; others that they grew in and around Sardis (the Greeks called them Sardian nuts). The Romans brought them to England. Chestnuts are supposed to have nourished and saved Zenophon's army during its retreat.

In Britain, chestnuts are called Spanish chestnuts; and all over the world, they are known by the French name marron. The local French name for chestnuts in general is *chatâigne*.

Many chestnut trees reach a venerable old age and are revered in a number of European countries. One on the grounds of Torwith Castle is said to be 1,000 years old. The Chinese ate and cooked with chestnuts in the 6th century A.D. By the 11th century, chestnuts appeared in France and Spain. In Catholic history, they were shown special favor by being used as a food on St. Simon's day; on St. Martin's feast day, chestnuts are distributed to the poor.

The chestnut grows up inside a prickly husk. Some of the nuts develop with 2 or 3 in a shell, but the finest type are single marrons. They used to grow extensively in the United States, but suffered a severe blight at the end of the 19th century when almost all chestnut trees were destroyed. Italy and France are now the main source for both fresh and dried chestnuts. In Great Britain, chestnuts are small and hard to shell yet still highly prized.

Unlike the other nuts in this book, the chestnut has a mealy-floury texture and no crunch or crackle. It is important as a food staple, particularly in the Apennine and Pyrenees mountainous areas of southern Europe, where yearly festivals celebrate the harvesting of the chestnuts. Chestnut flour is used extensively. Although their primary function is often in various pastries and as a confection, their general popularity is growing. They are being used boiled, roasted, steamed, and mashed, either by themselves or in combinations with other foods. Poultry stuffing has always been a natural for the addition of chestnuts, and they have a historic affinity with Brussels sprouts.

Chestnuts have a rich, slightly sweet taste. They are available in the shell; in jars or tins candied (glacé); puréed; as a spread; and whole, in simple syrup. A universal European favorite, especially in the streets of London, hot roasted chestnuts appear in profusion during the Thanksgiving and Christmas holidays. In some parts of Italy, they function as a substitute for the standard polenta. Nowadays nearly all chestnuts used for eating are imported from Italy and France. A new, small, soft-shelled chestnut appeared on the scene from the Orient, which is delicious and sweet when roasted and hot. A food both elegant and basic, the chestnut has been known and enjoyed for generations by royalty and common folk alike.

Chestnuts seem to be almost universally known and grown, given identifying names in special regions. *Castanea dentata* is the name of the American chestnut, so tragically devastated by blight; *Castanea sativa* is the name of the European chestnut, the one we use for the most part; *Castanea mollissima* is the name of the Chinese chestnut; and *Castanea crenata*, the name of the Japanese. An important worldwide food, the chestnut has come to the rescue, enabling whole communities to survive during periods of great food shortages.

 PURCHASE

Fresh chestnuts should be plump, shiny brown, and firm to the touch. They are available in most markets during fall and winter.

Dried chestnuts are available in specialty stores; they last a long time and after they are soaked and then cooked, they can be used just like fresh nuts.

 PREPARATION

There are several favorite ways of shelling chestnuts. With a sharp knife, cut a little cross in either the domed side or flat side. Cover with boiling water 15 minutes; remove from water; drain on paper towel; and proceed to remove shell, trying to keep chestnut whole—or boil 10 minutes to permit removal of shell.

Or arrange chestnuts in large frying pan in single layer with 1 or 2 tablespoons butter. Place in preheated 350° oven 20–25 minutes, shaking every 5 or 7 minutes. If you want them roasted for munching, keep them in at least 20 minutes longer—their flavor increases as does their tenderness. There are special chestnut pans with many holes or small openings and a long handle to shake over the fire to make roasting easy. Sometimes these roasted chestnuts, however prepared, can be shelled and peeled (blanched) without further bother, and will come out white and whole, ready for special use.

To blanch in general. Drop the shelled chestnuts in boiling water a few minutes; remove them with a slotted spoon. If it is hard to get the inner skin off with a knife or your fingers, drop chestnuts into cold water and back again into hot water, which seems to loosen the skin.

Most recipes are quite specific and will direct you, once you have shelled the chestnuts. Among the ways they can be cooked are boiling in milk, water, soup stock; sautéing in butter; kept whole, chopped, or pureed.

To use canned chestnuts. These are imported and fairly expensive, but save time and simplify cooking for special needs. Whole chestnuts, either in syrup or glacé (candied), can be found in specialty shops; spooned over ice creams or puddings, they make glamorous desserts.

Prepared chestnuts, whole and broken combined, come in 1- and 2-pound cans; drained, they are perfect to add to poultry stuffing and for other culinary uses. Puréed chestnuts in cans are ideal for recipes calling for unsweetened chestnuts.

Chestnut spread is a relatively new product in the United States, from France; it is made with chestnuts, sugar, and glucose. Sweetened, it is a perfect addition to desserts calling for chestnuts.

 AMOUNTS

1 pound chestnuts-in-the-shell equals 2½ cups nutmeats.

2½ pounds chestnuts-in-the-shell will serve as a vegetable for about 6 people, prepared in your favorite way.

 STORAGE

Fresh chestnuts are perishable at room temperature but keep several months in the refrigerator in loosely covered containers or ventilated plastic bags.

Freeze shelled, blanched chestnuts, whole or chopped, for longer storage, packed in tightly closed freezer containers. Use in cooking without defrosting.

ROASTED CHESTNUT SOUP

1 pound chestnuts in shell
4 tablespoons butter
4 green onions, chopped,
   or chives, chopped
3 cups chicken broth or
   beef broth
2 cups milk
1 tablespoon flour
salt to taste
pepper to taste
½ cup heavy cream

1. Preheat oven to 400°.

2. With point of sharp fruit knife, cut an X in skin of each nut. Roast nuts in oven about 15 minutes until tender—test with skewer.

3. When nuts are cool enough, peel off outer shell and remove inner skins (blanch). Chop nuts.

4. In large skillet, melt 2 tablespoons butter. Sauté nuts and onions in butter 6 minutes. Stir in chicken broth and milk and bring to a boil.

5. In small saucepan, make roux by blending remaining butter and flour. Cook 3 minutes.

6. Gradually add some soup mixture to roux, stirring. Pour this thickened mixture into hot soup, mixing thoroughly. Season with salt and pepper, stirring well.

7. Mix in cream thoroughly. Serve at once.

Serves 6

 CHESTNUTS IN CONSOMMÉ

1 pound chestnuts,
   shelled, blanched
1 stalk celery
1 can (10½ ounce)
   consommé, diluted with
   equal amount of water
2 tablespoons butter
   (optional)
salt to taste
pepper to taste

1. In large saucepan with a lid, cover nuts and celery with diluted consommé. Cook slowly until tender, covered.

2. Remove nuts from liquid and place in serving dish. Add butter, salt, and pepper to nuts. Serve as a vegetable.

Makes 1 pound

CHESTNUT PUREE

3–3½ pounds chestnuts,
   shelled, blanched
1 small celery root
salt to taste
1 cup boiling milk
2 tablespoons butter
3 tablespoons cream
pepper to taste

1. In large saucepan, put freshly blanched nuts with celery root, salt, and water to cover. Cook 30 minutes or until both nuts and celery root are tender.

2. Drain nuts and celery root and puree them in blender. Gradually add boiling milk bit by bit.

3. Blend in butter, cream, and pepper.

Serves 8

Hint: This is delicious served with poultry or roast pork.

 ## BRUSSELS SPROUTS WITH CHESTNUTS

4 tablespoons butter
2 teaspoons sugar
1 cup cooked chestnuts,
   blanched
4 cups boiled Brussels
   sprouts, sautéed in butter
⅓ cup chicken or veal
   stock

1. In large saucepan, cook butter and sugar until brown, blending thoroughly.

2. Add nuts and sauté until golden, stirring well.

3. Combine sprouts and stock with nut mixture; stir. Serve hot as a vegetable.

Serves 6–8

CHESTNUT STROGANOFF

3 tablespoons butter
1½ pounds fillet of beef,
  cut in 1-inch strips
2 tablespoons flour
½ teaspoon onion salt
½ teaspoon celery salt
½ teaspoon paprika
¼ teaspoon salt
1¼ cups beef bouillon or
  beef broth
½ cup sour cream
1 tablespoon sherry
1 cup mashed cooked
  chestnuts

1. In large skillet, melt 1 tablespoon butter. Over moderate heat, lightly brown beef in butter. Drain off any excess fat.

2. In medium saucepan, melt remaining butter. Blend in flour, onion salt, celery salt, paprika, and salt. Cook 3 minutes. Slowly add bouillon, stirring constantly. Cook until smooth and bubbly, stirring. Remove from heat.

3. Blend in sour cream, sherry, and nuts.

4. Add nut sauce to beef. Heat just until mixture bubbles, stirring constantly. Serve over potatoes, rice, or noodles.

Serves 4–6

 ## BRAISED OXTAIL WITH CHESTNUTS

2 oxtails
3 tablespoons butter
3 cups rich brown stock
1 onion, sliced, browned
1 can (14½ ounce) tomatoes
½ cup cooked barley
1 green pepper, sliced
3 carrots, sliced
2 teaspoons salt
6 peppercorns
pinch of basil
pinch of marjoram
pinch of thyme
1 teaspoon Worcestershire
  sauce
¾ cup claret wine
1½ cups chestnuts,
  shelled, blanched,
  braised in consommé

1. Preheat oven to 325°.

2. Cut oxtails in pieces at joints. Soak them 1–2 hours in salted water. Drain, rinse, and dry them.

3. In large skillet, melt butter. Quickly brown oxtails in butter. Put them into baking dish with a lid. In same browning skillet, add brown stock, browned onion, tomatoes, barley, green pepper, carrots, salt, peppercorns, basil, marjoram, thyme, Worcestershire sauce, and wine; bring to a boil. Pour over oxtails and cover.

4. Bake 3–4 hours, covered, testing tenderness of meat with a fork.

5. Remove joints, vegetables, and as much of barley as you can. Strain liquid, skim fat, and recombine liquid with other ingredients.

6. Just before serving, add nuts.

Serves 6

Hint: Consommé, bouillon, or commercial brown gravy can substitute for homemade brown stock.

CHESTNUT SOUFFLÉ

2 tablespoons butter
2 tablespoons flour
1 cup milk
1 cup unsweetened
  chestnut puree
½ cup sugar
2 squares (1 ounce) bitter
  chocolate, melted
4 eggs, separated
1 teaspoon vanilla
1 cup heavy cream, whipped,
  sweetened (optional)

1. In medium saucepan, melt butter. Stir in flour and cook 2–3 minutes. Set aside.
2. With rotary beater, beat milk with nut puree and sugar until smooth.
3. Gradually stir nut mixture into butter and flour. Cook over low heat, stirring constantly until thickened.
4. Preheat oven to 375°.
5. Melt chocolate and stir into nut mixture.
6. In medium bowl, beat egg yolks. Gradually stir hot sauce into egg yolks. Cool.
7. In small bowl, beat egg whites until stiff but not dry. Fold egg whites and vanilla into nut mixture.
8. Sprinkle well-buttered 1½-quart soufflé dish with sugar; pour in soufflé mixture.
9. Place soufflé dish in pan of hot water in oven. Bake 40–45 minutes. Serve at once with whipped cream.

Serves 6

 CHOCOLATE CHESTNUT CAKE

1 package (18½ ounce)
  devil's food cake mix
1 cup water
2 eggs
2 tablespoons freshly
  grated orange rind
1 cup drained, chopped
  canned chestnuts
1 cup heavy cream
whole chestnuts in syrup,
  drained, for garnish,
  with 2 tablespoons
  syrup reserved

1. Preheat oven to 325°.
2. In large bowl, combine cake mix, water, and eggs. Beat until smooth and well blended.
3. Fold in orange rind and chopped nuts.
4. Pour batter into buttered-and-floured 2-quart fancy mold. Bake 45–50 minutes until cake feels firm to touch.
5. Unmold cake and cool on a rack.
6. Place cake on serving platter. Whip cream until stiff; fold in 2 tablespoons reserved syrup. Pipe cream around cake with pastry tube, and spread over top.
7. Garnish cake with whole nuts.

Serves 8–10

Hint: Glacé chestnuts can substitute for chestnuts in syrup.

CHESTNUT ROLL

¾ cup sifted cake flour
1 teaspoon baking powder
¼ teaspoon salt
4 eggs
¾ cup sugar
1 teaspoon vanilla
¼ cup powdered sugar
1 recipe chestnut butter
   cream
½ cup shaved bitter
   chocolate

1. Preheat oven to 400°.

2. Line bottom of 12 x 10 x 1-inch jelly-roll pan with waxed paper or foil trimmed to fit; butter paper.

3. Sift together flour, baking powder, and salt.

4. In large bowl, beat eggs until light and foamy. Continue beating, adding sugar slowly until very thick and at least doubled in bulk. This will take about 10 minutes with an electric mixer.

5. Sprinkle sifted dry ingredients over egg mixture and fold in gently. Add vanilla to batter.

6. Pour batter into prepared pan, spreading evenly with rubber spatula. Bake 12–15 minutes until cake is delicately browned and top springs back when touched lightly.

7. Remove cake from oven. Loosen cake around edges with a knife and turn cake out on a tea towel sprinkled evenly with powdered sugar. Working quickly while cake is still warm, carefully remove paper. Cut off crisp cake edges with sharp knife.

8. Starting at long side, gently roll up cake along with towel, keeping cake from sticking to itself. Place roll, towel and all, on a rack to cool.

9. When cool, unroll cake and remove towel.

10. Spread cake top with half of chestnut butter cream.

11. Roll cake again. Place it on serving platter. Frost outside of roll with remaining chestnut butter cream.

12. Decorate top with chocolate.

Serves 8

 ## CHESTNUT BUTTER CREAM

2 cans (6 ounce) marrons
   glacés or 1 jar (10 ounce)
   marrons in vanilla
   syrup, drained
1 cup sweet butter, softened
½ cup sugar
⅓ cup light corn syrup
3 egg yolks
¼ cup dark rum

1. Finely chop marrons.

2. Cut butter in small pieces.

3. In small saucepan, combine sugar and corn syrup. Cook over medium heat until mixture comes to full, bubbling boil, stirring constantly. Remove from heat.

4. In large bowl, beat egg yolks until foamy and lemon colored.

5. Gradually add hot syrup, continuing to beat until mixture is cool. Beat in butter early in cooling process.

6. Stir in rum and marrons.

Serves 6–8

Hint: This is delicious as filling and frosting. It is especially tasty decorated with shaved bitter chocolate. Glacé chestnuts or preserved chestnuts are often called marrons.

COCONUT

Cocos nucifera

COCONUT

THE COCONUT IS the fruit of the coconut palm tree, *Cocos nucifera*. Considered native to tropical South America, in prehistoric times it was carried across the Pacific to the South Sea Islands. A far-flung traveler flourishing in many tropical and semitropical sites, the coconut is now grown in groves in the West Indies, Ceylon, and parts of India. The coconut industry in Hawaii and the Philippines is tremendous and still increasing. Some coco palms can be found in southern Florida too.

The coconut palm reaches great heights, straight, without branches but with a canopy of palm leaves at its crest, underneath which the coconuts grow close to the trunk. There are conflicting stories about the origin of the name coconut, and even the origin of the fruit itself. One well-documented source says that Vasco da Gama brought the coconut to Portugal from India in 1500, and it was given the name coconut stemming from the word known both in Portugal and Spain as coco, which refers to ghost or boogeyman. The strange appearance of the coconut in its shell with its "eyes" might have seemed like a boogeyman. Other sources say the word coco means grimace and, pushing its meaning still further, monkey, and that the coconut was so named because it somewhat resembles a monkey's face. Still another theory is that the Portuguese word for monkey, *macaco*, could have some bearing on it since monkeys have been professionally trained to climb the trees to harvest the coconuts in Brazil.

The harvested coconut is encased in a thick, furry, slightly straw-colored brown husk, which is angular and strangely modern looking. This husk is usually removed before the coconuts are exported; but at Thanksgiving and Christmas time, coconuts can be found still in their husks even in the supermarkets. Once the husk is removed, usually by hammer, the coconut emerges in its hard, round, brown shell, lightly covered with furry hair; at the stem end, there are three little declivities known as eyes.

Coconuts grow in bunches but ripen one at a time, falling to the ground when fully ripened. Mostly for native consumption, some are harvested green; these are especially delicious—the custardy insides can be eaten with a spoon. There is liquid inside all fresh coconuts; in the case of the green coconut, it is wonderfully rich, icy cold, and fragrant. This is the true coconut cream. Mature coconuts contain coconut water or liquid; both coconut milk and cream can be made from the actual coconut meat.

PURCHASE

Coconuts are available in most supermarkets, specialty shops, and health food stores. They are seldom seen with their outer husk except during the Christmas holiday. However, for children, it certainly would be fun to use a hammer to remove the husk and then examine the coconut as it emerges in its shell. If there is any doubt about the freshness of the coconut inside, ask the grocer to help remove the husk; if the husk is old and soft, it can be quite a chore to get it off.

Whether you are purchasing coconut in the husk or just in the shell, pick it up to test for weight—it should be heavy for its size. Shake it to hear a good slosh of liquid inside—otherwise it may be old and dried.

When you are buying coconut in the shell, be sure the eyes are neither moldy nor wet.

Coconut is packaged in plastic bags and in hermetically sealed cans. It is available shredded or threadlike especially for garnish, or flaked when intended for pies and cakes. Moist or very moist coconut comes in cans southern style; both are sweetened and most closely resemble fresh coconut.

 **PREPARATION**

Once the coconut is out of its husk, insert a sharp icepick or similar instrument in the softest of the three eyes; out of that opening, pour the liquid into a bowl and set it aside for later drinking or use as flavoring.

To obtain meat.　There are four methods to get to the coconut meat:

The easiest is to put the coconut on a baking sheet in a preheated 350° oven and leave it in the oven about 30 minutes until you see that the coconut has cracked open. Remove it from the oven, cool, and cut out the meat from the shell, using a knife, sharp pliable spatula, fork, or sturdy spoon. If you are impatient, you can take the coconut out of the oven after 15 minutes and tap it with a hammer.

Another system is to hold the coconut in your hand and estimate a line that will be a circle around its center. Hit the coconut with a hammer on that line, turning it; when you end up at the beginning of your hammering, the coconut should open.

Freezing the coconut for an hour prepares it for easy hammer opening.

There is still a fourth more meticulous way if you want to preserve the shells for serving or cooking and need an even edge. Have your butcher or grocer saw the coconut in two after having drained the liquid.

To prepare meat.　With a vegetable peeler, take off the brown inner skin. There is no other way to "blanch" the coconut. Use a hand grater, blender, or food processor to grate or shred the coconut meat. The coconut is now ready to use in all recipes, including my recipe for making milk and cream. To toast, spread it on a baking sheet in a 300° oven until it is golden color, stirring so it does not burn. Cool toasted coconut and put in an airtight jar.

The coconut tree is easily the most versatile tree around. There are infinite uses for the fruit, the wood, the flower, and even the roots! Coconuts have special properties suited to the many small tropical islands in the middle of the South Seas where they grow. Unhusked, they are buoyant in water and impenetrable, so that the nut itself remains safe. Their interior liquid stays cool and it can sustain anyone stranded without liquid. The fruit, ripe or unripe, raw or cooked, provides plentiful food. The terminal bud, called palm cabbage, is considered a delicacy. Coconut oil has multiple uses in cooking, industry, and in the field of pharmacy. The outside husks furnish coir, a fiber with varied usage for making matting, bristles, and rope. The fermented unopened flower stalks and sap are the basis of liqueurs. The coconut shells provide bowls, ladles, and ornamental containers. The leaves have multiple uses in house making, and even the roots are both chewed as narcotics and used ground up similar to tea and coffee, especially in southern India. The tree can satisfy almost all one's needs in its native land. The trees bear fruit around the seventh year; when well-cultivated, they produce 60–200 coconuts per year.

Copra is the dried or desiccated coconut from which the oil is made. The dried coconuts are available in our markets in cellophane packages or in hermetically sealed cans, sweetened or unsweetened. The domestically processed is usually sweetened; that labeled southern style is exceptionally moist and most closely resembles fresh coconut. In your cooking, be certain to take into account whether the coconut you use is sweetened or natural.

Whatever the form, coconut meat makes a luscious addition to any dish: cooked in food itself, sprinkled as a tasty and pretty garnish, or topping a fresh coconut cake, it is beautiful and equally delicious.

 STORAGE

Keep the plain white grated coconut in an airtight jar in the refrigerator and use within a few days because the coconut is quite perishable and gets a peculiar flavor quickly.

Tint coconut by tossing it with a few drops of food coloring mixed with a few drops of water and then spreading the tinted coconut on a piece of waxed paper until it is dry enough for storage, again in an airtight container placed in the refrigerator.

To keep coconut longer than three days, freeze it. This way the coconut is good indefinitely.

With or without meat in them, refrigerate shells.

COCONUT MILK

4 cups freshly grated
coconut
2 cups boiling water or
scalded milk

1. Tightly tie grated coconut in double piece of cheesecloth; place in deep bowl.
2. Pour boiling water over cheesecloth. Let coconut soak 30 minutes.
3. Squeeze coconut through cheesecloth bag, twisting and wringing to remove all liquid. Discard coconut meat or save it to use for decorations.
4. Place liquid in refrigerator, covered. Next day lift off thick top part, which is the "cream." Balance is coconut milk. Use each for their special recipes.

Makes scant 2 cups

Hint: Three cups boiling water can be used with same technique to provide more liquid, albeit less rich and less tasty.

Canned coconut can also be used: In medium saucepan, pour 2 cups milk over 1 standard can or package of coconut. Slowly bring to boil. Remove from heat and let stand 30 minutes. Strain through double thickness of cheesecloth.

TROPICAL COCONUT SOUP

4 cups freshly grated
coconut
2 cups boiling water
2 chopped green onions,
pressed through garlic
press
1 bay leaf
2 tablespoons butter,
melted
1½ teaspoons curry
powder (optional)
2 cups chicken broth,
homemade or canned,
undiluted
1 heaping tablespoon
cornstarch
½ bunch cilantro, washed,
dried

1. Soak coconut in boiling water 30 minutes.
2. Pour liquid into a bowl through fine strainer or double thickness cheesecloth, squeezing mixture to get out all liquid. Discard coconut residue. Remaining liquid is coconut cream to be used in soup.
3. In small saucepan, sauté green onions and bay leaf in melted butter. Remove bay leaf. Stir in curry powder.
4. In another small saucepan, mix 3 tablespoons chicken broth with cornstarch, stirring until smooth.
5. Heat remaining broth. Gradually add to cornstarch mixture, stirring constantly. Put in blender with sautéed green onions and blend until smooth.
6. Add coconut milk to mixture and blend once again. Correct seasoning.
7. Pour soup into saucepan, add washed cilantro, and heat thoroughly.
8. Serve in individual soup dishes with 1 or 2 sprigs of cilantro.

Serves 6

PORK CHOPS HAWAIIAN

4 medium pork chops
seasoned salt to taste
flour to dust
¼ cup butter
1 can (4 ounce) crushed
 pineapple
2 tablespoons lemon juice
3 tablespoons Chinese
 plum sauce
1 tablespoon cornstarch
¼ cup shredded coconut
2 tablespoons chopped
 almonds

1. Sprinkle pork chops with seasoned salt; dust with flour.

2. In large skillet with a lid, melt butter. Pan-fry pork chops in butter until golden brown.

3. Add 2 tablespoons water and cover. Cook slowly on top of stove or in 325° oven 50 minutes, covered. Meanwhile, make sauce.

4. Drain pineapple and add water to pineapple syrup to make 1 cup liquid.

5. In small saucepan, combine pineapple liquid, lemon juice, and plum sauce. Add a little water to cornstarch to make a smooth paste; pour into pineapple mixture.

6. Cook sauce until smooth and clear, stirring constantly. As sauce starts to thicken, add pineapple.

7. Preheat oven to 350°.

8. When pork chops are cooked, put them in 12 x 7-inch flat-bottom casserole. Pour sauce over them.

9. Bake 15 minutes until flavor penetrates pork chops.

10. Remove from oven. Sprinkle with coconut and almonds. Serve with boiled white rice.

Serves 4

 ## CURRIED SHRIMP IN COCONUT SHELLS

6 small fresh coconuts
⅓ cup butter
1 onion, chopped
1 stalk celery, chopped
1 tart apple, cored, chopped
6 tablespoons flour
2 tablespoons curry
 powder
2 cups chicken broth
1 cup heavy cream
¼ cup slivered almonds
3 cups medium shrimp

1. Saw coconuts about ⅓ from tops to form deep cups. Refrigerate until ready to use, then wrap in foil and bake at 350° about 30 minutes.

2. In large skillet, melt butter. Cook onion, celery, and apple in butter until tender, but not browned.

3. Stir in flour and curry powder. Add broth and bring to a boil, stirring until sauce is smooth.

4. Stir in cream and continue stirring until smooth.

5. Add almonds and shrimp. Heat thoroughly 10–15 minutes.

6. Spoon curried shrimp into hot coconut shells. Serve immediately.

Serves 6

Hint: Your butcher might saw coconuts for you.

CHICKEN WITH
COCONUT AND CARROTS

1 chicken, disjointed
salt to taste
pepper to taste
2 cups water
2 teaspoons chopped fresh
 ginger
1 tablespoon chopped
 garlic
2 teaspoons mint
3 tablespoons butter
1 cup sliced onion
2 cups shredded carrots
2 chilies, chopped
3 tablespoons flour
½ cup freshly grated
 coconut

1. Salt and pepper chicken and place in large saucepan with water, ginger, garlic, and mint. Cook 30 minutes or until tender.

2. Remove chicken from broth; skim fat from broth.

3. In medium skillet, melt butter. Sauté onion in butter a few minutes. Add carrots and chilies. Cook on low heat a few minutes, stirring constantly.

4. Stir in flour a little at a time, add broth, and cook until smooth and thickened. Add more water if necessary.

5. Sprinkle coconut over chicken.

Serves 4

COCONUT-VEAL CURRY

3 pounds veal stew, cut in
 small pieces
4 tablespoons butter
2 cans (10¾ ounce) cream
 of mushroom soup
1 cup coconut milk
3 tablespoons curry
 powder
10 green onions, chopped,
 using a little bit of
 green, sautéed
salt to taste
pepper to taste
1 can (8¼ ounce)
 pineapple tidbits
4 cups cooked rice
½ cup toasted flaked
 coconut
green onions, chopped
almonds
shredded coconut
raisins
bananas, chopped
chutney

1. In large skillet, melt butter. Brown veal in butter.

2. Stir in soup, milk, curry powder, 5 green onions, salt, and pepper. Simmer 25 minutes.

3. Stir in pineapple and 5 green onions. Simmer 20 minutes.

4. Serve over rice. Sprinkle with toasted flaked coconut. In separate small bowls, from which guests may help themselves, serve chopped green onions, almonds, shredded coconut, raisins, chopped bananas, and chutney as accompaniments.

Serves 6–8

Hint: If sauce is too thick, add ½ cup more milk, half-and-half, or sherry.

YAM BALLS HAWAIIAN

4 medium yams
2 tablespoons butter
1 teaspoon salt
1 teaspoon grated orange
  rind
1 tablespoon brown sugar
⅓ cup finely chopped
  macadamia nuts
1 cup shredded coconut
1 or more cups pineapple
  chunks

1. Peel yams and boil until tender; mash.
2. Preheat oven to 350°.
3. In small saucepan, melt butter. Stir in salt, orange rind, and brown sugar.
4. Add nuts to mashed yams; cool.
5. Form yam mixture into balls. Roll balls in melted butter mixture and then in coconut.
6. Put pineapple in bottom of buttered 9-inch square pan.
7. Arrange yam balls on top of pineapple, sprinkling with any remaining coconut and melted butter.
8. Bake 15 minutes.

Serves 6

 ## COCONUT PILAF

½ cup butter
½ cup raisins, soaked in
  sherry or water
½ cup grated coconut
¼ cup slivered almonds
½ cup brown sugar
2 cups steamed rice

1. In large skillet, melt butter.
2. Sauté raisins, coconut, and almonds in butter until raisins are plump and almonds and coconut are golden.
3. Add brown sugar and rice. Cook 2 minutes, stirring constantly.

Serves 6

BANANA-COCONUT BREAD

2 cups flour
2 teaspoons baking soda
½ teaspoon salt
3 eggs
½ cup butter, softened
1 teaspoon lemon extract
   or lemon juice
¼ cup sour cream
1 cup sugar
1 cup finely chopped nuts
1½ cups sliced bananas
½ cup shredded coconut

1. Preheat oven to 325°.
2. Into large bowl, sift together flour, baking soda, and salt; set aside.
3. Put eggs, butter, lemon extract, sour cream, and sugar in blender and mix.
4. Pour egg mixture into sifted dry ingredients, stirring thoroughly.
5. Fold in nuts, bananas, and coconut.
6. Pour batter into 2 lightly buttered 9 x 5 x 3-inch loaf pans. Bake 45–50 minutes.

Makes 2 loaves

 ## COCONUT-CORN BREAD

½ cup brown sugar
1¾ cups cornmeal
1 cup sifted flour
1½ teaspoons baking soda
1 teaspoon salt
1 teaspoon ginger
2 eggs, beaten
2 tablespoons butter,
   melted
2 cups buttermilk
¾ cup grated coconut

1. Preheat oven to 350°.
2. In large bowl, combine brown sugar and cornmeal.
3. Sift together flour, baking soda, salt, and ginger; add to cornmeal mixture.
4. Mix eggs, butter, and buttermilk; stir into dry ingredients.
5. Stir in ½ cup coconut.
6. Pour batter into well-buttered 8-inch square baking pan. Sprinkle top of batter with remaining coconut.
7. Bake 20 minutes or until it tests done.

Serves 8

RICE PUDDING

3 eggs, beaten
3 cups milk
1 teaspoon vanilla
½ cup brown sugar, packed
pinch of salt
2 cups raw brown or raw white rice
½ cup chopped mixed nuts
2 tablespoons currants
½ cup shredded coconut
¼ tablespoon nutmeg

1. Preheat oven to 325°.
2. In large bowl, mix together eggs, milk, vanilla, brown sugar, and salt; set aside.
3. Cook rice by boiling in salted water to cover until just tender; drain.
4. Mix rice into egg mixture.
5. Stir in mixed nuts, currants, and coconut well.
6. Pour pudding into well-buttered 2-quart casserole. Sprinkle with nutmeg.
7. Bake 30 minutes.

Serves 8

 # COCONUT SOUFFLÉ

This is delicate and subtle.

2 tablespoons butter, melted
4 tablespoons flour
¾ cup milk, perferably fresh coconut milk (See p. 71.)
¼ cup sugar
dash of salt
4 eggs, separated
1 tablespoon fresh lemon juice
2 tablespoons grated lemon rind
1 cup shredded coconut, preferably fresh
dash of salt

1. In top of a double boiler, melt butter. Add flour, stirring 3–5 minutes to avoid raw-flour taste.
2. Gradually add coconut milk, stirring until thick; do not boil.
3. Add sugar and salt, stirring until they dissolve.
4. Place coconut milk mixture over boiling water.
5. Beat egg yolks with lemon juice and lemon rind.
6. In the double boiler, combine coconut milk and egg yolk mixtures, beating thoroughly.
7. Stir in coconut.
8. Remove from heat and cool.
9. Preheat oven to 350°.
10. Beat egg whites with dash of salt until stiff but not dry. Fold into coconut mixture thoroughly.
11. Bake in buttered 1-quart soufflé dish or oven baking dish until a toothpick inserted in center comes out clean. Serve with favorite lemon sauce.

Serves 6

HAUPIA CAKE

1 package (1 pound 2½
ounce) white cake mix
⅔ cup coconut milk
⅔ cup water
2 egg whites
½ cup grated coconut,
canned or fresh

1. Preheat oven according to package directions.
2. Prepare cake mix as directed, using coconut milk, water, and egg whites.
3. Pour batter into 2 buttered 8-inch round layer pans, and bake.
4. Cool cake. Split layers.
5. Prepare Haupia filling.
6. Put layers together with filling. Chill until set.
7. Prepare frosting.
8. Frost cake and sprinkle with coconut.

Haupia Filling

2 cups coconut milk
½ cup sugar
¼ teaspoon salt
3 tablespoons cornstarch
½ cup water
1 teaspoon vanilla

1. In medium saucepan, heat coconut milk.
2. Mix sugar, salt, and cornstarch with water. Stir into hot coconut milk.
3. Cook mixture, stirring constantly until it thickens.
4. Stir in vanilla and cool.

Frosting

1 tablespoon gelatin
⅓ cup coconut milk
2 cups heavy cream
6 tablespoons sugar
1 teaspoon lemon extract

1. Soften gelatin in coconut milk and dissolve over hot water. Cool.
2. In medium bowl, whip cream; fold in gelatin mixture, sugar, and lemon extract.

Serves 10–12

Hint: Coconut milk is available frozen.
You can bake this cake as 13 x 9 x 2-inch sheet cake and cover it with whipped cream frosting and grated coconut.

FRESH COCONUT CAKE

½ cup butter
1 cup sugar
2 cups cake flour
3 teaspoons baking
   powder
⅔ cup coconut milk
1 teaspoon vanilla
3 large-egg whites
2½ cups freshly grated
   coconut (optional)

1. Preheat oven to 375°.
2. In large bowl, cream butter. Add sugar and continue beating.
3. Sift flour with baking powder 3 times. To butter mixture, add sifted dry ingredients alternately with coconut milk, beating well.
4. Stir in vanilla.
5. In medium bowl, beat egg whites until stiff but not dry. Gently fold into batter.
6. Fold in ½ cup coconut.
7. Pour batter into 2 well-buttered 9-inch round layer pans. Bake 25 minutes. Cool in pans on a rack.
8. Prepare frosting.
9. Spread frosting between layers; cover frosting heavily with 1 cup coconut. Cover top and sides with remaining frosting; sprinkle thickly with remaining coconut.

Frosting

1 cup sugar
½ cup pineapple juice
2 large-egg whites
½ teaspoon vanilla

1. Boil sugar and pineapple juice together until mixture spins a thread at 230–234°.
2. Beat egg whites until stiff but not dry. Slowly pour sugar syrup over egg whites, continually beating until cool.
3. Fold in vanilla.

Serves 8

Hint: If not used shortly, keep cake well covered and refrigerated as coconut milk and fresh coconut are very perishable.

 ## DOUBLE COCONUT PIE

1 cup heavy cream,
   whipped
1 tablespoon powdered
   sugar
1 teaspoon vanilla

1. Prepare baked coconut pie shell.
2. Prepare coconut cream filling
3. Pour filling into baked coconut shell.
4. Sweeten whipped cream with powdered sugar and flavor with vanilla. Cover top of pie. Chill pie if not served promptly.

Baked Coconut Pie Shell

3 tablespoons butter
1½ cups dry flaked coconut

1. Preheat oven to 300°.
2. Melt butter and mix with coconut.
3. Press coconut mixture into 8-inch pie plate.
4. Bake 30 minutes or until browned.

Coconut Cream Filling

3 tablespoons cornstarch
¼ cup sugar
½ teaspoon salt
2 cups milk
2 egg yolks, beaten
2 tablespoons butter
1 teaspoon vanilla
½ cup shredded coconut or
   flaked coconut

1. In heavy saucepan, mix cornstarch, sugar, and salt.
2. Gradually blend in milk. Stir over moderate heat 7 minutes or until mixture thickens.
3. Stir a little hot milk mixture into egg yolks; then stir egg yolks into remaining hot milk mixture. Cook 1 minute more, stirring constantly.
4. Add butter, vanilla, and coconut. Cool.

Serves 8

 ## PINEAPPLE PARTY PIE

4 egg whites
½ teaspoon cream of tartar
⅛ teaspoon salt
1 cup sugar
¾ cup heavy cream
2 tablespoons sugar
½ teaspoon vanilla
½ cup grated coconut

1. Preheat oven to 275°.
2. In medium bowl, beat egg whites until frothy. Add cream of tartar and salt. Beat until stiff, gradually adding 1 cup sugar.
3. Lightly spread meringue mixture in well-buttered, 9-inch, glass pie plate. Bake 1 hour.
4. Prepare filling.
5. Spread filling over meringue.
6. In small bowl, whip cream; blend in 2 tablespoons sugar and vanilla.
7. Spread topping over pineapple filling. Sprinkle with coconut.
8. Refrigerate at least 8 hours or overnight.

Filling

4 egg yolks, beaten
½ cup sugar
2 tablespoons lemon juice
¼ cup crushed pineapple
pinch of salt

1. In top of a double boiler, combine ingredients.
2. Cook over hot water, stirring constantly until thick and smooth. Cool.

Serves 8

CHOCOLATE MACAROONS

1 cup grated coconut
½ cup sweetened
    condensed milk
1 teaspoon vanilla
½ cup semisweet
    chocolate bits
½ cup chopped salted
    peanuts

1. Preheat oven to 350°.
2. In medium bowl, blend all ingredients together.
3. Drop cookies by teaspoonsful 1 inch apart on buttered baking sheets. Bake 10 minutes or until golden brown. Remove with spatula to a rack for cooling.

Makes 2 dozen

 ### APRICOT-COCONUT BALLS

1½ cups ground dried
    apricots
2¼ cups ground coconut
¼ cup powdered sugar
⅔ cup sweetened
    condensed milk
⅓ cup sugar

1. Mix together apricots, coconut, powdered sugar, and milk.
2. Form mixture into small balls and roll in sugar.
3. Store in covered container.

Makes 30

 ### WHITE COCONUT CANDY

1½ cups sugar
½ cup water
2 tablespoons light corn
    syrup
pinch of salt
1½ cups grated coconut
1 tablespoon butter
1 teaspoon vanilla

1. In medium saucepan, mix sugar, water, corn syrup, and salt; place over high heat and boil until it spins a long thread at 248°. Remove from heat.
2. Stir in coconut.
3. Boil mixture again until very thick at 236° and again remove from heat. Add butter and vanilla, stirring well.
4. Beat mixture until it becomes creamy and can be dropped from a spoon. Drop by teaspoonsful on buttered waxed paper. Cool.

Makes 2 dozen

FILBERT / HAZELNUT

Corylus avellana

FILBERT/HAZELNUT

THE HAZEL TREE, botanically known as *Corylus avellana* and found in Europe and North America, bears its nuts in clusters enclosed in a leafy husk. The small round nuts vary in color from a light to deep brown with a reddish cast. The filbert tree, technically speaking, is an improved and domestically cultivated hazel tree. In *Cooking with Nuts*, our recipes speak of hazelnuts and filberts interchangeably as by and large, and especially for cooking purposes, they are one and the same nut with the same appearance and flavor.

The hazel tree is a bushy shrub dating back to 4500 B.C.; it was said to have mysterious legendary qualities. Even the words *hazing* and *hazy* are supposedly derived from this tree. A Y-shaped branch of the hazel tree, grasped by hand at each end with the point kept toward the ground, is the divining rod of classical history. In some miraculous fashion, it was thought to find hidden springs and locate water that no one could have dreamed existed. This was the rod that Moses used to smite rocks from which came forth the water. Medieval sorcerers were never without their hazel wand. In recent history, its most famous role is as an integral part of the caduceus of Mercury, a hazel branch entwined with two serpents, the symbol of the medical profession standing for a combination of health, wisdom, mercy, and peace. According to a manuscript found in China about 3000 B.C., the hazelnut was classified as one of five sacred nourishments the Deity bestowed on mankind. In classical times, the Greeks put the nut to many medicinal uses.

The filbert tree derives its name from St. Philbert's Day, August 22, around which time the nuts become ripe and harvesting begins.

In England, there are three kinds of hazelnuts: white, red, and frizzled. In the United States, technically there are two kinds, known as the common and the beaked, with the common considered sweeter. Still another name for the nut is aveline. In Spain, there are two nuts very similar in flavor and texture known as the Barcelona nut and the cobnut.

Oregon is quickly becoming a major source of filberts, and cultivation in the state of Washington is accelerating. Other leading producers are Turkey, Sicily, and Spain. The hazelnut is also found wild in many parts of the United States and in parts of Great Britain. Like several other nuts, the green hazelnuts are popular on the Continent, particularly in salads.

Hazelnuts/filberts have high priority in European haute cuisine. Prized for their flavor and texture, the nuts are used extensively in tortes, pastries, and cookies; and they seem to have a natural alliance with chocolate, showing up in that combination in some of the most delicious European candies. Often they are used unblanched, and eaten raw or roasted that way too. Known as *noisettes* in France, these hazelnuts are highly prized. A most delicious flavoring is *beurre de noisette*, a hazelnut butter used for seasoning vegetables and meat.

PURCHASE

During summer, the nuts are still green on the tree; but a new crop of nuts is generally available in late fall.

In the shell, the nuts should be plump, shiny, characteristic reddish-brown, and smooth, not nicked or disfigured.

Shelled, in specialty stores, they are found in the bulk, unblanched, and in airtight cans and jars. The nuts are appearing in more and more supermarkets and small grocery stores. They should look round and plump and have on their red skin, which many cooking authorities feel should not be removed by blanching in order to preserve flavor and texture.

PREPARATION

To toast. For a rich, toasted flavor, spread shelled filberts in a shallow pan and toast in 275° oven 20 minutes or until the tender inner skins crack. Use skinned or unskinned.

To blanch.   To remove skins, rub nuts while warm with a rough cloth or between your palms.

To grind.   Place nuts in an electric blender jar and run blender until nuts are finely ground. Or put nuts through a food grinder using medium-fine blade.

To chop.   Working with a small handful at a time, place nuts on chopping board and chop with a sharp knife to desired degree of fineness. Or place nuts in jar of food chopper or other food processor, and chop to desired degree of fineness. Unroasted nuts are easiest to chop.

To slice.   Slicing nuts is easiest when they are unroasted. Hold the nut with the slightly flattened end against a cutting surface. Slice with a sharp knife.

AMOUNTS

1 cup whole nuts equals 1⅛ cups coarsely chopped nuts.
1 cup whole nuts equals 1¼ cups finely chopped nuts.
1 cup whole nuts equals 1½ cups sliced nuts.

STORAGE

Use properly sealed plastic bags or glass jars. Store in-shell nuts at 70° and below. In-shell nuts dried and stored under these conditions will keep satisfactorily about 14 months without serious weight changes or quality deterioration. They will be of substantially better quality than nuts stored under ordinary common storage conditions. Refrigerate for longer storage.

To refrigerate.   After drying, nuts can be stored at 32–35° 2 years packaged in sealed plastic or glass containers if the relative humidity is maintained at 60–65 percent and the nuts are stored away from odor-producing substances.

After storage, allow nuts to warm up in unopened containers to room temperature to avoid drawing moisture, which could cause mold and rancidity.

To freeze.   Freeze dried nuts successfully at 27° or lower 2 years with or without plastic containers. There is little danger of their absorbing odors, and it is not necessary to control humidity.

After freezer storage, allow nuts to warm up in unopened plastic bags, or in well-ventilated areas if plastic bags are not used, to prevent mold or rancidity.

HAZELNUT FRIED MUSHROOMS

2 eggs
½ teaspoon salt
⅛ teaspoon pepper
⅓ teaspoon nutmeg
⅓ cup ground hazelnuts
½ cup fine dry bread
  crumbs
1 pound mushrooms,
  washed, dried
2 cups vegetable oil

1. In small bowl, slightly beat eggs with salt, pepper, and nutmeg.
2. In separate bowl, mix together nuts and bread crumbs.
3. Dip mushrooms into egg mixture and then coat with nut mixture.
4. In deep pan, heat oil to 365°. Fry mushrooms a few at a time 6–7 minutes each or until golden brown on all sides.
5. Drain mushrooms on paper towel, and sprinkle with additional salt if desired.

 ## CAMEMBERT ROUND

1 box (8 ounce)
  Camembert cheese or 6
  individually wrapped
  pieces (1–1⅓ ounce)
  Camembert cheese
1 cup dry white wine
½ cup butter
1–1½ cups chopped
  toasted filberts

1. Soak cheese in wine overnight, turning occasionally. Drain; scrape any discolored parts off cheese, but do not remove rind.
2. In small electric-mixer bowl, cream butter; gradually add drained cheese and beat until smooth.
3. Chill cheese mixture about 1 hour.
4. Place cheese on waxed paper and shape into a ball.
5. Cover ball with ¾ cup nuts and shape into a flat round about 5 inches in diameter.
6. Turn round upside down onto serving plate; remove waxed paper; and coat top with remaining nuts. Chill.
7. Remove round from refrigerator about 30 minutes before serving time. Serve with French bread or heated crackers as an hors d'oeuvre or with fruit as a dessert.

Serves 6

CHEESE PUFFS

½ cup butter
¼ teaspoon salt
1 cup water
1 cup sifted flour
4 eggs

1. Preheat oven to 425°.
2. In large saucepan, heat butter, salt, and water together until mixture boils. Add flour all at once, stirring vigorously until mixture leaves sides of pan and adheres in a ball to mixing spoon.
3. Remove saucepan from heat; cool slightly. Add eggs 1 at a time, beating vigorously after each addition.
4. Drop egg mixture by ½ teaspoonsful on buttered baking sheet. Bake 10–15 minutes. Turn heat down to 300° and bake about 5 minutes more.
5. Meanwhile, prepare filling.
6. Cool cream puffs in pan on a rack. Cut off tops with sharp knife; fill each puff with ½ teaspoon prepared filling. Place tops back on puffs.

Filling

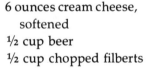

¼ pound Bleu cheese, softened
6 ounces cream cheese, softened
½ cup beer
½ cup chopped filberts

1. Vigorously mix together all ingredients.

Makes 48–60

Hint: Assemble these shortly before serving to eliminate need for refrigeration.
For a festive look, insert a sprig of watercress to peak out of each puff.

 CHEESE WAFERS

1 cup butter
2 glasses Old English sharp cheese
1 cup finely chopped hazelnuts
2½ cups flour
1 teaspoon salt
½ teaspoon cayenne

1. In medium bowl, cream butter with cheese.
2. Stir in nuts, flour, salt, and cayenne.
3. Form dough into long roll and chill several hours.
4. Preheat oven to 375°.
5. Thinly slice wafers and place on buttered baking sheet. Bake 12 minutes.

Makes 48

CREAM OF FILBERT SOUP

3 tablespoons butter
⅓ cup chopped onion
⅓ cup chopped celery
1 cup milk
1 cup heavy cream
1½ teaspoons freshly
  grated lemon rind
1½ cups chicken broth
1 cup ground filberts or
  grated filberts
⅛ teaspoon pepper
salt to taste
3 tablespoons chopped
  toasted filberts
¼ cup minced parsley

1. In large saucepan, melt butter. Sauté onion and celery in butter until crisp-tender, but not browned.
2. Meanwhile, scald milk and cream with lemon rind; discard rind.
3. Stir milk mixture into saucepan with sautéed vegetables; stir in chicken broth, ground nuts, pepper, and salt. Cover, bring to a boil, and simmer gently 15 minutes. Cool.
4. In electric blender, blend soup a little at a time.
5. Serve hot or cold garnished with toasted nuts. Sprinkle minced parsley on top.

Makes 4½ cups

 ## HAZELNUT SALAD

1 celery root
1 lemon
4 carrots
1 bunch of celery
4 firm tomatoes
2 thin slices ham, cooked
radishes
1 head favorite curly
  lettuce
5 tablespoons walnut oil or
  olive oil
3 tablespoons dry sherry
½ tablespoon wine
  vinegar
salt to taste
pepper to taste
1 tablespoon herb mustard
½ cup chopped hazelnuts
12 pimiento-stuffed green
  olives

1. Peel and grate celery root; sprinkle with a few drops of lemon juice to keep it white.
2. Grate carrots.
3. Cut celery in cubes, tomatoes in quarters, ham in thin strips, and radishes in slices.
4. Chop lettuce.
5. Prepare dressing by combining walnut oil, sherry, and wine vinegar. Add salt, pepper, herb mustard, and nuts.
6. Let dressing mellow a few minutes, then pour over salad. Add olives.
7. Toss salad and serve.

Serves 6–8

FILBERT-STUFFED ARTICHOKES

4 medium artichokes
½ cup chopped toasted
  filberts
½ cup seasoned dry bread
  crumbs
¼ cup chopped
  pimiento-stuffed green
  olives
1 garlic clove, pressed
2 tablespoons butter,
  melted
boiling water
1 teaspoon salt

1. Wash artichokes. Cut off stems at base and remove small bottom leaves. Trim tips of leaves with scissors and cut off about 1 inch from top of artichokes.

2. Combine nuts, bread crumbs, olives, garlic, and butter; stir with a tossing motion to coat mixture with butter. Spoon butter sauce between artichoke leaves.

3. Stand artichokes upright in deep saucepan large enough to hold them snugly. Add 1-inch boiling water and salt, pouring water around, not over, artichokes.

4. Cover and boil gently 35–45 minutes until base of artichokes can be pierced easily with a fork. Add more boiling water if needed.

5. Drain artichokes and serve with additional melted butter if desired.

Serves 4

 ASPARAGUS WITH FILBERT SAUCE

½ cup butter
¼ cup finely chopped
  filberts
1 teaspoon tarragon
  vinegar
2½ pounds fresh
  asparagus, cooked

1. In small saucepan, melt butter. Brown nuts in butter.
2. Remove browned nuts from heat and stir in vinegar.
3. Pour sauce over hot, cooked, drained, asparagus and serve.

Serves 6

 GREEN BEAN CASSEROLE

2 tablespoons butter
2 tablespoons finely
  chopped onion
2 tablespoons finely
  chopped celery
1 can (16 ounce) green
  beans
1 can (10½ ounce) cream
  of chicken soup
¾ cup coarsely chopped
  filberts
1 tablespoon grated
  Parmesan cheese
paprika to taste

1. Preheat oven to 350°.

2. In small saucepan, melt butter. Sauté onion and celery in butter until golden brown and tender.

3. Drain liquid from beans. Combine beans, undiluted chicken soup, and sautéed onion and celery with nuts in buttered casserole. Sprinkle on cheese and paprika. Bake 25 minutes.

Serves 6

LAMB SHOULDER CHOPS ON RICE

2 tablespoons butter
4 lamb shoulder chops, ¾ inch thick
1 small onion, chopped
¼ pound mushrooms, sliced
salt to taste
pepper to taste
2½ cups chicken broth or chicken bouillon
1 cup raw rice
¼ cup chopped parsley
dash of garlic powder
¼ cup chopped toasted filberts
¼ cup sliced black olives

1. In large skillet, melt butter. Brown lamb in butter; remove lamb.
2. Sauté onion and mushrooms in drippings until onion is crisp and tender.
3. Salt and pepper lamb; return to skillet.
4. Add ½ cup chicken broth. Simmer 45 minutes or until lamb is tender, covered.
5. Meanwhile, cook rice in remaining broth with parsley and garlic powder.
6. Remove lamb from skillet.
7. Toss onion and mushrooms with cooked rice, nuts, and olives. Serve lamb on rice mixture.

Serves 4

PORK CHOPS WITH HAZELNUT STUFFING

2 tablespoons butter
½ cup chopped hazelnuts
½ cup chopped celery
1 tablespoon chopped onion
1 tablespoon chopped green pepper
1 teaspoon grated orange rind
1 cup diced peeled orange
1 cup small bread cubes, cut from day-old bread
2 tablespoons raisins
1 teaspoon salt
dash of pepper
dash of ginger
dash of nutmeg
4 double-bone, center-cut pork chops, with pocket
½ cup orange juice

1. Preheat oven to 350°.
2. In large oven-proof skillet with a lid, melt butter. Sauté nuts, celery, onion, and green pepper in butter until nuts are toasted.
3. Combine nut mixture with orange rind, orange, bread, raisins, ½ teaspoon salt, pepper, ginger, and nutmeg; toss lightly.
4. Lightly spoon stuffing into pork chop pockets; secure with toothpicks or sew up. Sprinkle pork chops with remaining salt.
5. In same skillet, brown chops on both sides. Add orange juice.
6. Bake 1 hour, covered; uncover and bake 15 minutes more or until fork tender.
7. Remove chops to serving platter. Skim off excess fat from pan juices; serve juices over pork chops.

Serves 4

Hint: If oven-proof skillet is not available, transfer chops to casserole for baking.

TURKISH FISH FILLET

¼ cup flour
1 teaspoon paprika
1 teaspoon salt
¼ teaspoon pepper
2 pounds fillets of sole
¾ cup butter
1 cup thinly sliced filberts
¼ cup lemon juice
¼ cup chopped parsley

1. Combine flour, paprika, salt, and pepper.
2. Coat fillets with seasoned flour.
3. In large skillet, sauté fillets in ½ cup butter, using butter as needed. Remove fish; keep warm on a serving platter.
4. Add remaining butter and nuts to skillet; sauté nuts until lightly browned.
5. Stir in lemon juice and parsley. Heat sauce to serving temperature and pour over fish.

Serves 6

BROCCOLI WITH
TUNA-FILBERT SAUCE

¼ cup butter
¼ cup flour
¾ teaspoon salt
¼ teaspoon coarsely
  ground pepper
1½ cups milk
½ cup dry vermouth or
  white wine
2 cans (7 ounce)
  chunk-style tuna,
  drained
¾ cup chopped toasted
  filberts
1½–2 pounds fresh
  broccoli, trimmed,
  cooked until
  crisp-tender
½ cup grated Gruyère
  cheese or grated
  Parmesan cheese

1. Preheat oven to 375°.
2. In large saucepan, melt butter. Blend in flour, salt, and pepper. Gradually add milk and wine. Cook until sauce boils 1 minute and is thick and smooth, stirring constantly.
3. Stir in tuna and ½ cup nuts.
4. Arrange broccoli on oven-proof platter or in shallow 2-quart casserole.
5. Pour tuna sauce over broccoli, and sprinkle cheese and remaining nuts on top.
6. Lay strips of foil over any exposed broccoli. Bake 15–20 minutes until sauce bubbles.

Serves 6–8

OREGON FILBERT BREAD

1 egg
1 cup brown sugar
3 tablespoons vegetable oil
1½ cups buttermilk
2 cups sifted flour
1 cup whole wheat flour
1 tablespoon baking
   powder
½ teaspoon baking soda
1 teaspoon salt
1 cup chopped filberts

1. Preheat oven to 350°.
2. Beat egg until light; add brown sugar and beat until creamy.
3. Add oil and buttermilk; beat to blend.
4. Sift together flours, baking powder, baking soda, and salt; add to nuts.
5. Stir nut mixture into creamed ingredients just until mixed.
6. Pour batter into buttered 9 x 5 x 3-inch loaf pan. Bake 1 hour.

Makes 1 loaf (1½ pound)

 ## SOUTHERN COFFEE CAKE

¼ cup butter
½ cup brown sugar
2 eggs
2 cups sifted flour
3 teaspoons baking
   powder
½ teaspoon salt
1 teaspoon cinnamon
¾ cup milk
1 teaspoon vanilla

1. Preheat oven to 375°.
2. In large bowl, cream butter and brown sugar together.
3. Beat 1 egg and 1 egg yolk, reserving 1 egg white for topping; add to creamed mixture.
4. Sift together flour, baking powder, salt, and cinnamon.
5. To creamed mixture, add sifted dry ingredients alternately with milk. Mix batter until smooth. Stir in vanilla.
6. Pour batter into well-buttered, waxed-paper-lined 8-inch square baking pan. Bake 25 minutes.
7. Meanwhile, prepare topping.
8. Spread topping on coffee cake. Bake 5 minutes more.

Topping

2 tablespoons butter
1 egg white
½ cup powdered sugar
2 tablespoons brown sugar
   or molasses
½ cup chopped hazelnuts

1. Combine ingredients in order given and mix into smooth paste.

Serves 8

EGG-AND-HAZELNUT PANCAKES AU GRATIN

4 eggs
1¾ cups sifted flour
1 teaspoon salt
1 cup milk
¾ cup water
1 teaspoon vegetable oil
1 teaspoon butter
¼ cup coarsely chopped
   roasted hazelnuts

1. In large bowl, beat eggs thoroughly.
2. Sift flour with salt; add to eggs alternately with milk and water, mixing well with electric mixer or blender. Stir in oil. Let batter rest at least 30 minutes.
3. In 7-inch iron skillet, melt butter.
4. When skillet with butter is hot, pour in 1½–2 tablespoons butter. Tilt skillet from side to side so pancake batter spreads over bottom of whole skillet. Fry 1 minute and turn over carefully with spatula, cooking until slightly browned.
5. Turn out pancake on baking sheet for later assemblage. Continue making pancakes until you use all batter.
6. Prepare filling, then prepare sauce.
7. Preheat oven to 350°.
8. Put heaping tablespoon of filling in each pancake and roll up. Place seam-side down in oven-proof, flat-bottomed baking dish.
9. When all pancakes are in dish, cover them with cheese sauce, and sprinkle nuts on top.
10. Bake 10–15 minutes to heat through.

Sauce

2 tablespoons butter
1 tablespoon flour
1 teaspoon paprika
½ teaspoon ground mustard
salt to taste
dash of cayenne
2 cups milk
1 cup grated cheddar cheese

1. In medium saucepan, melt butter. Blend in flour, paprika, mustard, salt, and cayenne.
2. Gradually add milk; cook until thickened and bubbly, stirring constantly. Stir in cheese.

Serves 6–8

Filling

3 tablespoons mayonnaise
½ teaspoon salt
dash of pepper
¼ teaspoon ground
   coriander
⅛ teaspoon curry powder
2 eggs, hard-boiled, finely
   chopped
½ cup finely chopped
   hazelnuts
½ cup celery, diced in
   ¼-inch pieces

1. In small bowl, blend mayonnaise, salt, pepper, coriander, and curry powder.
2. Stir in remaining ingredients.

FILBERT CRÈME BRÛLÉE

2 cups light cream
1 cup brown sugar, firmly
   packed
⅛ teaspoon salt
7 egg yolks
1 tablespoon sherry
½ cup sliced toasted
   filberts

1. In top of a double boiler, scald cream with ⅓ cup brown sugar and salt.
2. Beat egg yolks with sherry.
3. Gradually stir hot cream into egg yolk mixture. Cook in top of double boiler until mixture thickens to consistency of a medium cream sauce, stirring constantly.
4. Pour sauce into 1 large or 6 small individual oven-proof dishes. Chill at least 12 hours.
5. About 2 hours before serving, preheat broiler.
6. Sprinkle top of cream with nuts.
7. Sift remaining brown sugar over top of cream to cover, about ⅓ inch thick. Make sure the surface is smooth.
8. Place dish or dishes under broiler 2–3 minutes or until sugar melts and begins to carmelize. Watch carefully so that sugar does not burn.
9. Return dessert to refrigerator until serving time.

Serves 6

Hint: If this is a new dish for your guests, instruct them to hit the hard brittle on top of crème with a spoon to break it open so they can reach the custard underneath.

 ## FILBERT PRALINE MOUSSE

1½ tablespoons gelatin
⅓ cup cold water
5 eggs, separated
½ cup sugar
1 tablespoon instant coffee
   powder
1½ cups hot milk
1 teaspoon vanilla
1½ cups filbert praline
   powder
1½ cups heavy cream,
   whipped

1. Soften gelatin in cold water.
2. In top of a double boiler, beat egg yolks with sugar until light and fluffy.
3. Combine coffee powder and hot milk; gradually beat into egg yolks. Cook over boiling water until mixture thickens and coats a metal spoon, stirring constantly.
4. Stir in gelatin until dissolved. Add vanilla.
5. Stir gelatin mixture over a bowl of ice or chill gelatin mixture until it begins to set.
6. Beat egg whites until stiff but not dry; fold into gelatin mixture.
7. Fold in 1 cup praline powder and whipped cream.
8. Fasten a 4-inch collar of doubled waxed paper around the side of 5-cup soufflé dish or 2-quart serving dish. Pour mousse into dish. Chill until set. If you use a soufflé dish, remove collar before serving.
9. Garnish with remaining ½ cup praline powder.

Serves 8

CHOCOLATE-HAZELNUT POTS OF CREAM

½ cup hazelnuts,
   blanched
1 cup light cream
4 tablespoons milk
1 package (6 ounce)
   semisweet chocolate bits
1 square (1 ounce)
   unsweetened chocolate
4 egg yolks
dash of salt
½ cup heavy cream,
   whipped
1 teaspoon powdered
   sugar

1. In blender, pulverize nuts.
2. In small saucepan, heat light cream and milk.
3. To milk mixture, add semisweet and unsweetened chocolates, stirring until melted.
4. In blender, combine nut and chocolate mixtures until smooth, using high speed.
5. Add egg yolks and salt and blend 1 minute longer.
6. Pour dessert into chocolate pots or custard cups and chill in refrigerator.
7. Remove from refrigerator about 1 hour before serving.
8. Sweeten whipped cream with powdered sugar. Serve dessert with a dab of sweetened whipped cream on top.

Serves 6

SIMPLE HAZELNUT CAKE

½ cup ground almonds
4 eggs
8½ tablespoons sugar
1 cup plus 2 tablespoons
   flour
¾ cup ground roasted
   hazelnuts
½ cup butter
2 tablespoons orange
   liqueur or anisette
½ cup apricot jam

1. Butter 9-inch round baking pan. Put in almonds and shake until they stick to butter, pressing on them if necessary. Refrigerate to make them hold.
2. Preheat oven to 350°.
3. In medium bowl, beat eggs well.
4. Mix in sugar, flour, and hazelnuts.
5. Bring butter to point of melting and stir into flour mixture.
6. Stir in orange liqueur.
7. Pour batter into prepared pan. Bake 40 minutes.
8. Remove from oven and invert cake onto a rack.
9. In small saucepan, heat apricot jam. Paint it onto cake with pastry brush.

Serves 8

Hint: This delicious cake is even better 24 hours after it has been made.

BLACK-TOP PIE

1 tablespoon gelatin
3 tablespoons water
2 eggs, separated
6 tablespoons sugar
1½ cups milk
1 teaspoon rum flavoring
½ cup chopped toasted
 filberts

1. Prepare crust.
2. Soften gelatin in water; dissolve over hot water.
3. In medium bowl, beat egg yolks until thick and lemon colored; beat in 4 tablespoons sugar.
4. Add milk and flavoring; continue beating while adding dissolved gelatin.
5. Chill gelatin mixture until slightly thickened.
6. In large bowl, beat egg whites; gradually add remaining sugar and beat until stiff but not dry.
7. Whip thickened gelatin mixture until fluffy; fold into beaten egg whites.
8. Pour mixture into prepared crust and chill until firm.
9. Prepare frosting.
10. Spread frosting on top of pie; sprinkle with nuts. Chill.

Crust

½ cup chopped filberts
⅓ cup butter, melted
1 cup graham cracker
 crumbs
3 tablespoons sugar

1. Preheat oven to 350°.
2. Combine ingredients; press into bottom and sides of 9-inch pie plate.
3. Bake 12 minutes.

Frosting

½ cup semisweet
 chocolate bits
¼ cup powdered sugar
1 tablespoon butter
2 tablespoons cream

1. In top of a double boiler, melt chocolate over hot water.
2. Add powdered sugar, butter, and cream; stir until smooth.

Serves 8

FROSTY FILBERT PIE

3 egg yolks
⅔ cup brown sugar
1 cup sieved pumpkin
½ teaspoon cinnamon
¼ teaspoon nutmeg
¼ teaspoon ginger
⅛ teaspoon ground cloves
¼ teaspoon salt
½ cup hot milk
½ cup chopped toasted
 filberts
1 cup heavy cream,
 whipped
3 egg whites
2 teaspoons lemon juice
6 tablespoons sugar
½ teaspoon grated lemon
 rind
1 vanilla crumb pie shell
 (9 inch)

1. In medium saucepan, combine egg yolks, brown sugar, and pumpkin; stir in cinnamon, nutmeg, ginger, cloves, salt, and hot milk.
2. Cook milk mixture over low heat until it boils; cook 1 minute more. Cool.
3. Pour cooled mixture into freezing tray, and freeze until mixture is frozen ½ inch from edge of tray.
4. Turn into chilled bowl. Whip with rotary beater until smooth.
5. Stir in nuts along with whipped cream. Return mixture to refrigerator tray and freeze.
6. Prepare meringue by beating egg whites with lemon juice until stiff. Gradually add sugar and continue beating until sugar dissolves. Mix in lemon rind.
7. When ready to serve, preheat oven to 450°.
8. Spoon frozen cream into crust and spread meringue over its top, making sure that all ice cream is covered. Bake 3–4 minutes. Serve immediately.

Serves 8

Hint: You can put filling into prepared pie shell to freeze. When ready to serve, cover with meringue and brown.

HAZELNUT COOKIES

½ cup finely chopped
 hazelnuts
2 cups flour
1 cup sugar
1 cup butter, softened
2 eggs
1 teaspoon vanilla
1 egg yolk, thinned with 1
 tablespoon water

1. Preheat oven to 350°.
2. Mix together nuts, flour, sugar, butter, 2 eggs, and vanilla. If dough is too soft after mixing, refrigerate ½ hour.
3. Roll out dough on lightly floured board, using as little flour as possible.
4. Cut dough with cookie cutter. Put cookies on well-buttered baking sheet. Brush with egg yolk. Bake 15–20 minutes.
5. Cool on a rack.

Makes 3 dozen

Hint: You can put cookies together with jam between them, but they will not keep well this way.

CHOCOLATE-FILBERT CORNUCOPIAS

1 package (6 ounce)
  semisweet chocolate bits
⅔ cup finely chopped
  toasted filberts
Filbert Praline Cream or
  favorite ice cream

1. In top of a double boiler, over hot, not boiling, water, partially melt chocolate bits.

2. Cover 9 metal cone forms, 3–4 inches long, with foil—or use sugar ice cream cones in place of metal forms. Thinly spread melted chocolate over foil and then roll in nuts. Stand covered cones on tray with pointed ends up.

3. Chill about 30 minutes until chocolate sets. Gently lift out cone forms and peel foil from chocolate, making sure no bits of foil stick to chocolate.

4. Chill. When ready to serve, fill with Filbert Praline Cream.

Serves 9

BUTTERSCOTCH-FILBERT BALLS

1 package (6 ounce)
  butterscotch bits
⅓ cup sweetened
  condensed milk
½ teaspoon vanilla
1 cup finely chopped
  filberts
1 egg white, slightly
  beaten

1. In top of a double boiler, melt butterscotch bits over hot water.

2. Stir in condensed milk and vanilla.

3. Mix in ½ cup nuts.

4. Chill mixture until it can be handled. Form into ½-inch balls.

5. Roll balls in egg white and then in remaining nuts.

Makes about 30

FILBERT PRALINE POWDER

¾ cup sugar
¼ cup water
1 teaspoon light corn
  syrup or ⅛ teaspoon
  cream of tartar
¾ cup filberts

1. In small saucepan, combine sugar, water, and corn syrup. Stir over medium heat until sugar dissolves and mixture boils.

2. Stir in nuts. Cook over high heat until mixture is color of molasses, without stirring.

3. Pour onto oiled baking sheet. Cool.

4. Break in pieces. Whirl in blender until powdered, or put pieces of praline through food grinder using fine blade.

5. Store praline powder in covered container in refrigerator. Use as topping for puddings, pies, cakes, ice cream, and fruit.

Makes 2–2½ cups

MACADAMIA

Macadamia ternifolia

MACADAMIA

NATIVE TO Australia, the macadamia nut is also called the Queensland nut. Although the Australians had tried to promote it for years, it was not until the nut was introduced to Hawaii that it became well known.

Now a favorite of many in the United States who first saw and tasted the nut during Hawaiian travel, it is prized as a dessert nut and for snacks, eaten salted and unsalted. That it is relatively expensive does not seem to dampen the enthusiasm of its fans.

The macadamia is a member of the Proteaceae family. Although it reached Hawaii around 1880, the first commercial trees were not planted until 1949; since it takes 7 years from planting until the grafted tree bears its first crop, it was not commercially harvested until 1956. The industry has grown fast. Originally, jungles had to be cleared and rough lava land leveled to make way for what we now know as the Royal Hawaiian Orchard. The trees reach a full height of 40 feet at about 20 years of age.

Since the flower of the macadamia tree contains both pistil and stamen and is self-pollinating, an isolated tree can produce fruit. In the last 60 years, this beautiful evergreen tree has been planted in southern California primarily for landscaping. Here the tree thrives in the same climate and conditions as the avocado and is becoming an industry in California. The nuts grow on pendulous racemes that bear 200–300 small flowers. There are two species, one flowering only once a year and one flowering almost the whole year long. Their husks are similar to the walnuts'. The macadamia tree should not be shaken; the nuts fall to the ground naturally. The nuts start falling from the trees in late July, and harvesting continues until March.

To avoid mildew, the husks should be removed promptly. The nuts-in-shell are small, shaped like a marble, with a smooth brown cover. They look surprisingly dull and uninteresting in their shell, but out of the shell, they are fat, round, and creamy white, with a fine crisp texture and a smooth elegant taste and aroma. The macadamia makes a marvelous nut butter.

To shell your own, place the nuts in the oven 1 hour at about 200° because the shell is hard to crack. California-grown nuts are now available in 1-pound plastic bags containing a hand nut-cracker, which is efficient with nuts of commercial quality. In addition, there are special nutcrackers available through a newly organized California Macadamia Society, P.O. Box 1352, Vista, California 92083.

Specialty confections have pyramided, especially chocolate-covered macadamia and brittle. Macadamia ice cream is new and popular. A great new favorite, the macadamia is at home in all kinds of simple and complicated recipes. It deservedly bears the Luther Burbank description, "the perfect nut."

PURCHASE

Imported whole nuts or whole and pieces mixed are available in vacuum-packed cans and jars in supermarkets, specialty shops, and drugstores. In selecting them, consider their size and creamy color.

The deluxe nut is whole and plump, available raw, roasted, and roasted salted. For cooking purposes and economical reasons, it is wise to look for the packed mixtures that contain some pieces and some whole nuts.

Macadamias in the shell are found mostly in specialty shops—sometimes packaged with a special nutcracker, as in the case of the California macadamia.

PREPARATION

To shell—an impractical procedure, place the nuts in a 200° oven 1 hour; this makes cracking possible.

STORAGE

For short storage, place macadamias in airtight containers in the refrigerator.

For long storage, freezing in airtight containers is the safest method.

MACADAMIA APPETIZER

1 package (3 ounce) cream cheese
⅓ cup chopped roasted macadamia nuts
¼ cup sweet pickle relish
⅛ teaspoon Tabasco sauce
½ teaspoon salt
½ teaspoon horseradish
1 teaspoon mayonnaise
⅛ teaspoon paprika
watercress or parsley to garnish
16 crackers

1. In small bowl, cream the cheese.
2. Add nuts, relish, Tabasco sauce, salt, horseradish, mayonnaise, and paprika, creaming well to blend thoroughly. Chill.
3. Serve as a ball or in small bowl. Crown with watercress. Serve with crisp crackers.

 ## MACADAMIA APPETIZER

1 jar (6 ounce) marinated artichoke hearts
2 tablespoons mayonnaise
1 teaspoon sour cream
1 teaspoon anchovy paste
⅓ cup chopped, salted macadamia nuts
8 slices any favorite thin bread, cut into 2-inch circles

1. Preheat oven to 325°.
2. Drain artichoke hearts, saving liquid for other use. Chop finely.
3. Blend together mayonnaise, sour cream, and anchovy paste and stir into chopped artichokes.
4. Add nuts and mix well.
5. Butter miniature muffin pans (1½ inch diameter) and nestle bread rounds into them.
6. Bake bread nests in oven till light brown and crisp.
7. Remove bread nests from tin and place on rack to cool.
8. Fill each with heaping teaspoon of artichoke mixture.
9. Decorate with parsley or ½ macadamia nut.

Hint: Small cherry tomatoes may be used. Cut off tops, scoop out insides, and turn upside down to drain. When ready to stuff, turn right side up and fill as in bread nests.

CREAMY AVOCADO-MACADAMIA SOUP

2 ripe avocados, peeled, seeded
1 cup macadamia nuts
1 cup chicken broth
1½ teaspoons lime juice or lemon juice
1 small garlic clove, peeled, pressed
¼ teaspoon salt
2 cups heavy cream

1. In blender, blend avocados, ½ cup nuts, broth, lime juice, garlic, and salt until smooth.
2. Pour this into large bowl, and stir in 1½ cups cream. Chill thoroughly.
3. At serving time, whip remaining cream and put a dollop on each serving.
4. Chop remaining nuts and sprinkle on top of servings.

Serves 6

 ## FRUITED CHICKEN SALAD MACADAMIA

¼ cup mayonnaise
¼ cup sour cream
2 tablespoons finely chopped green onions, with tops
1 teaspoon lemon juice
1½ cups chicken, cooked, diced
1 cup seedless green grapes, fresh or canned, drained
1 cup coarsely chopped macadamia nuts
salt and pepper to taste
1 head crisp lettuce

1. In large bowl, combine mayonnaise, sour cream, green onions, and lemon juice.
2. Add chicken, grapes, and nuts; toss.
3. Sprinkle with salt and pepper.
4. Arrange combination on crisp lettuce.

Serves 4–5

Hint: Decorate with parsley or watercress and slices of drained mandarin oranges.

 ## MACADAMIA LEMON BUTTER

½ cup butter
2 tablespoons fresh lemon juice
dash of pepper
½ cup macadamia nuts

1. In small pan, heat butter until it foams and then browns lightly.
2. Stir in lemon juice, pepper, and nuts.
3. Pour sauce over hot cooked vegetable.

Makes 1 cup

COCONUT-MACADAMIA CHICKEN

5 whole frying chicken
  breasts, split, boned
salt to taste
freshly ground pepper to
  taste
4 tablespoons butter
½ cup thinly sliced green
  onions, with part of tops
1 tablespoon brown sugar
dash of salt
⅛ teaspoon dried
  crumbled thyme
1 jar (4 ounce) pimientos,
  sliced
⅔ cup golden raisins
2 tablespoons fresh lemon
  juice
¾ cup macadamia nuts

1. Prepare coconut crust.

2. Generously season chicken with salt and pepper to taste. Fold under loose corners of each chicken piece to form compact pieces.

3. Preheat oven to 375°.

4. In large skillet, melt butter. Gently brown chicken on all sides in butter.

5. Arrange single layer of pieces in 18 x 12-inch baking dish at least 2 inches deep.

6. Add green onions to skillet, and stir to coat with drippings. Stir in brown sugar, dash of salt, thyme, pimientos, raisins, and lemon juice. Evenly spoon combination over chicken.

7. Cover with foil, and bake 45 minutes or until chicken is tender.

8. Remove foil. Sprinkle coconut crust over chicken; top with nuts.

9. Bake 10 minutes more, uncovered. Spoon juices over chicken.

Coconut Crust

5 tablespoons butter,
  melted
2 tablespoons fresh lemon
  juice
¼ teaspoon salt
¼ teaspoon freshly
  ground pepper
1½ cups flaked coconut
2 tablespoons chopped
  fresh parsley

1. Toss ingredients together thoroughly.

Serves 8

VEAL CORDON BLEU

8 veal cutlets, ⅛ inch thick
8 thin slices boiled ham
8 thin slices Swiss cheese
8 tablespoons butter, melted
½ cup cornflake crumbs
1 can (10¾ ounce) cream of mushroom soup, undiluted
½ cup light cream
2 tablespoons sauterne
wine to taste
½ cup chopped macadamia nuts

1. Preheat oven to 350°.
2. With meat hammer, pound each cutlet to thin 7½ x 4½-inch rectangle.
3. Cut ham and cheese slices in half; stack 2 half slices of each in center of each cutlet. Fold veal over to cover ham and cheese.
4. Brush veal combination with butter and roll in cornflake crumbs.
5. Place veal in unbuttered 11 x 7 x 1-inch baking dish. Bake 30 minutes.
6. Combine soup, cream, and sauterne; pour over top of veal.
7. Cover and bake 20 minutes more. While cooking, add wine to taste.
8. Sprinkle nuts on top of each portion. Serve with rice.

Serves 6–8

TROPICAL CRAB SALAD

¾ pound fresh crab meat (preferably mostly legs) or 2 cans (7 ounce) crab meat rinsed, drained
2 small grapefruits, peeled, cut in sections
1 large avocado, peeled, sliced
crisp lettuce leaves

1. Chill 4 plates.
2. Prepare dressing.
3. On chilled plates, arrange crab meat, grapefruits, and avocado on lettuce.
4. Spoon on half of dressing, and serve remaining dressing in separate bowl.

Dressing

1 cup vegetable oil
¼ cup fresh lemon juice
1 teaspoon grated lemon rind
½ teaspoon salt
½ teaspoon dry mustard
¼ teaspoon pepper
1½ cups chopped macadamia nuts

1. Shake or beat together oil, lemon juice, lemon rind, salt, dry mustard, and pepper.
2. Just before serving, add nuts. Shake or beat together again.

Serves 4

MACADAMIA-CRUSTED RED SNAPPER

½ cup butter, softened
½ cup shredded Parmesan
  cheese or grated
  Parmesan cheese
4 red snapper fillets (about
  1½ pounds total)
1 teaspoon seasoned salt
½ cup finely chopped
  macadamia nuts
freshly ground pepper to
  taste

1. Preheat oven to 400°.
2. Spread ¼ cup butter over bottom of 8-inch square shallow baking pan; sprinkle with ¼ cup cheese.
3. Dust fish with seasoned salt and arrange in single layer over cheese.
4. Dot with remaining butter, sprinkle with remaining cheese, and top with nuts.
5. Bake 15 minutes. Just before serving, spoon pan drippings over fish and sprinkle lightly with pepper.

Serves 4

 ## SALMON LOAF

½ cup coarsely chopped
  macadamia nuts
2 cups flaked salmon,
  canned or fresh
1 egg, beaten
½ teaspoon salt
½ teaspoon celery salt
¼ teaspoon pepper
1 cup dry bread crumbs or
  cracker crumbs
⅔ cup milk
2 tablespoons butter
2 tablespoons finely
  minced onion

1. Preheat oven to 350°.
2. Combine ingredients well.
3. Pack mixture into buttered 8 x 4 x 4-inch loaf pan, or shape by hand into oblong loaf or oval ring in buttered shallow baking pan.
4. Bake 35 minutes.
5. Prepare sauce.
6. Serve loaf on hot platter with hot sauce in separate bowl.

Sauce

¼ cup chopped
  macadamia nuts
1 can (10½ ounce) cream of
  celery soup, undiluted
2 tablespoons sherry
2 tablespoons cream
½ cup chopped pimiento-
  stuffed green olives

1. Combine all ingredients.
2. In a double boiler, heat sauce.

Serves 4 generously

CORN-NUT PUDDING

2 tablespoons butter
1 large Spanish onion,
  chopped
2 eggs, separated
1 cup canned creamed
  corn
dash of paprika
1 teaspoon seasoned salt
3 tablespoons flour
1 cup warm milk
½ cup chopped toasted
  macadamia nuts
1 tablespoon sugar

1. Preheat oven to 350°.
2. In small saucepan, melt 1 tablespoon butter. Sauté onion in butter until tender and golden.
3. In large bowl, beat egg yolks; mix in corn, sautéed onion, paprika, and seasoned salt.
4. In small saucepan, melt remaining butter; stir in flour and cook 2 minutes.
5. Gradually add warm milk, stirring until creamy and thick.
6. Combine with corn mixture. Correct seasoning.
7. In small bowl, beat egg whites until stiff but not dry.
8. Fold nuts, sugar, and egg whites into corn mixture.
9. Pour pudding into well-buttered 1-quart casserole. Bake 30–40 minutes until mixture is set and golden.

Serves 4–5

Hint: Nutmeg, curry, and chili are possibilities for seasoning variations.

 ## POTATOES WITH MACADAMIAS

2 slices bread, cubed
4 tablespoons olive oil
2 garlic cloves, minced
1 bay leaf
2 tablespoons minced
  onion
¼ pound ground
  macadamia nuts
1 teaspoon saffron
1 pound potatoes
salt to taste
pepper to taste
dash of powdered cloves
¼ cup bread crumbs,
  buttered

1. In small saucepan, fry cubed bread in olive oil with garlic, bay leaf, and onion.
2. Combine fried bread mixture with nuts; season with saffron.
3. Preheat oven to 350°.
4. Peel and thinly slice potatoes. Place them in medium well-buttered casserole.
5. Pour nut mixture over potatoes. Moisten with a little milk if necessary.
6. Add enough boiling water to cover potatoes; sprinkle combination with salt, pepper, cloves, and bread crumbs. Bake 30–40 minutes until potatoes are tender and brown.

Serves 6

CINNAMON-CRUMB COFFEE CAKE

2½ cups flour
1 cup brown sugar, firmly
  packed
¾ cup sugar
¾ cup butter, melted
2 teaspoons cinnamon
1 teaspoon baking powder
1 teaspoon baking soda
1 cup buttermilk
1 egg, beaten
½ cup chopped
  macadamia nuts

1. Preheat oven to 350°.
2. In large bowl, stir together flour, brown sugar, sugar, butter, and 1 teaspoon cinnamon to make a crumbly mixture.
3. Measure ¾ cup crumb mixture and set aside.
4. To ingredients in mixing bowl, add baking powder, baking soda, buttermilk, and egg; combine thoroughly (batter will not be smooth).
5. Pour batter into buttered 9-inch square baking pan.
6. Mix nuts and remaining cinnamon with reserved crumb mixture; sprinkle over top of batter.
7. Bake 45 minutes. Cut in squares and serve warm.

Makes 20 squares

 MACADAMIA EGGS

4 large slices Swiss cheese
4 eggs
dash of salt
dash of pepper
8 tablespoons finely
  chopped macadamia
  nuts
1 tablespoon butter
8 tablespoons heavy
  cream, scalded
¼ cup finely chopped
  fresh parsley

1. Preheat oven to 350°.
2. Place cheese over bottom of buttered 8-inch square pan or in 4 individual ramekins.
3. Gently break 1 egg onto each cheese slice.
4. Sprinkle eggs with salt, pepper, and nuts; dot with butter.
5. Pour cream around eggs, and bake 10 minutes.
6. Lightly sprinkle eggs with parsley.

Serves 4

SUGAR-NUT CRUSTED FRUITS

4 cups sliced bananas and
   pineapple or other sliced
   fresh fruits
1 cup chopped macadamia
   nuts
4 tablespoons butter
¾ cup brown sugar, firmly
   packed
1 pint vanilla ice cream or
   ½ cup heavy cream,
   whipped

1. Arrange fruits in 8-inch square dish which can go from broiler to table.
2. Sprinkle fruits with nuts, dot with butter, and sprinkle with brown sugar.
3. Broil 6 inches below heat until sugar melts and bubbles.
4. With serving spoon, tap crusty top on fruits to break it. Spoon hot fruits and sugar crust into serving bowls.
5. Top each serving with ice cream.

Serves 6

 ## PUDDING FOR A FEAST

2 cups milk, scalded
5 cups 2–3-day-old bread,
   cut in cubes
¾ cup sugar
2 eggs, beaten slightly
½ teaspoon cinnamon
1 teaspoon vanilla
6 tablespoons butter,
   melted
½ cup chopped
   macadamia nuts
½ cup flaked coconut
1 cup heavy cream
2 tablespoons powdered
   sugar
1 tablespoon vanilla

1. Preheat oven to 300°.
2. In large bowl, pour milk over bread cubes.
3. Mix in sugar, eggs, cinnamon, vanilla, 5 tablespoons butter, macadamia nuts, and coconut thoroughly.
4. Pour pudding into 8-inch square baking pan. Dot with remaining butter and bake 40–50 minutes until knife inserted in center comes out clean.
5. Whip cream; stir in powdered sugar and vanilla.
6. Serve pudding warm or cold with sweetened, flavored cream in separate bowl.

Serves 6

Hint: You can decorate pudding with glacé or marischino cherries.

HUSBAND'S CAKE

¾ cup butter
1½ cups sugar
1 cup tomato soup
¾ cup water
1 teaspoon baking soda
3 cups flour
¾ teaspoon salt
3 teaspoons baking
  powder
1½ teaspoons cinnamon
1½ teaspoons nutmeg
1 teaspoon ground cloves
1½ cups raisins
1½ cups chopped
  macadamia nuts
¼ cup powdered sugar

1. Preheat oven to 350°.
2. In large bowl, cream butter and sugar.
3. Combine soup with water and baking soda.
4. Sift together flour, salt, baking powder, cinnamon, nutmeg, and cloves.
5. Into butter mixture, stir sifted dry ingredients alternately with soup combination.
6. Mix in raisins and nuts.
7. Pour batter into well-buttered 9-inch tube pan. Bake 1 hour.
8. Cool on a rack. Invert cake on serving plate and sprinkle with powdered sugar.

Serves 8-12

 ## FRESH PINEAPPLE BREAD-CAKE

1¾ cups flour
2 teaspoons baking
  powder
¼ teaspoon baking soda
½ teaspoon salt
¾ cup coarsely chopped
  macadamia nuts
¾ cup brown sugar, firmly
  packed
3 tablespoons butter,
  softened
2 eggs
1 cup finely chopped fresh
  pineapple, firmly
  packed (Do not squeeze
  out natural juice.)
2 tablespoons sugar
½ teaspoon cinnamon

1. Preheat oven to 350°.
2. Into medium bowl, sift together flour, baking powder, baking soda, and salt.
3. Add nuts to sifted dry ingredients.
4. In large bowl, cream together brown sugar, butter, and eggs until mixture is fluffy.
5. Stir in half of flour mixture. Mix in pineapple. Blend in remaining flour mixture.
6. Pour batter into well-buttered 9 x 5 x 3-inch loaf pan.
7. Combine sugar and cinnamon for topping.
8. Sprinkle topping over bread-cake mixture. Bake 1 hour or until done.

Makes 1 loaf

MACADAMIA NUT PIE

3 eggs
⅔ cup sugar
1 cup light corn syrup
3 tablespoons butter,
   melted
1 teaspoon vanilla
1½ cups chopped
   macadamia nuts
1 pie shell (9 inch)
2 tablespoons powdered
   sugar
2 tablespoons sherry or 1
   tablespoon sherry and 1
   tablespoon vanilla
1 cup heavy cream,
   whipped

1. Preheat oven to 350°.
2. In medium bowl, beat eggs, sugar, syrup, butter, and vanilla thoroughly.
3. Stir in nuts.
4. Pour filling into pie shell. Bake 40 minutes. Cool.
5. Blend powdered sugar and sherry into whipped cream. Serve in separate bowl.

Serves 8

MACADAMIA-BUTTER COOKIE BALLS

1 cup butter, softened
1 cup sifted powdered
   sugar
1 teaspoon vanilla
2½ cups flour
¼ teaspoon salt
1 cup finely chopped
   macadamia nuts
powdered sugar to coat

1. Preheat oven to 400°.
2. In large bowl, cream butter and sifted powdered sugar together thoroughly. Beat in vanilla.
3. Into creamed mixture, sift together flour and salt; beat thoroughly. Stir in nuts.
4. Pinch off small portions of dough and shape into 1-inch balls. Place on unbuttered baking sheet. Bake 9 minutes.
5. Remove balls to a rack. While still warm, roll them in powdered sugar.

Makes 50

Hint: These keep well in airtight container with powdered sugar between layers.

MACADAMIA NUT BARS

2 eggs
1 teaspoon vanilla
1½ cups light brown
  sugar, firmly packed
2 tablespoons flour
½ teaspoon salt
¼ teaspoon baking
  powder
¼ cup flaked coconut or
  shredded coconut
1 cup chopped macadamia
  nuts
¾ cup sifted powdered
  sugar

1. Prepare butter crust.
2. Keep oven at 350°.
3. In large bowl, beat eggs with vanilla.
4. Stir in brown sugar. Add flour sifted together with salt and baking powder. Mix in coconut and nuts.
5. Spread mixture evenly over butter crust. Bake 20 minutes.
6. Cool on a rack and cut in bars. Roll bars in powdered sugar.

Butter Crust

1 cup flour
¼ cup sugar
½ cup butter

1. Preheat oven to 350°.
2. Into medium bowl, sift together flour and sugar.
3. Cut in butter until particles are fine.
4. Press mixture over bottom of 9-inch square baking pan. Bake 20 minutes.

Makes 30 bars

 # MACADAMIA-ICE CREAM DESSERT

1¼ cups plain chocolate
  wafer crumbs
½ cup butter, melted
½ gallon chocolate ice
  cream
1½ cups chopped
  macadamia nuts

1. Mix chocolate crumbs and butter thoroughly.
2. Press mixture into 13 x 9 x 2-inch baking pan.
3. Cut ice cream in 1½-inch-thick slices; lay slices close together over crumb crust, blending slices together with a knife as ice cream melts slightly until it is spread evenly over entire pan. Top with nuts. Freeze.
4. Cut in squares to serve.

Serves 8

Hint: This dessert is delicious plain, but it can be made more festive by serving with chocolate or caramel sauce.

MACADAMIA SAUCE
TOPPING FOR ICE CREAMS

2 egg yolks
1 cup powdered sugar
1 cup chopped macadamia
　nuts
1 cup heavy cream,
　whipped

1. Beat egg yolks with powdered sugar until smooth and thick.
2. Fold powdered sugar mixture and nuts into whipped cream.
3. Serve sauce immediately.

Makes topping for 6–8 scoops ice cream

Hint: You can refrigerate sauce, but you must blend it immediately before serving.

 ## DATE CONFECTION

1 cup sherry
1 pound pitted dates
whole roasted macadamia
　nuts (same number as
　dates)

1. Pour sherry over dates. Let stand in refrigerator 24 hours.
2. Remove dates from sherry marinade. Place macadamia nut in the center of each date.
3. Store dates up to 1 month, covered.

Makes 25–35

 ## MACADAMIA TOFFEE

1 cup butter
1¼ cups sugar
¾ cup whole macadamia
　nuts
4 squares (1 ounce)
　semisweet chocolate,
　melted
¾ cup finely chopped
　macadamia nuts

1. In heavy skillet, melt butter.
2. Add sugar. Cook over high heat until mixture foams vigorously, stirring; cook over low heat 5 minutes more, stirring.
3. Add whole nuts; stir over high heat until mixture begins to smoke. Reduce heat to low; cook 7 minutes more, stirring. (If mixture darkens too quickly, remove it from heat, but still stir full 7 minutes.)
4. Quickly pour mixture into 13 x 9 x 2-inch pan; cool.
5. Spread half of chocolate over candy; sprinkle with half of chopped nuts; cool.
6. Flip candy sheet out of pan. Spread second side with remaining chocolate; sprinkle with remaining nuts.
7. Cool. Break in pieces.

Hint: Store candy pieces in covered waxed-paper-lined metal container.

PEANUT

Arachis hypogaea

PEANUT

FIRST INTRODUCED to North America in the 19th century, this nut is said to be a native of South America. It is hard to imagine the peanut having a history before Americans became addicted to it, but jars shaped like peanuts and other items with peanut designs have been found in Inca Indian tombs, leading historians to believe that peanuts were grown and treasured by the Incas of Peru. Around 1630, Spanish conquistadors came to South America for gold and discovered peanuts. They took the peanuts back to Spain, where they became an important crop. Later, carried to Africa on Spanish and Portuguese ships, they were traded for spices and elephant tusks and were given the name goobers by the Africans.

Their travels were long and circuitous. During the 18th century, slave ships en route to America used peanuts as a staple because they were considered the cheapest food available in Africa, the point of departure. As early as the 1800s, peanuts were being grown in the South. During the Civil War, both northern and southern troops used peanuts as part of their diet.

France was the first major country to import peanuts from Africa and crush and extract their oil. Soon other European countries were establishing crushing mills and making peanut oil. Commercial production did not take place in the United States until long after the Civil War. By 1968, world production had reached 19 million tons—enough to encircle the earth with a band of peanuts 90 feet wide! While the South has a tremendous peanut industry, it still raises only about 3.2 percent of the world's peanut acreage. The largest growers are in Asia; India and China account for about half the world's acreage.

In the United States, Georgia is the leading producer; Virginia, Alabama, the Carolinas, Oklahoma, and Texas have substantial production; Florida and New Mexico have entered the field too.

There are a variety of strains. Spanish peanuts, the pride of Oklahoma, are small, almost always round, and usually sold shelled with their red skins on. They are considered to have a lower fat content than other peanuts. The Virginia-type peanut, found in Virginia and the Carolinas, is large, grows in clusters near the taproot of the plant, and is sometimes called the cocktail nut. Alabama produces both the runner peanut, which is used mostly in peanut butter and candies, and the large-seeded florigiant, which is sold in the shell or as salted peanuts.

The peanut plant has a growing season of 140–175 days. Being a legume, the plant looks somewhat like a pea vine with yellow blossoms; but the peanuts grow in the ground. At harvesttime, the peanuts are dug from the ground.

The peanut is not really a nut, but a low-growing annual leguminous plant with two peas (what we call peanuts) to a pod. The shell is corrugated looking, straw colored, and soft; when the nuts are roasted in shells, the salt is easily absorbed into the kernels. Adults as well as children can easily crack the shells.

The name peanut is closely associated with George Washington Carver, a brilliant southern American who found 200 to 300 important uses for the peanut at a time of economic distress in the South. Its many functions now rival those of the coconut. The popularity of the nut stems from the Civil War. The soldiers stationed in the South tasted peanuts, found them to be a delicious food, and by now the whole world knows salted peanuts, peanut butter, and peanut oil. Hogs and cattle as well as human beings are nourished by this widespread nut, which is still very southern in its growing habits and its reputation—it is not successfully cultivated commercially north of Washington, D.C.

The peanut has an assortment of names: goober, earth-nut, groundpea, pinder, and groundnut, which is its name in Europe. Peanuts have been converted into flour. Peanut oil is greatly prized as it has a very high smoking-burning tolerance, is brilliantly clear, neutral in terms of intruding into or absorbing flavors or tastes, and does not spoil without refrigeration. In many European countries, peanut oil is more desirable than olive oil for salad dressings and cooking.

In the Orient and countries of the Far East, peanuts are used in soups, sauces, and accompaniments to curry. Indonesia has its peanut specialty, saté—with an exotic peanut sauce. When not directly part of cooking, peanuts are often sprinkled on top of a finished dish. Peanut meal and flour are used by bakers and candy-makers, and the peanut is even used as a coffee substitute. Whole nuts and less desirable parts of peanuts end up as nourishing animal feed; peanut-fed hams command special enthusiasm.

We all know of peanuts roasted, double roasted, deep-fat fried, and candied; smooth or crunchy peanut butter; and candies using peanuts and peanut butter. The peanut has infinite possibilities in cooking, and its derivatives have become staples in American life. Industry has found both the nutmeat and the plant of inestimable value. The nonfood products, such as shaving cream, adhesive, paper, ink, plastics, cosmetics, and shampoo, have great importance to us. From the shells alone come such industrial products as insulation filler, buffing for steel mills, floor-sweeping compound, and wallboard.

Although the peanut is in the family of legumes and not a true nut, no one who has ever been a child in the United States and gone to a circus or baseball game has escaped the seductive call, "fresh hot roasted peanuts," and bags of the tan nuts-in-shells to munch on, salted or not.

While it is almost impossible to imagine Americans without peanut butter, it was only in 1890 that a doctor in St. Louis, looking for high-protein food that could be easily digested by his patients, tried an experiment. He put roasted shelled peanuts and some salt through a meat grinder. The result was peanut butter. Soon hospitals were serving it for ailing and undernourished patients. In the 1920s, it emerged from the exclusive health food category into a delicious spread beloved by millions. With the advent of stabilizers, which keep the natural oil from separating within the jar, peanut butter became a staple in 4 out of 5 American homes. The smooth versus the crunchy is a matter of personal taste and family debate.

One of the special virtues of the peanut is its relatively low price and its high protein content. It is an excellent food, high in protein, calcium, and iron. Raw peanuts have become an essential part of the health food diet and are used in many substitute meat dishes. The peanut has truly made the world scene. Its contributions are myriad. And as Channing Pollock once said in a most quotable quote, "It's impossible to eat only one. . . ."

 PURCHASE

Peanuts are available all year but are especially plentiful in all varieties during major holiday seasons. They are in vending machines, nut shops, grocery stores, chain stores, and drugstores.

Peanuts can be found in many forms that are suited to individual dietary needs. They are in bulk in specialty shops and are elsewhere in vacuum-packed cans, tight-lidded jars, and plastic bags. They are available in the shells, plain or salted, and shelled, salted, unsalted, double roasted, partially defatted, and specially seasoned.

Shelling raw peanuts and roasting them at home has been a southern tradition, and now shelled raw peanuts, usually unblanched in their red skins, are available in packages. They are used raw in cooking or roasted for eating and cooking, either unsalted or seasoned.

There is a new peanut product available, known as nu-nuts, which are walnut- and pecan-flavored peanut pieces, at peanut prices.

PREPARATION

To blanch. Put shelled raw peanuts in boiling water and let them stand 3 minutes. Drain, slide skin off with your fingers, and spread nuts on absorbent paper towel to dry. Roasting will also loosen the skins of shelled or unshelled peanuts.

To oven roast. Place peanuts in single layer in shallow pan. Cook at 350° 15–20 minutes until golden brown, stirring occasionally for even roasting. Garnish with butter and salt to taste.

To french fry. Using a good vegetable oil, preferably peanut oil, cook in deep oil with wire basket or in shallow oil with no basket but in enough oil to easily cover blanched peanuts. Heat to 300° and add peanuts, stirring occasionally to ensure even cooking. When peanuts begin browning, remove from the oil as they will continue to brown while cooling. Drain off excess oil, place peanuts on brown paper for further draining, and salt immediately according to taste.

To roast in the shell. Place peanuts 1 or 2 layers deep in shallow pan. Cook in moderately hot oven 20–30 minutes, stirring occasionally. Shell and sample the nuts during the last few minutes of cooking time to ensure roasting to the desired color.

STORAGE

Because of the high fat content and susceptibility to rancidness, keep shelled peanuts in tightly closed containers and refrigerate.

Peanuts in the shell and unsalted peanuts have better keeping qualities.

Refrigerate peanut butter but take it out a little before using to soften at room temperature.

AMOUNTS

1½ pounds Virginia-type peanuts in the shell equals 1 pound shelled.

From the point of view of practicality and economics, the shelled peanuts function better if the nuts are to be used to any extent in cooking.

MYSTERY MARVEL APPETIZER

1 package (3 ounce) cream
  cheese
½ pound chunky peanut
  butter
½ cup imported chutney,
  finely cut up
½ teaspoon seasoned salt
red wine for moistening
⅓ cup finely chopped
  peanuts
⅓ cup finely chopped
  parsley or finely
  chopped watercress

1. Mix cream cheese, peanut butter, chutney, and seasoned salt together with just enough red wine to moisten sufficiently to mold into a round ball.
2. Roll ball in nuts and parsley.
3. Serve with toast rounds or unsalted crackers.

Makes 1 large ball

Hint: For a distinctive Indian flavor, reduce amount of peanut butter by 2 ounces and add 1 teaspoon curry powder.

DEVILED HAM APPETIZER

⅓ cup chunky peanut
  butter
1 can (2¼ ounce) deviled
  ham
¼ cup mayonnaise or
  salad dressing
3 tablespoons chopped dill
  pickle

1. Combine peanut butter, ham, mayonnaise, and pickle, mixing thoroughly.
2. Arrange appetizer in a bowl on a tray, with cocktail crackers and melba toast.

Makes 1 cup

CREAM OF PEANUT BUTTER SOUP

¼ stalk celery
½ small onion
1 tablespoon butter
1 tablespoon flour
¾ cup peanut butter
1 cup milk
2 cups chicken broth
¼ teaspoon
   Worcestershire sauce
salt to taste
pepper to taste

1. Finely chop celery and onion.
2. In large saucepan, melt butter. Sauté celery and onion in butter until tender, stirring.
3. Mix flour and peanut butter into celery mixture.
4. Slowly add milk, stirring until smooth. Add remaining ingredients.
5. Bring soup to a boil and lower heat, stirring as needed to keep from sticking. Cook and stir 1 minute longer.

Serves 6

Hint: Two chicken bouillon cubes and 2 cups water can substitute for chicken broth.

 SQUASH BISQUE

2 medium butternut
   squash (about 2 pounds)
3 cans (10¾ ounce)
   chicken broth
1 cup water
¼ teaspoon nutmeg
1 tablespoon butter
1 medium onion, chopped
½ teaspoon curry powder
⅛ teaspoon crushed red
   pepper
1 small garlic clove,
   chopped
1 teaspoon Worcestershire
   sauce
2 tablespoons creamy
   peanut butter
½ cup heavy cream

1. Pare, seed, and cube squash.
2. In heavy saucepan, place squash, chicken broth, water, and nutmeg. Cover and bring to a boil over medium heat. Reduce heat and boil gently until squash is tender.
3. In small skillet over medium-low heat, melt butter. Sauté onion, curry powder, and red pepper in butter until almost tender.
4. Add garlic to onion mixture and cook slowly 3–4 minutes, stirring constantly. Add onion mixture to boiling squash and cook 10 minutes more. Remove from heat. Stir in Worcestershire sauce and peanut butter.
5. Pour soup into blender container with cream and blend until smooth. Reheat to serve.

Serves 8

Hint: Amount of peanut butter can be increased according to taste.

BOMBAY CURRY SALAD

½ cup mayonnaise
¾ teaspoon salt
1 teaspoon curry powder
1 tablespoon lemon juice
1 can (1 pound) peach
   slices, drained
2 cups turkey, cooked,
   cubed or julienne-cut
1 cup coarsely sliced celery
¼ cup sliced green onions,
   with tops
crisp greens
¼ cup salted peanuts

1. Combine mayonnaise, salt, curry powder, and lemon juice.
2. In large bowl, gently toss mayonnaise mixture with peaches, turkey, celery, and green onions.
3. Heap turkey salad into center of a platter lined with greens. Sprinkle with nuts.

Serves 5–6

Hint: As an alternate way to serve, arrange all salad ingredients in piles on a tray and pass dressing separately.

 ## SOHO SALAD

1½ cups shredded
   cabbage
½ cup grated carrots
1 cup crushed pineapple
1 cup shredded coconut
3 tablespoons vinegar
2 tablespoons water
1 tablespoon cornstarch
½ cup pineapple juice
1 egg yolk
¾ cup mayonnaise
1½ cups heavy cream,
   whipped
1 cup chopped peanuts

1. In large bowl, mix together cabbage, carrots, pineapple, and coconut.
2. Mix vinegar with water and stir into cabbage mixture. Chill.
3. In medium saucepan, mix cornstarch with pineapple juice; cook until thick. Stir in egg yolk well, and cook 2 minutes; cool.
4. With hand beater, stir mayonnaise into pineapple juice solution. Fold in whipped cream.
5. Add cream solution to cabbage mixture, mix, and chill. At serving time, sprinkle nuts on top of salad.

Serves 6

CREAMY ORANGE DRESSING

½ cup evaporated milk
½ cup smooth peanut
  butter
1 tablespoon grated orange
  rind
¼ cup orange juice

1. In small bowl, combine ingredients, blending until thoroughly mixed and smooth. Chill.
2. Serve on any fruit or cottage cheese salad.

Serves 6

 ## PEANUT BUTTER

1 cup salted roasted
  Spanish peanuts
1 tablespoon peanut oil

1. Place ingredients in blender. Blend several minutes until mixture becomes spreadable. It may be necessary to add more peanut oil.
2. Store peanut butter in tightly covered container. Refrigerate.
Makes scant cup

Hint: Homemade peanut butter will separate on standing. Stir before using.

You can make this in a special peanut butter machine or food processor without the oil.
For a salt-free diet, use unsalted roasted peanuts.

 ## PEANUT SAUCE

2 tablespoons grated onion
2 tablespoons sesame oil
2 tablespoons brown sugar
1 tablespoon lime juice
2 tablespoons peanut
  butter
1 cup coconut milk
½ teaspoon salt

This is an Indonesian staple.

1. In small skillet, sauté onion in sesame oil 3 minutes.
2. Add brown sugar, lime juice, and peanut butter to onions, mixing well.
3. Blend in coconut milk slowly, stirring constantly. Add salt and simmer until sauce thickens.

Makes 1⅓ cups

Hint: Serve on barbecued pork or use as basting sauce. There are many versions of this Indonesian favorite.

PEANUT-CORN SCALLOP

¼ cup peanut butter
1 can (16 ounce) creamed
    corn
2 eggs, beaten
2 slices bacon, cooked,
    crumbled
⅛ teaspoon pepper
salt to taste
paprika to taste

1. Preheat oven to 325°.
2. In medium bowl, stir peanut butter to soften. Blend in corn, then eggs.
3. Stir in bacon, pepper, and salt.
4. Pour mixture into 1-quart casserole. Sprinkle with paprika. Bake 45 minutes or until firm in center.

Serves 4–5

 ### SOUTHERN GREEN BEANS

⅓ pound bacon
⅔ cup thinly sliced onion
⅓ cup bacon fat
4 cups green beans,
    cooked
2 tablespoons wine
    vinegar
1 teaspoon salt
¼ teaspoon pepper
½ cup dry roasted salted
    peanuts

1. Slice bacon in ½–¾-inch pieces. In large skillet, sauté bacon until crisp. Remove bacon and reserve ⅓ cup fat.
2. Sauté onion in bacon fat until golden.
3. Add green beans, wine vinegar, salt, and pepper to onion. Simmer 12 minutes.
4. Place beans with sauce in warm serving dish. Sprinkle with bacon bits and nuts.

Serves 6

BEEFSTEAK WITH TOMATO-PEANUT SAUCE

2 pounds beef round
  steak, sliced ¾ inch
  thick
¼ cup flour
1 teaspoon salt
⅛ teaspoon freshly
  ground pepper
4 tablespoons vegetable oil
¾ cup chopped onion
1½ cups solid pack
  tomatoes
1 cup chicken or beef stock
½ cup peanut butter

1. Cut steak in 6 servings. Mix flour with salt and pepper and coat meat.

2. In large skillet with lid, heat oil. Brown meat on both sides in oil.

3. Remove meat and sauté onion until tender, but not browned.

4. Return meat to skillet with tomatoes and stock. Cook over low heat 15 minutes, covered.

5. Stir in peanut butter. Cook 15 minutes more or until meat is tender. Serve with rice.

Serves 6

 ## EL RANCHO CHILI

1 pound ground beef
2 cups chopped celery
1 cup chopped onion
1 cup chopped green
  pepper
2 medium garlic cloves,
  crushed
1 can (1 pound) tomatoes
2 cans (8 ounce) tomato
  sauce
1 cup chunky peanut
  butter
2 cans (1 pound) red
  kidney beans, drained
2 tablespoons chili powder
ground cumin to taste
2 teaspoons salt

1. In large saucepan with lid, brown beef, celery, onion, green pepper, and garlic.

2. Stir remaining ingredients into beef mixture. Simmer chili 30 minutes, covered, stirring every 10 minutes.

Serves 6–8

PEANUT MEAT LOAF

1½ cups ground beef (¾
  pound)
3 tablespoons finely
  chopped onion
1 teaspoon dry mustard
1 teaspoon Worcestershire
  sauce
1 teaspoon salt
1 cup finely chopped
  salted peanuts
¾ cup fine bread crumbs
2 eggs
½ cup tomato juice

1. Preheat oven to 350°.
2. Lightly mix ingredients together.
3. Place mixture in buttered 9 x 5 x 3-inch loaf pan. Bake 1 hour. Serve with tomato sauce.

Serves 6

 PEANUT BUTTER-FILLED FRANKFURTERS

½ cup peanut butter
½ cup cream cheese
1 tablespoon chutney
1 tablespoon curry powder
1 tablespoon
  Worcestershire sauce
8 frankfurters

1. In small bowl, combine peanut butter and cream cheese.
2. Blend in chutney, curry powder, and Worcestershire sauce.
3. Spread filling on split frankfurters. Grill filled frankfurters.

Serves 8

Hint: This filling is delicious piled on bread rounds, put under broiler until bubbly, and served as an appetizer.

 PEANUT BUTTER-HAM SQUARES

½ cup peanut butter
2 teaspoons grated onion
6 slices boiled ham
1 egg, beaten
2 tablespoons water
½ cup bread crumbs
½ cup peanut oil

1. Mix together peanut butter and onion well.
2. Spread mixture on 3 slices boiled ham. Top each with second slice of ham, and wrap slices in waxed paper.
3. Chill about 1 hour, then cut slices in 1-inch squares.
4. Mix egg with water. Dip squares into egg and then into bread crumbs.
5. Fry squares in hot peanut oil about 2 minutes until golden brown. Serve at once on toothpicks.

Makes about 5 dozen

INDONESIAN SATÉ

1 large onion, coarsely
  chopped
½ cup vegetable oil
1½ cups lime juice or
  lemon juice
⅓ cup soy sauce
1 tablespoon crushed
  cumin seed
1 tablespoon crushed
  coriander seed
2 tablespoons brown sugar
1 teaspoon ginger
1½ teaspoons pepper
2 garlic cloves, pressed
3 pounds pork tenderloin
  or any lean pork

½ cup peanut butter,
  smooth or crunchy
¾ cup hot water
2 garlic cloves, pressed
2 tablespoons brown sugar
¼ cup soy sauce
¼ cup lemon juice or lime
  juice
¾ teaspoon crushed red
  pepper
1 small onion, finely
  chopped
2 onions, sliced in rings,
  French-fried in oil

1. Combine all ingredients except pork; blend in blender or food processor.

2. Cut pork in bite-size pieces for skewers, and place in large bowl.

3. Pour blended marinade over pork and marinate 3–4 hours.

4. Preheat oven to 325°. Thread pork on skewers. Bake pork pieces 30 minutes, basting several times.

5. Meanwhile, prepare saté sauce.

6. Remove pork, and place on shallow pan on a rack. Baste again.

7. Serve with saté sauce.

Saté Sauce

1. In small saucepan over low heat, stir peanut butter into hot water, cooking until smooth. Stir in garlic, brown sugar, soy sauce, lemon juice, and red pepper, blending thoroughly.

2. Spoon sauce over roasted meat. Sprinkle with chopped raw onion and decorate with fried onion rings.

Serves 6

Hint: This is a somewhat lazy version of the sauce; usually 1 cup peanuts are ground with the water, and the seasonings are blended into this. However, commercial peanut butter works beautifully.

The French-fried onions are optional, but their crunch is a delightful addition.

CROWN ROAST OF PORK WITH CURRY STUFFING

1 large crown roast of pork
   (5 pound)
1 tablespoon seasoned salt
2 tablespoons butter
1 garlic clove, minced
1 onion, chopped
2 tart apples
¼ pound prunes, stewed,
   with stones removed
2–3 teaspoons curry
   powder
½ cup chopped peanuts
½ cup chopped, pitted
   black olives
¼ cup shredded coconut
1 cup bread crumbs,
   toasted

1. Preheat oven to 325°.
2. Season roast inside and outside of crown with seasoned salt.
3. In large skillet, melt butter. Sauté garlic and onion in butter.
4. Core apples and chop in coarse pieces. Add to onion mixture with remaining ingredients. Cook slowly 5 minutes.
5. Fill center of crown with dressing. Protect rib ends from burning by capping them with foil.
6. Bake 35–40 minutes per pound.

Serves 8

Hint: For visual splendor, remove foil and put paper frills on rib ends.

CHICKEN QUENELLES WITH SAUCE PROVENÇALE

1 pound chicken breasts,
   boned, skinned
1 teaspoon salt
2 egg whites
2 ice cubes, cracked
2 cups heavy cream
¼ cup butter
1 onion, minced
1 garlic clove, minced
¼ cup peanut butter
¼ cup flour
2 cups tomato juice
salt to taste
pepper to taste

1. Cut chicken in ½-inch strips.
2. In blender, place chicken, salt, egg whites, and ice cubes. Whirl at top speed, turning motor on and off several times and pushing contents down from sides until mixture is smooth. While blender is whirling, slowly pour in cream. Mixture will be thick and creamy.
3. Fill large skillet with 1½ inches of salted simmering water. Drop chicken mixture by egg-shaped spoonfuls into simmering water. Simmer 15 minutes. Remove quenelles with slotted spoon and drain on absorbent paper.
4. In medium saucepan, melt butter. Sauté onion and garlic in butter until golden. Stir in peanut butter and flour. Gradually stir in tomato juice. Cook over low heat until sauce bubbles and thickens, stirring. Season with salt and pepper.
5. Place quenelles on serving platter. Pour hot sauce over them. Serve at once.

Serves 4–6

ORANGE-PEANUT DUCKLING

1 duckling (4 pound)
seasoned salt to taste
1 can (6 ounce) frozen
    concentrated orange
    juice, thawed
1 small onion, minced
¼ cup peanut butter
1 cup water
2 teaspoons grated orange
    rind
1 tablespoon cider vinegar

1. Preheat oven to 325°.
2. Wash duckling thoroughly and dry. Rub inside and out with seasoned salt. Prick entire skin with a fork, at a horizontal angle to avoid piercing the meat.
3. Roast duckling, breast-side down, on a rack in a shallow pan 1½ hours.
4. Brush duckling heavily with concentrated orange juice every 20 minutes; prick skin often too.
5. Roast 30 minutes more until tender, brushing duckling heavily with orange juice every 10 minutes. Duck takes about 2–3 hours roasting before it is fork tender. Remove it to platter breast-side up and keep warm.
6. Drain fat from drippings in roasting pan.
7. In separate pan, sauté onion in 2 tablespoons of duckling fat. Stir in peanut butter.
8. Add water to pan drippings. Boil to loosen all particles.
9. Stir drippings into peanut mixture. Add orange rind and cider vinegar.
10. While stirring, cook about 5 minutes until sauce thickens slightly. Season to taste with additional salt. Serve sauce separately.

Serves 4

Hint: As an accompaniment, use orange halves scooped out, filled with whipped sweet potatoes, and baked. Sprinkle filled halves with chopped salted peanuts. On the platter, alternate filled orange halves with sugared purple grapes. Garnish with parsley sprigs.

POTATO-PEANUT CASSEROLE

2 cups hot mashed
  potatoes
1 cup bread crumbs
½ teaspoon pepper
½ teaspoon salt
4 tablespoons butter,
  melted
2 tablespoons onion juice
1 cup ground peanuts

1. Preheat oven to 350°.
2. Combine all ingredients. Place in buttered casserole.
3. Bake 30 minutes, uncovered.

Serves 4–6

 ## MAPLE-PEANUT RING

2¾–3¼ cups flour
¼ cup sugar
¾ teaspoon salt
1 envelope dry yeast
4 tablespoons butter,
  softened
¾ cup warm water
1 egg, room temperature
¾ cup chopped peanuts
¼ cup dark brown sugar,
  packed
1 teaspoon maple flavoring
1 tablespoon peanut oil
½ cup powdered sugar,
  mixed with 1 teaspoon
  milk

1. In large bowl, mix 1 cup flour, sugar, salt, and undissolved yeast thoroughly. Add 2 tablespoons butter.
2. Gradually add warm water to dry ingredients, and beat 2 minutes at medium speed of electric mixer.
3. Add egg and ½ cup flour. Beat at high speed 2 minutes. Stir in enough additional flour to make a soft dough.
4. Turn out dough onto lightly floured board; knead until smooth and elastic. Cover dough with plastic wrap, then a tea towel. Let dough rise 20 minutes.
5. Punch dough down on lightly floured board and roll into 16 x 8-inch rectangle.
6. Melt remaining butter. Brush dough with butter.
7. Combine nuts, brown sugar, and maple flavoring. Sprinkle mixture over dough.
8. Roll up from long side to form a ring. Place on buttered baking sheet.
9. Cut ⅔ way into ring with scissors at 1-inch intervals; turn each section on its side.
10. Brush ring with peanut oil and cover loosely with plastic wrap. Refrigerate 2–24 hours.
11. When ready to bake, uncover and let stand 10 minutes.
12. Preheat oven to 375°.
13. Bake 20–25 minutes or until done. Drizzle with powdered sugar frosting.

Serves 8–10

SWEET-POTATO NUTBURGERS

2 cups mashed cooked
   sweet potatoes
½ cup chopped peanuts
¼ cup sugar
½ teaspoon cinnamon
1 cup finely ground
   peanuts
¼ cup butter

1. Preheat oven to 400°.
2. Mix together sweet potatoes, chopped nuts, sugar, and cinnamon.
3. Shape potato mixture into flat patties. Roll in ground nuts.
4. Place patties on buttered baking sheet. Dot with butter. Bake 15–20 minutes or until nuts are toasty brown.

Serves 6–8

PRIZE PEANUT BREAD

½ cup finely chopped
   dried apricots
1 egg
1 cup sugar
2 tablespoons butter,
   melted
2 cups sifted flour
3 teaspoons baking
   powder
¼ teaspoon baking soda
¾ teaspoon salt
½ cup orange juice
¼ cup water
1 cup chopped roasted
   peanuts
cream cheese to taste
crushed pineapple to taste,
   well drained

1. Soak apricots in water 2 hours; drain and dry on paper towels.
2. In large bowl, mix egg, sugar, and butter.
3. Sift together flour, baking powder, baking soda, and salt. To butter mixture, add sifted dry ingredients alternately with orange juice and water, beginning and ending with dry ingredients.
4. Preheat oven to 350°.
5. Stir apricots and nuts into batter. Beat until well blended.
6. Pour batter into buttered 9 x 5 x 3-inch loaf pan. Bake 1 hour and 15 minutes or until bread tests done in the center.
7. Turn loaf out on a rack to cool. When cool, cut in thin slices with serrated knife. Spread with cream cheese and top with well-drained crushed pineapple.

Makes 1 loaf

SOUTHERN PEANUT BUTTER PIE

½ cup sugar
¼ cup cornstarch
2 cups milk
3 egg yolks
2 tablespoons butter
1 teaspoon vanilla
3 egg whites
4 teaspoons sugar
1 cup powdered sugar
1½ cups smooth peanut
   butter
1 pie shell (9 inch),
   baked

This recipe was graciously sent to author by First Lady Rosalynn Carter, who originally received it from Mrs. Frank Dean of Jacksonville, Florida.

1. Preheat oven to 325°.
2. Mix together ½ cup sugar and cornstarch.
3. Add milk and egg yolks. Cook over low flame, stirring constantly.
4. When mixture is thick, add butter and vanilla. Put filling aside.
5. Beat egg whites and add sugar. Put aside.
6. Mix together powdered sugar and peanut butter.
7. Put ⅔ of peanut butter mixture in baked 9-inch pie shell.
8. Put filling on top, and top with meringue. Sprinkle remainder of peanut butter mixture on top of meringue.
9. Bake about 10 minutes or until light brown.

Serves 6–8

PEANUT-BANANA-OATMEAL COOKIES

1½ cups sifted flour
½ teaspoon baking
   powder
¾ teaspoon salt
¾ teaspoon cinnamon
¼ teaspoon nutmeg
½ cup butter
½ cup smooth peanut
   butter or crunchy
   peanut butter
1 cup sugar
1 egg
1 ripe banana, mashed
1½ cups raw
   quick-cooking oatmeal

1. Preheat oven to 375°.
2. Sift together flour, baking powder, salt, cinnamon, and nutmeg. Set aside.
3. In large bowl, cream butter, peanut butter, and sugar together until light and fluffy.
4. Beat egg and banana into creamed mixture.
5. Into egg mixture, fold flour mixture and oatmeal until just blended.
6. Drop batter by teaspoonsful on buttered baking sheet. Bake 8–10 minutes.

Makes 4½ dozen

135

THE CLASSIC CRISSCROSS COOKIES

1 cup butter
1 cup peanut butter
1 cup sugar
1 cup brown sugar, firmly
 packed
2 eggs
2 cups flour
1 teaspoon baking soda

1. Preheat oven to 350°.
2. In large bowl, cream butter and peanut butter together. Gradually add sugars, creaming until blended.
3. Add eggs 1 at a time, and beat until smooth.
4. Sift flour, measure, then sift again with baking soda into peanut butter mixture; blend.
5. Shape mixture into 1-inch balls and place about 2 inches apart on buttered sheet. Flatten with a fork in crisscross pattern.
6. Bake 10-15 minutes.

Makes 6 dozen

Hint: Use 1 package (6 ounce) semisweet chocolate bits as a delicious addition.

PEANUT BUTTER-MOLASSES SQUARES

1½ cups sifted flour
1½ teaspoons baking
 powder
¼ teaspoon baking soda
1 teaspoon cinnamon
½ teaspoon ground cloves
½ teaspoon salt
⅓ cup butter, softened
½ cup peanut butter
½ cup sugar
1 egg
½ cup light molasses
½ cup hot water
½ cup chopped peanuts

1. Preheat oven to 350°.
2. Butter a 13 x 9 x 2-inch baking pan; line with waxed paper; and butter and flour paper.
3. Sift together flour, baking powder, baking soda, cinnamon, cloves, and salt.
4. In large bowl, blend butter and peanut butter until creamy; add sugar, beating well. Add egg and molasses, beating until well blended.
5. To creamed mixture, add hot water alternately with sifted dry ingredients; mix well after each addition.
6. Pour mixture into prepared pan. Sprinkle with nuts. Bake 30–35 minutes. Cool slightly and remove from pan to a rack.
7. Cool and cut in bars.

Makes 30 bars

INSTANT PEANUT BRITTLE ICE CREAM

1 pint vanilla ice cream,
  very soft
1 cup coarsely chopped
  peanut brittle

1. Mix ingredients together until well blended.
2. Pack into airtight container, cover, and place in freezer.

Makes more than 1 pint

 INSTANT PEANUT BUTTER ICE CREAM

1 pint vanilla ice cream,
  very soft
¾ cup chunky peanut
  butter

1. Mix ingredients together until well blended.
2. Pack into airtight container, cover, and place in freezer.

Makes more than 1 pint

 PEANUT BUTTER FUDGE

4 cups sugar
¼ teaspoon salt
1½ cups milk or
  half-and-half
4 tablespoons light corn
  syrup
½ cup peanut butter
2 teaspoons vanilla

1. In large saucepan, combine sugar, salt, milk, and corn syrup.
2. Cook sugar mixture to soft-ball stage at 236°. Cool to lukewarm and beat in peanut butter and vanilla until creamy.
3. Pour candy into lightly buttered 8-inch square pan. Let stand to cool. Cut in squares.

Makes 30 pieces

PECAN

Carya illinoensis

PECAN

THE PECAN IS strictly an American nut. George Washington carried pecans in his pockets all through the Revolutionary War. His great-nephew planted two pecan trees at Mount Vernon about 1858, which still bear nuts.

The pecan is a species of the hickory nut family, whose existence allegedly goes back to Cretaceous times. The nut is in two parts, each part pillowing a little in a convoluted shape. Pecans have a thin, clinging, inner brown skin, which seems immovable.

The smooth shell of the pecan is all of a piece, and the nuts-in-shell are shaped somewhat like olives, brown colored in general. Some of the strains vary in shape and color, from long and pointed to almost rectangular. The shells, some artificially colored a reddish brown and even polished for marketing, range from being hard to "paper-shelled," the latter are often a grayish beige or tan.

While the paper-shell variety are known to be easy to crack and shell, all pecans are relatively easy to crack with the use of a nutcracker or hammer or by squeezing two nuts together. They can come out of their shells whole with a thin layer of brown fibrous material between the two halves; but when this inedible material is removed, the pecan becomes two halves, usually perfect halves; the halves are graded and priced according to size.

Pecans are the fruit of a big tree that originally grew wild throughout the Mississippi Valley and the river valleys of its tributaries. The tree is also found in the river valleys of Texas all the way down to Mexico. Long before the advent of the European explorer, Indian tribes used pecans as food, even making flour from the nuts. Although many trees are still wild in the South, today the cultivated pecan industry flourishes in Georgia, Texas, and many other southern states. While there is some uncertainty about the date domestic cultivation of the pecan started, George Washington was planting pecans in 1775, calling them Mississippi nuts, which he likened to a pig-nut. Over 300 varieties have been described, propagated from wild seedlings.

The pecan has a very sweet, oily, rich-tasting meat and a warm, lovely brown color. Pecans are nutritious, remarkably high in polyunsaturated fats, and low in sodium. The pecan is considered the most valuable of the nut trees in the United States, for the wood is used extensively in furniture. Although the pecan is native to restricted areas of the South and Mexico, it is now grown in California. However, it rarely thrives above the 39th parallel. The nuts are delicious right out of the shell and are prized for their taste and texture in cakes and candies. They are increasingly being used in all kinds of cooking, whether in halves, chopped, ground, roasted, or toasted. There does not seem to be any relationship between their size and shape and their flavor and aroma.

Pecan trees grow to a lofty height of 100 to 160 feet. Although a single tree has been known to bear 3,000 pounds of nuts in a year, the average pecan tree bears 25 to 100 pounds yearly.

While the pecan nut does not have the glamorous and romantic history of world travel that many other nuts have had, the name pecan has a special romantic aura of its own, conjuring up visions of charming southern dishes. A delicious nut, sweet and yet mild, it blends in and enhances many foods without dominating them. Its fame as part of the pecan pie tradition and as part of the New Orleans famous praline family is unchallenged. Once only the darling of the South, the pecan is now used and prized throughout the world.

 PURCHASE

Pecans are available in supermarkets and specialty shops in halves, pieces, and finely chopped. The specialty shops feature halves, which are found in bulk, in cans, and in 5–10-pound tins.

Pecans are available ground at special nut stores, which feature nut meal. They can be ground at home (See Preparation).

Look for well-formed, unblemished nuts in the shell and plump, nut-brown, well-formed and convoluted, shelled nuts.

The size classifications of pecan halves are determined by the U.S. Dept. of Agriculture. They are based on the number of halves it takes to make a pound, as follows:

Mammoth	under 250 halves per pound
Jr. Mammoth	250–300 halves per pound
Jumbo	300–350 halves per pound
Large	450–550 halves per pound
Topper	650–800 halves per pound

Pecans are also commercially available in pieces, finely or coarsely chopped, packaged both in plastic bags and hermetically sealed cans. They are marketed raw or roasted, salted and unsalted.

Pecans in the shell keep in a cool place for months. Shelled, they keep best for any length of time in airtight containers either in the refrigerator or freezer.

PREPARATION

To shell pecans, if you are careful, using a nutcracker with skill you can obtain perfect pecan halves which never need blanching.

To toast. Spread halves or pieces in a single layer in shallow pan, and place in 350° oven about 15 minutes, stirring every 5 minutes. Remove, cool, and store in airtight container, either salted or unsalted.

For cooking, in order to achieve a richer taste, toast pecans in the oven or on top of the stove in 1 teaspoon or 1 tablespoon butter before using in a recipe.

To grind. For tortes or special dishes, grind pecans in a meat grinder, nut mill, blender, or food processor. The meat grinder makes the most oily product, mealy tasting as well as crunchy and full flavored. This is ideal for certain foods, especially for coating the outside of candies.

AMOUNTS

2 pounds in-shell pecans reduce to 1 pound shelled nutmeats.
1 pound shelled pecans equals 4 cups nutmeats.

PLAINS SPECIAL CHEESE RING

1 pound grated mild
  cheese
1 cup chopped pecans
1 cup mayonnaise
1 small onion, grated
black pepper to taste
dash of cayenne

This is a favorite of President Jimmy Carter's family.

1. Mix thoroughly and mold with hands into desired shape. Place in refrigerator until chilled.
2. When ready to serve, serve with strawberry preserves.

Serves 6–8

 ## COCKTAIL DELIGHTS

1 cup butter, softened
4 cups shredded sharp
  cheese
2 cups finely chopped
  pecans
2 cups flour
1 teaspoon cayenne
2 teaspoons salt

1. Preheat oven to 325°.
2. In large bowl, cream butter and cheese together thoroughly.
3. Add remaining ingredients and mix well.
4. Roll mixture into long roll and refrigerate several hours.
5. Slice roll in thin rounds. Place slices on slightly buttered baking sheet.
6. Bake 20 minutes or until edges brown.

Serves 8–10 along with other appetizers

 ## TV PARTY SNACKS

⅓ cup butter, melted
1 tablespoon
  Worcestershire sauce
¼ teaspoon salt
⅛ teaspoon garlic salt or
  garlic powder
2 cups Wheat Chex
2 cups Rice Chex
2 cups Cheerios
2 cups thin pretzel sticks
½ cup pecan halves

1. Preheat oven to 300°.
2. In large bowl, combine butter, Worcestershire sauce, salt, and garlic salt.
3. Add Wheat Chex, Rice Chex, Cheerios, pretzel sticks, and nuts, mixing until all pieces are coated with butter. Pour onto baking sheet.
4. Bake 30 minutes, stirring every 10 minutes. Let cool.

Makes 7 cups

PECAN SOUP

2 tablespoons butter
2 heaping teaspoons
  instant minced onions
1 tablespoon flour
1 teaspoon seasoned salt
1 can (13¾ ounce) chicken
  broth, undiluted
1 heaping teaspoon
  seasoned chicken stock
  base
¾ cup half-and-half
¼ cup heavy cream
⅓ cup sherry
1 cup pecans, pulverized
  in food processor
sour cream or whipped
  cream to garnish
  (optional)

1. In saucepan, melt butter. Stir in instant onions, blending well and cooking 1 minute.
2. Add flour, seasoned salt, and ½ cup chicken broth. Cook until slightly thickened.
3. Gradually stir in remaining chicken broth and seasoned chicken stock base.
4. Add half-and-half and cream; then stir in sherry. Correct for seasoning. Add nuts.
5. Simmer 20 minutes to blend flavors and thicken soup.
6. Serve hot with small dollop of sour cream.

Serves 6.

PECAN-VEGETABLE ASPIC

1⅓ tablespoons gelatin
⅔ cup chicken broth
2 cups tomato juice
¼ cup lemon juice
2 tablespoons sugar
¾ teaspoon salt
dash of pepper
¼ cup minced green onion
¾ cup diced cooked green
  beans
⅔ cup grated cabbage
¼ cup sliced cucumber
⅓ cup chopped green
  pepper
¾ cup diced raw
  cauliflower
⅔ cup chopped pecans

1. Pour gelatin into chicken broth and let stand 10 minutes.
2. In large saucepan, bring tomato juice to a boil; add broth, stirring until gelatin dissolves.
3. Mix in lemon juice, sugar, salt, and pepper.
4. Chill gelatin until it begins to thicken. Stir in remaining ingredients.
5. Place gelatin mixture in oiled 6-cup mold or pan of same volume. Chill until set.
6. Unmold on cold serving plate.

Serves 8

Hint: Mayonnaise seasoned with a hint of chopped chives or dill weed is excellent with this.

CRANBERRY TIP-TOP MOLD

1 can (16 ounce) whole
   berry cranberry sauce,
   strained
2½ tablespoons lemon
   juice
½ pint heavy cream
1 package (3 ounce) cream
   cheese
¼ cup mayonnaise
¼ cup powdered sugar
½ cup chopped pecans
1 teaspoon vanilla

1. Mash cranberry sauce with lemon juice and pour into oiled mold.
2. In medium bowl, whip cream.
3. In another medium bowl, mix together cream cheese, mayonnaise, and powdered sugar.
4. Fold cheese mixture into whipped cream with nuts and vanilla.
5. Spread cream mixture over cranberry layer in mold.
6. Freeze. Serve salad in mold in which it was frozen, or unmold only when ready to use as it should be served still frozen.

Serves 6–8

 ## SOUTHERN SWEET SALAD

1 package (3 ounce) cream
   cheese, at room
   temperature
2 tablespoons heavy cream
⅓ cup mayonnaise
2 tablespoons lemon juice
½ teaspoon salt
2 tablespoons sugar
1 can (20 ounce) white
   cherries, pitted
1 can (8 ounce) sweetened
   apricots, coarsely cut
1 can (8 ounce) pineapple
   chunks
1 cup seeded green grape
   halves or seeded purple
   grape halves
½ cup coarsely chopped
   pecans
1 cup chopped
   marshmallows
1 cup heavy cream,
   whipped
1 cup shredded green leaf
   lettuce

Apricots, nuts, grapes, and other fruits give this salad an exotic flavor.

1. In large bowl, mix cheese with cream.
2. Blend mayonnaise, lemon juice, salt, and sugar into cheese mixture.
3. Fold in cherries, apricots, pineapple, grapes, nuts, and marshmallows. Add whipped cream and mix together well.
4. Pour mixture into refrigerator tray and freeze.
5. Unmold on cold serving dish and surround with shredded lettuce.

Serves 6–8

STUFFED BREAST OF VEAL

1 large breast of veal, with
  pocket cut in for
  stuffing, or 2 small
  breasts of veal, each
  with pocket cut in for
  stuffing
4 tablespoons butter,
  softened
seasoned salt to taste
3 tablespoons flour
1 onion, chopped
1 cup hot water
3 tablespoons water
⅓ bunch parsley sprigs

1. Preheat oven to 325°.
2. Wash veal and dry thoroughly. Prepare stuffing.
3. Lightly season pocket; stuff with dressing; sew up. Bake extra stuffing in separate dish.
4. Rub stuffed veal all over with butter, sprinkle with seasoned salt, and dust with 1½ tablespoons flour.
5. Place veal in roaster with onion and 1 cup hot water.
6. Roast 3 hours. Leave uncovered first hour until a
7. Decorate with parsley. Serve extra gravy in a sauceboat.

Stuffing

1 small loaf egg bread,
  sliced, lightly toasted
½ cup butter
1 onion, finely chopped
4–6 stalks celery, chopped
3 tablespoons finely
  minced parsley
seasoned salt to taste
1 cup chopped pecans

1. Soak toasted bread in water 1 minute; squeeze out all liquid.
2. In large saucepan, melt butter. Sauté onion and celery in butter until softened.
3. Add parsley, seasoned salt, and "squeezed-out" bread to onion mixture, mixing thoroughly to evenly distribute vegetables.
4. Stir in nuts. Fry slowly until dressing becomes golden and flavors permeate.

Serves 6–8

Hint: Whipped, creamy, mashed potatoes go well with this dish.

PECAN STUFFED PEPPERS

6 green peppers, tops cut
   off, cored, seeded
1½ cups cooked rice
1½ cups chopped pecans
1½ teaspoons salt
¾ cup tomato juice
3 tablespoons butter,
   melted
2 pounds ground beef
1½ tablespoons minced
   onion
3 tablespoons finely
   chopped celery
¾ cup water or ¾ cup
   additional tomato juice

1. Preheat oven to 350°.
2. Boil green peppers 10 minutes. Drain and keep warm.
3. In large bowl, mix rice, nuts, salt, and tomato juice.
4. In large skillet, melt butter. Sauté beef, onion, and celery in butter.
5. Mix beef mixture with rice mixture, stirring thoroughly without handling too much. Lightly stuff peppers and place in buttered baking pan large enough to accommodate them. Pour ¾ cup water into pan around peppers. Bake 30 minutes.

Serves 6

 BUTTERMILK-PECAN CHICKEN

1 cup buttermilk
1 egg, slightly beaten
1 cup flour
1 cup finely chopped
   pecans
½ cup sesame seed
1 tablespoon salt
1 tablespoon paprika
⅛ teaspoon pepper
2 broiler-fryers (3 pound),
   disjointed
½ cup vegetable oil
¼ cup pecan halves
parsley to taste
1 cup cherry tomatoes
   (optional)

1. Preheat oven to 350°.
2. Mix buttermilk with egg.
3. On heavy-duty foil, stir together flour, chopped nuts, sesame seed, salt, paprika, and pepper.
4. Dip chicken into buttermilk mixture and then into flour mixture.
5. Place oil in large, shallow, foil-lined roasting pan.
6. Place chicken in pan skin-side down; then turn pieces skin-side up.
7. Put nut halves on each piece of chicken.
8. Bake 1 hour and 15 minutes or until tender and golden brown. Serve garnished with parsley and cherry tomatoes.

Serves 6–8

YAM-NUT PIE

1½ cups flour
½ teaspoon salt
½ cup butter
3 tablespoons water
1½ cups mashed yams,
  canned or cooked
⅓ cup brown sugar
¾ teaspoon cinnamon
¾ teaspoon ginger
dash of salt
¾ cup half-and-half,
  scalded
2 eggs, well beaten

1. Preheat oven to 375°.
2. In medium bowl, combine flour and salt; cut in butter.
3. Mix in water to form dough. Roll out dough for 9-inch pie shell. Fit rolled dough into pie plate. Set aside.
4. In another medium bowl, mix yams, brown sugar, cinnamon, ginger, and salt.
5. Vigorously stir scalded half-and-half and eggs into yam mixture to blend. Mixture should be thoroughly mixed and aerated.
6. Pour filling into unbaked pie shell. Bake 20 minutes.
7. Meanwhile, prepare topping.
8. Spread topping over pie filling. Bake 25 minutes more.

Topping

¼ cup butter
¾ cup chopped pecans
½ cup brown sugar

1. Mix ingredients together well.

Serves 8

Hint: This yam mixture needs personal tasting. Some cooks like to add ⅓ cup granulated sugar for a definite sweet taste.
You can use a commercial pie shell of the deep-dish variety.

 # TEXAS RICE

⅓ cup butter
1 large onion, finely
  chopped
1 cup finely chopped
  pecans
6 cups cooked brown rice
salt to taste
pepper to taste
sprinkle of garlic salt

1. In large skillet, melt butter. Sauté onions in butter.
2. Add nuts. Sauté 2 minutes more.
3. Lower heat. Gently stir in rice, salt, pepper, and garlic salt. If rice is dry, add more butter. This is good served with poultry.

Serves 8

Hint: You can keep this in refrigerator overnight and heat it in 350° oven 15 minutes or until warmed thoroughly.

CRANBERRY BREAD

2 cups sifted flour
½ teaspoon salt
1½ teaspoons baking
  powder
½ teaspoon baking soda
1 cup sugar
1 egg, beaten
4 tablespoons butter,
  melted
½ cup orange juice
2 tablespoons hot water
½ cup chopped pecans
1 cup raw cranberries, cut
  in half

1. Preheat oven to 325°.
2. Into large bowl, sift together flour, salt, baking powder, baking soda, and sugar.
3. Beat together egg, 2 tablespoons butter, orange juice, and hot water.
4. Stir egg mixture into dry ingredients.
5. Mix in nuts and cranberries.
6. Pour batter into 9 x 5 x 3-inch loaf pan. Bake 1 hour and 10 minutes.
7. Brush hot bread with remaining butter.
8. Wrap hot bread in waxed paper and refrigerate 3 hours.
9. Remove waxed paper; wrap bread in a towel, and store in refrigerator.

Makes 1 loaf

 ## RHUBARB BREAD

⅓ cup sugar
¾ cup chopped pecans
2 tablespoons butter
½ teaspoon cinnamon
1½ cups brown sugar
⅔ cup butter, melted, or
  vegetable oil
1 egg
1 cup sour milk
1½ teaspoons baking soda
2½ cups flour
1 teaspoon salt
1½ cups raw rhubarb, cut
  in small pieces
1 teaspoon vanilla

1. Combine sugar, ¼ cup nuts, 2 tablespoons butter, and cinnamon, blending well. Set aside for topping.
2. Preheat oven to 350°.
3. In large bowl, mix together brown sugar, melted butter, egg, sour milk, and baking soda.
4. Into brown sugar mixture, sift together flour and salt; blend.
5. Fold rhubarb, vanilla, and remaining nuts into flour mixture.
6. Place batter in 2 buttered 9 x 5 x 3-inch loaf pans.
7. Sprinkle with topping. Bake 45 minutes.

Makes 2 loaves

CHOCOLATE SUNDAE PUDDING

1 cup sifted flour
2 teaspoons baking
 powder
¼ teaspoon salt
¾ cup sugar
5½ tablespoons cocoa
½ cup milk
2 tablespoons butter,
 melted
1 cup chopped pecans
1 cup brown sugar
1¾ cups hot water
1 cup heavy cream,
 whipped, or 1 pint
 vanilla ice cream

1. Preheat oven to 350°.
2. Into medium bowl, sift together flour, baking powder, salt, sugar, and 1½ tablespoons cocoa.
3. Stir in milk, butter, and nuts; beat by hand or electric mixer until well blended.
4. Pour batter into well-buttered 8-inch square baking pan.
5. Mix remaining cocoa with brown sugar; sprinkle over top of batter.
6. Carefully pour hot water over whole mixture.
7. Bake 45 minutes. Cool on a rack, but serve warm with whipped cream.

Serves 8

Hint: Make this at least 1 hour before serving and cool on a rack. This will insure that the sauce becomes thick and delicious. Do not refrigerate before serving.
 This is also tasty with heavy cream poured on individual servings rather than whipped.

 CORNFLAKE RING

¾ cup pecan halves
⅓ cup brown sugar
⅔ cup white sugar
½ cup light corn syrup
⅓ cup water
1 teaspoon salt
¼ cup butter
1 teaspoon vanilla
cornflakes measured by
 filling ring mold with
 them
1 quart ice cream

1. In small saucepan, cook together ½ cup nuts, sugars, corn syrup, water, salt, and butter to soft-ball stage at 236°. Stir in vanilla.
2. Preheat oven to 300°.
3. Butter small ring mold well.
4. In large bowl, add remaining nuts to cornflakes.
5. Pour just less than half of syrup mixture over cornflakes, tossing with 2 large forks or spoons.
6. Pack this mixture into small, buttered ring mold.
7. Prepare cornflake ring for unmolding by standing it in 300° oven 5 minutes. Remove from oven. Run knife around cornflake ring and quickly invert on large serving plate.
8. Fill center of ring with ice cream balls.
9. Heat remaining syrup mixture and serve separately to spoon over ice cream balls.

Serves 6

Hint: For larger mold and more guests, double recipe.

SCHNECKEN

This old family favorite is a little complicated, but worth every minute.

Dough

1 cake yeast
¼ cup sugar
1 cup half-and-half
1 cup butter
2 eggs, beaten
1 egg yolk
3 cups flour
1 teaspoon salt
butter, melted

1. Dissolve yeast and 1 teaspoon sugar in 2 tablespoons warm half-and-half.

2. In medium saucepan, scald remaining half-and-half. Add 1 cup butter and remaining sugar.

3. Cool to lukewarm. Stir in eggs, egg yolk, and softened yeast.

4. Into large bowl, sift together flour and salt; gradually beat in yeast mixture. The dough often climbs the beaters of an electric mixer that does not have a dough hook, but persistence will pay. Mix as well as you can, and then knead dough on lightly floured board a few minutes.

5. Place dough in large buttered bowl, and brush top of dough with melted butter. Cover bowl with tea towel; tie tea towel onto bowl. Refrigerate overnight. Dough will rise.

6. Next morning, work on half of dough at a time. Roll half of dough on lightly floured board into large 12½ x 10-inch rectangle about ½ inch thick.

Filling

6 tablespoons butter, melted

6 tablespoons dark brown sugar

6 tablespoons chopped pecans

3 tablespoons grated unsweetened chocolate

1. Assemble filling ingredients. Spread dough rectangle with 3 tablespoons butter, sprinkling 3 tablespoons brown sugar and 3 tablespoons nuts over this.
2. Sprinkle 1½ tablespoons chocolate on top. Roll up jelly-roll fashion, manipulating it into a 15-inch roll.
3. Prepare pans.
4. Cut rolls into ¾-inch slices and place cut-side down in prepared pans.
5. Brush tops of pieces with melted butter. Let rise in warm place until dough is light.
6. Preheat oven to 350°.
7. Bake Schnecken 20 minutes, watching carefully. Take out; let stand 2 minutes; and then place plate or pan on top and turn out upside down, replacing nuts or syrup if necessary. Cool on a rack.

Pan Preparation

2 cups butter

¾ cup light brown sugar, tightly packed

¾ cup dark brown sugar, tightly packed

¼ teaspoon cinnamon

2 tablespoons water

2 cups pecan halves

1. In medium saucepan, melt butter. Stir in brown sugars, cinnamon, and water. Cook over low heat about 3 minutes.
2. Liberally butter muffin pans; place 2 nut halves in bottom of each muffin pan and cover with 1 tablespoon of mixture.

Makes 2 dozen large rolls or about 3 dozen small rolls.

PECAN PIE SHELL

1¼ cups flour
½ cup butter, softened
3 tablespoons sugar
¼ cup finely chopped
  pecans

1. Preheat oven to 400°.
2. Combine ingredients well.
3. Roll mixture between 2 waxed-paper sheets. Place crust evenly in 9-inch pie plate. Prick crust all over with fork so it will bake evenly.
4. Bake 10–15 minutes until golden brown. Cool.

Makes 1 pie shell (9 inch)

 ## GEORGIA PECAN PIE

1 cup pecan halves
1 pie shell (9 inch),
  unbaked
3 eggs, well beaten
2 tablespoons butter,
  melted
1 cup dark corn syrup
½ teaspoon vanilla
1 cup sugar
1 tablespoon flour

1. Preheat oven to 350°.
2. Arrange nuts in bottom of pie shell.
3. In small bowl, beat eggs until frothy. Blend in butter, corn syrup, and vanilla well.
4. In medium bowl, combine sugar and flour. Blend in egg mixture thoroughly.
5. Pour filling over nuts in pie shell. Let stand until nuts rise to surface.
6. Bake 45 minutes. Cool on a rack. Serve warm or completely cooled.

Serves 8

 ## DERBY PIE

½ cup butter
1 cup sugar
2 eggs, beaten
1 teaspoon vanilla
½ cup flour
1 cup pecans
1 package (6 ounce)
  semisweet chocolate bits
1 pie shell (9 inch),
  unbaked

1. Preheat oven to 325°.
2. In large saucepan, melt butter. Stir sugar into butter.
3. Blend eggs, vanilla, and flour into sugar mixture. Stir in nuts and chocolate bits.
4. Pour filling into pie shell. Bake 1 hour or until silver knife comes out clean.

Serves 8

Hint: There are many variations of Derby Pie served with pride and fanfare in the South. Serve this excellent one warm or cold with flavored, sweetened whipped cream.

PECAN DOATES

¾ cup butter
1 cup sifted flour
2 cups powdered sugar
1 cup oatmeal
2 eggs
1 cup chopped pecans
1 teaspoon vanilla

1. Preheat oven to 300°.
2. In large bowl, blend butter, flour, powdered sugar, and oatmeal with fingertips until crumbly.
3. Mix in eggs.
4. Stir in nuts and vanilla thoroughly.
5. Drop batter by teaspoonsful on buttered baking sheet 2 inches apart.
6. Bake cookies 20 minutes. Loosen cookies and cool before removing from pan.

Makes 4–5 dozen

 ## MARSHMALLOWS CHICAGO STYLE

2 envelopes (1 tablespoon)
  unflavored gelatin
½ cup cold water
2 cups sugar
¾ cup water
dash of salt
¼ cup powdered sugar
1 egg white
4 cups finely ground pecans

1. In large electric–mixer bowl, dissolve gelatin in cold water.
2. Cook sugar with ¾ cup water and salt 12 minutes or until syrup spins a thread.
3. Pour hot syrup over dissolved gelatin; let cool partially.
4. With electric mixer at high speed, beat 15 minutes or until mixture is of marshmallow consistency.
5. Dust 9-inch square pan thickly with powdered sugar; spread marshmallow mixture over bottom of pan. Brush top with egg white.
6. Immediately press 1½ cups nuts over top, covering it completely and using more nuts if you need them.
7. Put nutted marshmallow in cool place to rest at least 30 minutes.
8. Turn out nutted marshmallow on waxed paper sprinkled with powdered sugar. Lightly brush or spoon egg white over exposed side.
9. Again immediately press thick coat of remaining nuts into marshmallow mixture. Let rest 1 hour.
10. Cut marshmallows in 1–inch squares and dip each side into egg white and remaining nuts until all sides are coated. Let stand at least 1 hour to adhere, and then individually wrap squares in waxed paper.

Makes 81

Hint: Mix the nuts with ½ cup light brown sugar to coat the marshmallow more easily.

BOURBON BALLS

1 cup powdered sugar
2 teaspoons cocoa
1 cup vanilla wafer crumbs
1 cup finely chopped
  pecans
½ tablespoon light corn
  syrup
½ cup bourbon
powdered sugar to coat

1. In large bowl, mix together 1 cup powdered sugar and cocoa. Add crumbs and nuts.
2. Combine corn syrup and bourbon, and vigorously stir into dry ingredients.
3. Form mixture into small balls; roll balls in powdered sugar.
4. Store in tightly covered jar.

Hint: These are best if they are made 3–4 days before serving.

 FANTASY-COME-TRUE FUDGE

4½ cups sugar
1 can (13 ounce)
  evaporated milk
1 cup butter
1 jar (8 ounce)
  marshmallow cream
3 packages (6 ounce)
  semisweet chocolate bits
3 cups chopped pecans

1. In large saucepan, mix together sugar and milk. Bring to a boil; boil rapidly 10–15 minutes to soft-ball stage at 236°, stirring constantly to prevent burning.
2. Remove mixture from heat and mix in remaining ingredients.
3. Pour fudge into buttered 15 x 10-inch dish or 2 smaller ones. Set aside to cool.
4. When cool, cut this delicious fudge in squares.

Makes 5 pounds

 PRALINES

1 can (5⅓ ounce)
  evaporated milk
2 cups sugar
2 teaspoons vanilla
2 tablespoons butter
2 cups pecan halves

1. Add enough water to milk to make ¾ cup.
2. In large saucepan, add sugar to milk mixture and bring to a boil, stirring constantly. Cook to firm-ball stage at 244°. Remove from heat.
3. Add vanilla, butter, and nuts to candy, stirring but not beating.
4. Drop candy by tablespoonsful on well-buttered waxed paper. Let cool.

Makes 18–20

 PINE NUT

Pinus pinea/Pinus edulis

PINE NUT

THE PINE NUT is the fruit of the pine tree. Throughout the world, both the tree and its fruit have frequently been endowed with strange magical properties. The very small nut has a soft, smooth, brown shell and is found in pine cones. The cones are often heated to spread their scales so the nuts can be more easily dislodged.

The pine nut comes in many sizes and shapes and has a variety of names. It has no inner skin. The nut is white, smaller than a tiny white bean, varying roughly from ¼ to ¾ inch in length, and is generally the size of a single puffed rice, only solid. It is sweet, oily, slightly mealy, high in protein content, and has been highly prized through the ages in various parts of the world.

In Italy, the tall stone pine tree, known as *Pinus pinea*, furnishes the domestic nuts and also those to export to many parts of the world. France is also a large exporter, and in haute cuisine recipes, these fancy nuts are called pignolias. The largest pine nuts known are from the Araucanian pines of Brazil and Chile, where they often grow two inches long.

Among the Indians and Mexicans, the nuts are known as pinons, pignolas, Indian nuts, pignons, and stone nuts. They are referred to as stone nuts in the Bible, described as coming from the green fir tree. These names are applied quite casually to the nuts of all species of pine trees.

Historically, the ancient Greeks added pine nuts to their grape leaves recipes for flavor and thickening. When the colonists arrived in the United States, they found most Indian tribes using pine nuts as a salted, roasted snack and food staple: in soups, in meat dishes, for flour, and for baby food. They are now frequently part of South American and Mediterranean cooking. The Italians use them fried in butter and salted as an appetizer and in fish and meat dishes. In China, the city of Soochow specializes in pine nut confections: the nuts are made into a brittle; some are dipped into a thin syrup and sprinkled with coarse crystallized sugar.

The legends connected with the pine tree and then extended to its fruit, the pine nut, have fascinated historians. In the Balkan countries, it is believed that the oil in the pine nuts makes the eater bulletproof, providing the ultimate in protection. Medicinally, the nut is supposed to cure gout, cataracts, and certain cattle diseases. The name pine allegedly comes from the word *pinus*, a raft, because primitive peoples could easily cut the wood into rafts and boats; this must account for the early Greeks considering the pine tree sacred to the sea god. The pine tree appears on the state seal of Massachusetts, and Maine is known as the Pine Tree State. Among the attributes given the pine tree are constancy and loving shelter; in the Orient, the pine symbolizes friendship and long endurance.

 PURCHASE

Pine nuts are available in specialty food shops, nut shops, health stores, and some markets. They are fun to eat in the shell, and years ago they were most popular sold that way; but currently in the United States, they are mostly sold shelled. Presently expensive, they still provide a lot of eating pleasure and, because they are light in weight, you get a lot of nut for your money, adding immeasurably to the deliciousness of a dish.

PIZZA RISSOLES

1 cake yeast
3 tablespoons warm water
pinch of salt
1¾ ounces lard
3½ cups sifted flour
2 cups vegetable oil

1. Dissolve yeast in warm water.
2. Add salt and lard; work in flour, kneading lightly with fingertips. When completely blended, let dough rest 3 hours in warm place. It will rise to approximately double its size.
3. Prepare filling.
4. When it is time to use dough, knead it a little again to remove air.
5. Divide dough in 24 small balls. Roll out each ball in circle about 4 inches in diameter.
6. Place some spinach mixture in center of each circle; fold and press together dampened edges to form a roughly semicircular pillow.
7. Deep fry pillows in hot, but not smoking, oil until they become cooked inside and golden outside. Serve very hot.

Filling

2 packages (12 ounce)
  frozen spinach, thawed,
  or 2 bunches fresh
  spinach
1 tablespoon olive oil
salt to taste
pepper to taste
1 garlic clove, pressed
2–3 cans (2 ounce)
  anchovies preserved in
  oil
2 egg yolks
3 tablespoons capers
½ cup pine nuts
1 can (2¼ ounce) black
  olives, chopped
1 tablespoon raisins

1. Blanch fresh spinach. Drain and chop coarsely.
2. Heat spinach in pan with olive oil, salt, pepper, and garlic until all water evaporates.
3. Chop anchovies.
4. Beat egg yolks and combine with spinach mixture, anchovies, and remaining ingredients. Mix thoroughly to blend seasonings.

Makes 24

Hint: More vegetable oil may be needed. Fry only 4 or 6 at a time to allow each enough room. Drain and place on absorbent paper before serving.

EASY ELEGANT SOUP

½ cup pine nuts, finely
   blended in blender
½ cup half-and-half
1 tablespoon sherry
½ teaspoon seasoned salt
2 cups chicken broth,
   homemade or canned,
   undiluted
1 cup heavy cream,
   whipped
¼ cup chopped toasted
   pine nuts

1. Combine blended nuts, half-and-half, sherry, seasoned salt, and broth.
2. Heat soup in a double boiler and serve hot, or serve chilled with spoonful of whipped cream sprinkled with chopped nuts. Use crisp crackers or melba toast as accompaniment to this delicate, delicious soup.

Serves 6

Hint: If you prefer a little stronger chicken flavor, add 1 teaspoon seasoned chicken-stock base to hot soup.

 SALMON SALAD

2 cans (6 ounce)
   water-packed salmon
1½ cups finely diced
   celery
1 cup spiced grapes
1 tablespoon minced onion
1 jar (2 ounce)
   pimiento-stuffed green
   olives, sliced
mayonnaise
6 lettuce leaf cups
½ cup chopped pine nuts
1 tablespoon butter

1. Drain salmon and coarsely flake.
2. Add celery, grapes, onion, olives, and mayonnaise, using enough mayonnaise to moisten to proper consistency.
3. Mound salad in individual lettuce cups.
4. Toast nuts in butter until golden. Sprinkle nuts on top of each salmon salad.

Serves 6

CARROT HALWA

1 pound carrots
pinch of saffron
⅓ cup milk
2 tablespoons butter
2 whole cloves
4 whole cardamom
½ cup sugar
½ cup pine nuts

1. Scrape and grate carrots.
2. In medium saucepan, combine saffron and milk.
3. Stir in carrots. Cook them in milk over low heat until reduced to paste.
4. In another medium saucepan, melt butter. Sauté cloves, cardamom, and carrot mixture in butter until light brown.
5. Add sugar and continue stirring until well dissolved and carrots are golden brown.
6. Add nuts. Transfer halwa to a bowl and chill.

Serves 6

NEAR EAST SPINACH

2 pounds spinach
4 tablespoons butter, melted
3 garlic cloves, minced
½ teaspoon salt
dash of cayenne
4 tablespoons raisins
½ cup pine nuts
½ cup freshly grated Romano cheese

1. Steam spinach; drain and chop.
2. In small saucepan, combine 2 tablespoons butter, garlic, salt, and cayenne. Stir in raisins and nuts. Cook slowly 5 minutes.
3. Blend mixture well with spinach and place in 8-inch square baking dish, which preferably can go from broiler to table.
4. Top with cheese and remaining butter. Put under broiler until nicely browned.

Serves 4

MIDDLE EASTERN STUFFED TOMATOES

12 large tomatoes
1 large Spanish onion, minced
2 large garlic cloves, minced
1 cup olive oil
1 cup cooked rice
½ cup chopped pine nuts, sautéed in butter
3 tablespoons currants
salt to taste
freshly grated pepper to taste

1. Preheat oven to 350°.
2. Cut top off each tomato and carefully scoop out pulp.
3. In medium saucepan, sauté onion and garlic in 2 tablespoons olive oil. Mix with rice, nuts, and currants. Season well with salt and pepper.
4. Stuff tomato shells with mixture.
5. In large casserole with a lid, heat remaining olive oil; when well heated, arrange stuffed tomatoes in it. Bake 25 minutes, covered. Serve warm.

Serves 12

Hint: During baking, check tomatoes after 15 minutes to be sure they do not fall apart. If they look suspiciously soft and bulging, remove lid.

LAMB WITH ORIENTAL SAUCE

⅓ cup raisins
⅓ cup golden raisins
2 tablespoons warm water
   or wine
4 tablespoons butter
salt and pepper to taste
pinch of cayenne
1 leg of lamb (6 pounds)
2 tablespoons olive oil
2 small onions, finely
   chopped
4 tablespoons pine nuts
6 tablespoons extra-dry
   vermouth
1 tablespoon boiling water

1. Soak raisins and golden raisins in warm water.

2. Cream butter with salt, pepper, and cayenne. Rub leg of lamb thoroughly with seasoned butter. Allow lamb to rest 30 minutes before putting it in oven.

3. Preheat oven to 450°.

4. Roast lamb 30 minutes; then reduce oven to 350° and roast 2–3 hours more at rate of 30 minutes per pound. For pink and juicy meat, properly gauge with meat thermometer, heating to 170°.

5. While meat is roasting, make sauce. In small saucepan, heat 1 tablespoon olive oil. Add onions to warm oil. Add nuts to onions. Drain raisins. Add them to onions.

7. After roast is done, pour excess fat out of roasting pan

8. Correct seasoning of sauce. Serve in sauce boat. Rice is an excellent accompaniment to leg of lamb.

Serves 6–8

Hint: If you like a thicker sauce, make a roux of 1 tablespoon melted butter and 1 tablespoon flour, adding this to sauce and cooking it a few minutes to thicken.

NUTTED VEAL STEAKS

4 thin veal steaks
salt to taste
pepper to taste
3 tablespoons butter
4 tablespoons dry sherry
1 cup sour cream
½ cup pine nuts

1. Lightly season veal on both sides with salt and pepper.
2. In large skillet, melt butter. Sauté veal over medium-high heat about 3 minutes on each side until golden brown and tender. Remove from pan and keep warm.
3. Add sherry to pan. Cook until slightly reduced. Reduce heat to low.
4. Add sour cream and nuts. Slowly heat through, stirring to blend.
5. Return veal to pan and spoon sauce over it. Heat thoroughly.

Serves 4

Hint: This is delicious with steamed white rice or fine noodles.

CHICKEN DIVINE

1 tablespoon chopped
  green onions
4 tablespoons butter
½ cup dry white wine
3 tablespoons flour
1 cup milk
1 cup chicken stock
1 whole clove
1 bay leaf
½ cup raisins
3 pounds chicken, cooked,
  diced
½ cup toasted pine nuts
3 egg yolks
½ cup heavy cream
¼ cup sherry
cumin seeds to taste

1. In large skillet, sauté green onions in 1 tablespoon butter.
2. Add wine to green onions.
3. In small saucepan, melt remaining butter. Stir in flour until bubbly and gradually add milk, stirring over medium heat until mixture becomes a thick white sauce.
4. Stir white sauce into onion mixture.
5. Add chicken stock, clove, and bay leaf to mixture. Cook 5 minutes. Add raisins, chicken, and nuts.
6. Beat together egg yolks, heavy cream, and sherry. Add to chicken mixture.
7. Cook mixture 1 minute. Serve with a sprinkle of cumin seeds over rice or noodles.

Serves 6

CHICKEN VERA CRUZ

3 tablespoons vegetable oil
1 tablespoon butter
1 roasting chicken (4 pound), disjointed
2 red onions, chopped
1 cup diced green tomatoes
1 cup pine nuts
½ cup chopped parsley
2 garlic cloves, minced
1½ cups chicken broth
½ cup dry vermouth
1 teaspoon cumin
2 oranges, peeled, sectioned

1. In large skillet with a lid, heat oil and butter. Brown chicken on all sides. Remove chicken from pan and set aside.
2. In same pan, cook onions until soft.
3. Puree tomatoes, nuts, and parsley in blender or mince very fine.
4. Combine chicken, onions in oil and butter, puree mixture, and remaining ingredients; mix well.
5. Simmer 60 minutes or longer, covered, basting occasionally.

Serves 6

 ## CRAB CAKES

1 pound crab meat (2⅔ cups)
2 eggs, slightly beaten
3 cups soft bread crumbs
1 teaspoon mustard
1 teaspoon seafood seasoning
1 tablespoon minced parsley
½ cup pine nuts
2 tablespoons butter

1. Combine crab meat, eggs, 2¾ cups bread crumbs, mustard, seafood seasoning, and parsley; mix well.
2. Shape mixture into 6-8 patties.
3. Mix nuts with remaining bread crumbs.
4. Dip patties into nut mixture.
5. In large skillet, melt butter. Fry patties in butter until golden, turning.

Serves 6

Hint: Although a sauce is optional, these crab cakes are particularly delicious with a wine-flavored cream sauce.

STUFFED GRAPE LEAVES

1 jar grape leaves, washed, gently dried
2 small onions, finely diced
¾ cup olive oil
⅔ cup raw rice
3 tablespoons fresh lemon juice
½ cup minced parsley
1 teaspoon chopped mint
1 teaspoon chopped fresh dill
½ cup plain pine nuts or toasted pine nuts
1 cup boiling water, used in 2 parts

1. Spread grape leaves out flat, ready for filling.
2. In medium saucepan, sauté onions in 2 tablespoons olive oil until golden; remove from heat.
3. Add rice, 1 tablespoon lemon juice, and ⅓ cup olive oil; mix.
4. Place mixture back over heat and stir until all is slightly golden.
5. Add parsley, mint, dill, and sufficient boiling water to cover. Cook 20–30 minutes until rice is dry, covered. Gently mix in nuts.
6. Place 1 rounded teaspoon filling in center of underside of leaf. Fold each side toward center and roll tightly.
7. Place a few leaves in bottom of heavy Dutch oven-type pot. Arrange stuffed leaves close to each other in layers.
8. Add remaining olive oil and lemon juice. Add remaining boiling water, weighing down dolmas (stuffed grape leaves) with heavy plate.
9. Simmer 45 minutes, covered. Serve cold.

Serves 6–8

 MUSHROOM BARLEY

2 tablespoons butter
1 cup raw pearl barley
1 small onion, minced
2 cans (10¾ ounce) beef broth, undiluted
1 can (4 ounce) mushroom pieces, with liquid, or 4 ounces fresh mushrooms
¼ teaspoon nutmeg
¼ cup lightly toasted pine nuts
salt to taste

1. Preheat oven to 350°.
2. In large saucepan, melt butter. Cook barley and onion in butter, stirring often, until barley is lightly toasted and onion is tender, but not browned.
3. Mix in beef broth, mushrooms with their liquid, nutmeg, nuts, and salt.
4. Turn into 1½-quart casserole. Cover tightly and bake 1 hour or until barley is tender and liquid absorbed.

Serves 6

FLEMISH LACE COOKIES

¾ cup chopped pine nuts
½ cup butter
½ cup sugar
1 tablespoon flour
1 tablespoon cream
1 tablespoon milk

1. Preheat oven to 350°.
2. In small heavy-bottomed pan, combine all ingredients. Cook slowly until butter melts, stirring carefully constantly.
3. Remove pan from heat; beat contents well.
4. Drop mixture by heaping tablespoonsful on buttered baking sheet, keeping cookies at least 3 inches apart and doing only a few at a time as you must work quickly with these.
5. Bake about 9 minutes until cookies are brown around edge and still bubbly in center.
6. With a spatula, remove cookies. Immediately wrap or fold each cookie around handle of wooden spoon and slide off. These are delicious as is, but can be filled with sweetened, flavored whipped cream.

Makes 18–20

Hint: Do not make cookies in damp or extra-warm weather. Pack loosely in tin or airtight glass container.

 PINE NUT-STUDDED CRESCENTS

3 tablespoons powdered sugar
¼ teaspoon vanilla
2¼ pounds almond paste, uncooked
3 egg whites
1 grated lemon rind
flour
2 cups pine nuts

1. Combine powdered sugar and vanilla.
2. On a board, knead almond paste, gradually adding 1 egg white, lemon rind, and the vanilla sugar.
3. When mixture is supple and totally blended, add 1 egg white and mix well.
4. Divide dough in little balls the size of a large lemon. Roll each ball into 1-inch-diameter sausage shape.
5. Preheat oven to 450°.
6. Cut sausage shapes in 2-inch pieces. Roll each piece on a floured board.
7. Moisten hands with remaining egg white. Form each piece into crescent shape with both ends pointed.
8. Dip crescents into nuts, which will stick to egg coating.
9. Bake 10–15 minutes. Cool on a rack.

Makes 5 dozen

PISTACHIO

Pistacia vera

PISTACHIO

THE PISTACHIO NUT, whose special glamour is its color, is perhaps the most elegant of all the nuts, the name alone conjuring up visions of exotic and special food. Its green beauty adds to its distinctiveness, albeit some pistachios have a creamy yellow color, particularly those from Iran. For holiday use, especially for Christmas and St. Patrick's Day, when green has special significance, grated or chopped pistachios are both delicious and effective. Even displays of the nuts in their shells have built-in visual drama—the whites, encrusted in salt; the reds, dyed that color and without any salt; and the beige, natural and salt-free. The nuts are oval, smaller than an olive, with a smooth, thin brittle shell which is often slightly open. To shell them, use the shell of one nut to pry open the slightly opened shell of another. The kernel itself has an inner skin, which is reddish. To blanch, parboil the nuts 1 minute, drain, and rub in a towel to remove the skin.

Pistachios grow on a small, 20-foot tall, deciduous tree, a species of turpentine. Native to western Asia and Asia Minor, they are now cultivated in all Mediterranean countries and California. In their natural state, the nuts come from the tree in a gummy husk, which is removed by a special soaking process. In this crude state, they can be kept safely 2 years, but they are not exported this way. They do not leave their native habitat until they are out of their husks and roasted in their shells. Although sold mostly in the shell, specialty shops do carry shelled pistachios, usually the ones from Turkey having the prized green color. If a recipe calls for a quantity of pistachios, it is wise to try to find them shelled.

As far back as 20000 B.C., the pistachio found its way from Persia to China. At the beginning of the Christian era, pistachios were introduced to Mediterranean Europe as green almonds. The Bible mentions them, and most historians now agree that the nuts of Jacob were pistachio nuts. Many of the rocky parts of Lebanon and Palestine bear pistachio trees. The

Arabs learned to use nuts lavishly from the wonderful cooking of the Persians. The Greeks prized pistachios, believed that they were not only delicious served as appetizers, but also were an effective way of promoting the desire for drink. In the days of Plato, the nuts were used layered in special pâtés. The gorgeous Persian pilaus were studded with whole pistachio nuts, and some of the world's finest ice creams likewise contained whole pistachios.

Pistachio nuts were introduced to the United States through vending machines. The red pistachios* seen everywhere were first conceived by venders as colorful and appealing, able to capture the interest of potential buyers. Colored, they made their debut. Now in the 70s, our increasing sophistication in cookery has affected even this: knowledgeable people now prefer the natural, untreated beige nuts because they know the desirability and deliciousness of the nut itself and because of the growing interest in natural foods. The red color tends to rub off onto fingers and is gradually losing its appeal. White pistachios, thickly encrusted with salt, find their greatest popularity in the cold states, particularly New England and the Middle West where people like to suck on the salty shell. They have the shortest shelf life because before the nuts are coated with salt, they are covered with cornstarch—if they are kept on the shelf long, they will germinate.

Like many other nuts, pistachios historically have been used as a thickening agent. In the Middle Ages, they were used to make gruel, ground up, then mixed with cereals. Among the nuts used for nut butter, pistachios have always been desirable because of their fresh and lovely color. Pistachios are still a favorite of the Italians and Persians; some connoisseurs say that the pistachio nuts imported from Sicily are the finest, while others endorse those from Turkey.

Prized for its looks, taste, and texture, the pistachio nut has traveled far. It is equally at home in plebeian sausages and the elegant baklava pastry, beloved of the Middle East and now growing in popularity on the Continent, in England, and in the United States. European sausage makers and those in the state of Wisconsin often use whole pistachios in various wursts and many other sausages, including liver sausage. The presence of pistachios immediately conveys a touch of elegance, and the fanciest of ice cream and pastry makers cherish the pistachio for its delicacy of taste and the beauty of its appearance.

The pistachio adds luster wherever it is used and is truly a nut of distinction.

PURCHASE

Since pistachio nuts become stale quickly, they should be purchased when you plan to use them. The larger and plumper the nut, the better. Nuts with shells slightly open at time of purchase are the easiest to handle.

 PREPARATION

To blanch.   Plunge shelled pistachios into boiling water for only 1 minute, drain, and rub in a tea towel. The red skin will immediately come off. Dry them in a single layer on a baking sheet. If they seem too soft, crisp them either in the oven 15 minutes at 300° or on top of the stove. Stirring and the addition of a little butter seem to improve their flavor and texture.
   To fry.   For eating as a snack or serving as an appetizer with drinks, a most cosmopolitan touch is to fry them in butter with salt and pepper.

 **FOR APPEARANCE AND FUN**

There is a new liqueur, Pistasha, which is artificially colored green. It does not capture the delicious taste of the nut. From my cooking and tasting experience, its greatest value is for use in coloring desserts that feature the pistachio. Like most of the nut liqueurs, the actual taste of the nut is overpowered by the alcohol.

AMOUNTS

Pistachios lose about ⅓ of their weight by being shelled.

STORAGE

Shelled pistachios, and those blanched for special recipes, keep well in the refrigerator in airtight storage jars. They keep best for any length of time in the freezer.

172

 CHEESE BALLS SOUTH AMERICAN

1 package (8 ounce) cream cheese
8 ounces Roquefort cheese
2 tablespoons sherry or cream
1 teaspoon seasoned salt
½ teaspoon Worcestershire sauce
1½ tablespoons finely minced onion
2 tablespoons finely minced green pepper
2 tablespoons chopped pimiento
1 cup coarsely chopped pistachios

1. Soften cheeses at room temperature. Blend together.
2. Mix in sherry, seasoned salt, Worcestershire sauce, and onion thoroughly.
3. Fold in green pepper and pimiento.
4. Form into large ball and chill. Just before serving, roll ball in nuts.

Serves 8

Hint: Serve with crisp, bland crackers to enhance full flavor of cheeses.

 POOR MAN'S PATÉ

1 envelope (1 tablespoon) unflavored gelatin
1 can (10½ ounce) consommé, undiluted
2 tablespoons sherry
6 ounces liver sausage
3 ounces cream cheese
½ cup chopped pistachios
parsley to garnish

1. Dissolve gelatin in 2 tablespoons consommé.
2. Simmer remaining consommé, and combine with gelatin mixture and 1 tablespoon sherry.
3. Pour enough consommé liquid into small round or ring mold to cover bottom; refrigerate.
4. Cream liver sausage and cheese with sherry until pliable. Mix in nuts and press liver mixture into mold. Pour remaining consommé liquid on top of this.
5. Chill again until gelatin sets.
6. Unmold and garnish with parsley. Serve with thinly sliced dark rye bread or rye melba toast.

Serves 6–8

COLD CUCUMBER SOUP

2 medium white potatoes
2 medium cucumbers
1 cup chicken stock,
  undiluted
salt to taste
pepper to taste
½ teaspoon onion juice
2 cups milk
1 cup sour cream
1 cup heavy cream,
  whipped
½ cup finely chopped
  pistachios

1. Boil potatoes in just enough salted water to cover.
2. When potatoes are tender, put them in blender with water in which they were cooked along with cucumbers cut in chunks. Blend thoroughly.
3. Add chicken stock, salt, pepper, and onion juice; blend. Add milk, blending once more.
4. Stir in sour cream.
5. Chill thoroughly before serving. Correct seasoning.
6. Serve each portion with a dollop of whipped cream and heavy sprinkling of nuts.

Serves 6–8

 RICE SALAD MEDITERRANEAN

7 tablespoons olive oil
3 tablespoons fresh lemon
  juice
dash of cinnamon
dash of coriander
salt to taste
pepper to taste
1½ cups raw long grain
  rice
3 cups water
¾ teaspoon salt
1 tablespoon butter
¾ cup chopped pistachios
½ cup currants or raisins
½ cup sliced mushrooms,
  fresh or canned, drained
¼ cup finely chopped
  mint leaves

1. Combine olive oil, lemon juice, cinnamon, coriander, salt, and pepper. Set this dressing aside.
2. In medium saucepan with a lid, cover rice with water; add salt and butter.
3. Steam, covered, over moderate heat 20–30 minutes until dry and fluffy.
4. While hot, toss rice with dressing. Add remaining ingredients. Serve lukewarm or cold.

Serves 6–8

174

CAULIFLOWER CROWNED WITH PISTACHIOS

1 head cauliflower
3 tablespoons butter
2 tablespoons minced
  parsley
¼ cup chopped pistachios

1. Wash cauliflower; remove tough leaves and stalk from bottom.
2. Cook cauliflower whole 15–20 minutes until tender; drain well.
3. In small saucepan, melt butter. Add parsley and nuts.
4. Pour nut mixture over cauliflower.

Serves 4–6

Hint: This is festive surrounded by a circle of buttered peas or carrots.

SYRIAN EGGPLANT

3 small eggplants
4 tablespoons butter
3 tomatoes, peeled,
  chopped
1 chopped garlic clove
¼ cup chopped parsley
salt to taste
pepper to taste
1 onion, chopped
½ cup whole pistachios
1 green pepper, diced
½ teaspoon sweet basil
½ teaspoon marjoram
1 cup bread crumbs,
  buttered
¾ cup grated Romano
  cheese
½ cup chopped pistachios
2 tablespoons butter

1. In salted water to cover, parboil unpeeled eggplants only 15 minutes. Remove from water and drain.
2. Preheat oven to 350°.
3. Cut eggplants in half and scoop out pulp of each half. In large skillet, melt butter. Sauté pulp in butter 10 minutes.
4. Mix tomatoes, garlic, parsley, salt, pepper, onion, whole nuts, green pepper, basil, marjoram, and ½ cup bread crumbs with scooped-out eggplant. Sauté 30 minutes, stirring frequently.
5. Fill shells with mixture; cover with remaining bread crumbs and cheese. Top with chopped nuts. Dot with butter.
6. In large baking pan, bake filled eggplant 20–30 minutes.

Serves 6

PISTACHIO CHICKEN IN CREAM

1 frying chicken (2½ pound), cut in serving pieces
dash of salt
dash of pepper
4 tablespoons butter
2 tablespoons lemon juice
1 cup heavy cream
2 tablespoons sherry
1 cup chopped pistachios
¼ cup chopped fresh parsley

1. Season chicken with salt and pepper.
2. In large skillet, melt butter. Slowly brown chicken on all sides in butter.
3. Sprinkle chicken with lemon juice; tightly cover skillet; and simmer 30 minutes or until tender.
4. Remove chicken from skillet and keep warm.
5. Add cream and sherry to skillet. Cook a few minutes, stirring to loosen and blend pan drippings.
6. Stir in nuts and parsley and heat them thoroughly. Serve sauce over warm chicken pieces.

Serves 4

 TURKISH MEATBALLS

1 onion, finely chopped
¼ cup olive oil
½ pound finely ground lamb
½ pound finely ground pork
dash of garlic salt
½ teaspoon cinnamon
½ cup whole pine nuts
1 cup cooked rice
1 cup chopped pistachios
vegetable oil for frying

1. In large skillet, brown onion in 3 tablespoons olive oil until soft.
2. Add ground lamb and pork, stirring to brown all over and blend.
3. Add garlic salt and cinnamon. Cook gently 10–15 minutes until there is no pink appearance to meat.
4. Remove mixture from stove and cool in large bowl.
5. Stir in pine nuts and rice.
6. Moisten hands with remaining olive oil and form mixture into small balls. Roll balls in pistachios to coat.
7. Either fry coated balls in shallow vegetable oil until brown and crisp all over or deep fry them in vegetable oil, removing them with slotted spoon when brown and placing them on paper towels to drain. Serve hot.

Serves 6

Hint: These can be served with cocktails or as an entrée over a bed of rice cooked in chicken broth.

ORANGE-NUT BREAD

2¼ cups sifted flour
1½ teaspoons baking powder
½ teaspoon baking soda
¾ teaspoon salt
1 cup sugar
¾ cup chopped pistachios
1 egg, beaten
2 tablespoons butter, softened
¾ cup orange juice
1 tablespoon grated orange rind

1. Preheat oven to 350°.
2. Into large bowl, sift together flour, baking powder, baking soda, salt, and sugar; add nuts.
3. Combine egg, butter, orange juice, and orange rind; beat until well blended.
4. Pour liquid ingredients into flour mixture; stir only until smooth.
5. Place batter in buttered 9 x 5 x 3-inch loaf pan. Bake 60–65 minutes.

Makes 1 loaf

 PISTACHIO PANCAKES

2 cups flour
2 cups milk
3 egg yolks
1 tablespoon butter, melted
2 tablespoons brandy
⅛ teaspoon salt
½ cup ground pistachios

1. In large bowl, mix flour and milk. Stir in egg yolks and butter.
2. Blend in brandy, salt, and nuts. Batter must be thin; adjust it by adding a little more milk if necessary.
3. Butter 6-inch skillet and place over medium heat. Pour in enough batter to cover bottom. When pancake is golden on both sides, butter and roll up.
4. Serve with favorite topping.

Serves 6–8

BAKLAVA

4 cups coarsely chopped
   pistachios
¼ cup sugar
½ teaspoon cinnamon
dash of ground cloves
1 pound of phyllo
   (commercial strudel
   dough)
2 cups sweet butter,
   melted

This is the Jewel Pastry of the Middle East.

1. In large bowl, combine nuts, sugar, cinnamon, and cloves.
2. Preheat oven to 350°.
3. Butter baking sheet or jelly-roll pan well. Brush 5 sheets of phyllo dough with melted butter, and place them on top of one another in pan.
4. On top of fifth layer, spread thick layer of nut mixture. On top of that, place 2 sheets of phyllo dough, each spread with melted butter.
5. Using remaining phyllo sheets, spread thin layer of nut mixture on each, reserving 3 plain sheets of dough for topping, each one layered with melted butter alone.
6. Liberally brush whole top with melted butter.
7. With small sharp knife, cut the pastry into diamond-shaped pieces prior to baking.
8. Bake 45–60 minutes on middle shelf of oven. When pastry appears golden brown, it is sufficiently baked.
9. Meanwhile, prepare syrup.
10. Remove pan from oven and place on a rack. While pastry is still hot, pour cooled syrup over it.

Syrup

2 cups sugar
1½ cups water
½ cup honey
2 tablespoons rose water or
   orange blossom water
1 tablespoon lemon juice

1. In medium saucepan, cook sugar and water together until they begin to thicken and spin a thread.
2. Add honey to water and bring to a boil. Cook over medium heat 20–25 minutes until thick and syrupy.
3. Add rose water and lemon juice. Skim foam off syrup and allow to cool.

Makes about 2 dozen

Note: Baclava is a personal as well as ethnic offering, and there is great competition even in choice of nuts. Contenders are walnuts and hazelnuts, but I choose pistachios, albeit they are more expensive.

Use baking sheet or jelly-roll pan for both baking and assemblage. Have everything ready including damp tea towel to cover phyllo sheets because they dry out very quickly. Take out individual phyllo sheets as needed. They are thin and fragile.

ELEGANT RICE MOLD

¾ cup raw rice
½ teaspoon salt
1½ cups water
⅔ cup brown sugar
1 cup chopped toasted
    pistachios
1 cup chopped toasted
    almonds, blanched
½ cup dates
½ cup glacé cherries (set
    aside 3.)
½ cup golden raisins
½ cup glacé pineapple
1 tablespoon powdered
    sugar
1 tablespoon sherry
1 cup heavy cream,
    whipped

1. Steam rice in salted water 20 minutes, covered. Drain. Stir in brown sugar.

2. Oil 3-cup ring mold or other fancy mold with tasteless oil. Cover thickly with pistachios.

3. Over the pistachios, place a layer of rice, a layer of almonds, a layer of fruits, another layer of rice, another of almonds, and another of fruits.

4. Cover mold with well-buttered foil. Steam over gently boiling water 35 minutes.

5. Unmold and decorate with 3 glacé cherries.

6. Blend powdered sugar and sherry into whipped cream. Serve in separate bowl with rice mold.

Serves 6–8

 VENETIAN COFFEE TORTONI

2 tablespoons instant
    coffee
¼ teaspoon salt
2 egg whites
4 tablespoons sugar
2 cups heavy cream
½ cup sugar
2 teaspoons vanilla
¼ teaspoon almond
    extract
¾ cup finely chopped
    toasted pistachios

1. In medium bowl, combine coffee and salt with egg whites and beat until stiff but not dry.

2. Gradually beat in 4 tablespoons sugar, continuing to beat until stiff and satiny.

3. Whip cream; add ½ cup sugar, vanilla, and almond extract, continuing to beat until stiff.

4. Fold whipped cream mixture and ½ cup nuts into egg white mixture.

5. Spoon mixture into 12 paper cups inserted in muffin pans. Sprinkle remaining nuts on top. Freeze quickly.

6. Remove cups from freezer and individually wrap each Tortoni in transparent freezer wrap.

7. Return to freezer until needed.

Serves 12

STRAWBERRY CREAM PIE SULTANA

2¼ cups rich milk
3 tablespoons cornstarch
⅓ cup sugar
¼ teaspoon salt
3 egg yolks, lightly beaten
1 teaspoon vanilla
½ cup apricot preserves
1 pie shell (9 inch), baked
1 quart ripe strawberries
   washed, kept whole,
   dried
1 cup heavy cream,
   whipped
½ cup chopped pistachios
1 pie shell (9 inch), baked

1. In top of a double boiler, scald 2 cups rich milk.
2. In small bowl, mix cornstarch, sugar, and salt.
3. Combine egg yolks with remaining ¼ cup rich milk, mixing thoroughly.
4. Stir egg yolk mixture into cornstarch mixture, blending thoroughly.
5. Pour scalded milk into this mixture, stirring well. Then scrape it all back into top of the double boiler.
6. Place double boiler top over boiling water; cook, stirring constantly, until mixture thickens and coats the mixing spoon.
7. Remove top of double boiler from over boiling water. Add vanilla to custard, and stir vigorously with metal whisk.
8. Pour custard into medium bowl, and place on a rack to cool.
9. Place apricot preserves in small saucepan over hot water; stir until it softens and liquefies. Keep hot.
10. Pour custard into baked pie shell, and place whole strawberries close together in pleasing pattern to cover pie.
11. Brush berries carefully with pastry brush dipped generously in hot apricot preserves. This makes an elegant glaze.
12. Through a pastry tube, pipe whipped cream around edge of pie; or with a spoon, shape a border of cream to encircle edge of pie.
13. Sprinkle this edge of cream with chopped pistachios.
14. Keep pie chilled until it is served.

Serves 8

PISTACHIO LACY WAFERS

1¾ cups half-and-half
1 tablespoon cornstarch
2 tablespoons flour
¼ cup milk
4 egg yolks, beaten
¼ teaspoon salt
1 tablespoon butter
1 teaspoon pistachio liqueur
  or vanilla
½ cup chopped pistachios

1. Preheat oven to 350°.
2. In small saucepan, combine butter, sugar, flour, milk, and salt. Cook, stirring until smooth.
3. Add nuts.
4. Drop dough by tablespoonsful on baking sheet 4–6 at a time. Bake 6–8 minutes until lightly browned.
5. Cool slightly on baking sheet; carefully lift with wide spatula and wrap around handle of wooden spoon. If rolled tightly, wafers can be filled with pistachio cream.

Pistachio Cream

1. In top of a double boiler, heat half-and-half.
2. In small bowl, mix cornstarch and flour with milk.
3. Stir egg yolks and salt into flour mixture.
4. Pour a little hot half-and-half into egg yolk mixture, stirring vigorously; return mixture to top of double boiler, stirring constantly.
5. When it starts to thicken, place pan over hot water, stirring until very thick. Remove from heat; add butter and liqueur.
6. Cool and spoon into wafers. Fold in nuts.
7. Cool thoroughly. Fold in nuts. Use this cream to fill pistachio wafers, or serve separately in little custard cups with a dab of whipped cream.

Makes about 2 dozen

WALNUT

Juglans regia

WALNUT

THE ENGLISH WALNUT is really Persian. Although it found its way to England less than 375 years ago, it has been transported all over the world by English trading ships and become famous as an English nut.

One of the most ancient of nuts, native to Persia and still known in many European countries by its correct name, the Persian nut, it was a favorite émigré from its first home. It bears a most romantic historical mantle, with legend asserting that from Persia the walnut found its way to Greece about 400 B.C., thence across the desert to Egypt, and around A.D. 400 the Romans introduced the nut all over continental Europe. For centuries B.C., it had been firmly established as the nut of the gods, and given such colorful names as Jupiter's nuts and Jupiter's acorns; it was also known as the royal nut, ball nut, and Welsh nut. Some of these names properly reflect the long-enduring reverence for the walnut, which was singled out as a nut for royalty. Even as long ago as 100 B.C., walnuts were highly prized in China.

The Persians used walnuts for barter; the Phoenicians traded in them; the Greeks dedicated the walnut to Diana, whose feasts were held beneath walnut trees. Many myths have grown up about the magical properties attributed to the walnut and the walnut tree, said to be capable of both curing diseases and warding them off. Because they were thought to make a couple fertile, walnuts were strewn at wedding parties. The Bible refers to them in the Songs of Solomon, and King Solomon's Nut Garden has been described as a walnut bower, many-splendored and highly prized. Walnut trees grew profusely in Palestine.

Traditionally, walnut trees are esteemed for their beauty and majesty, their delicious and nourishing fruit, their tasty nuts, and their wood, which is used to make fine furniture. On the Continent an excellent liqueur called Brou is made from the walnuts' shucks, the fleshy green casing of the nut; another liqueur named Nociana comes from walnuts. France has its own walnut liqueur, known as Eau-De-Nois, with the Périgord region providing its own special version. An Italian-style liquor named Liquore di Noce is increasingly popular in the United States.

Walnut oil, too, is especially prized in Germany and Switzerland. In California where there is a growing walnut industry, all parts of the walnut are supplying various industrial as well as dietary needs. Industrially, walnut oil is used in making paints because it has an ingredient that promotes fast drying; walnut mash, the cake residue from extracting the oil, is used for feeding poultry; and every part of the walnut, including its shells, now has some industrial or commercial use.

The walnut trees bloom in May and the small fruits appear in July. It is in England, and really all of Great Britain, where there is no actual commercial walnut industry but where the walnut trees grow wild and where there is private cultivation and enormous interest, that the young green walnuts with their immature shells are used for pickling and making walnut catsup. In the Balkan countries, the immature walnuts are gathered for pickling and also for preserving in a sweet syrup.

The nut or kernel itself has a tightly attached inner covering or skin, which is brown and somewhat wrinkled; the nutmeat is cream colored. Its wheat-colored, hard, woodlike outer shell is further covered in the growing stages by a heavy rubbery green husk known as the shuck. The nuts are easily shelled with a hammer or nutcracker; with a little care, you can have perfect halves. The shell itself is sort of bisected and appears to be in two parts, but the parts of the shell are not separated. The walnut is one of the easiest nuts to crack and shell.

Walnuts have a more biting pungent tang than other nuts discussed in this book. They do not require the conventional blanching to remove the inner skin, technically known as the pellicle, which protects the walnut kernel against oxidation, a cause of breakdown in flavor and texture that hastens rancidity. In the commercial shelling process, especially in packaging pieces of nuts rather than perfect halves, the breaking of the pellicle is unavoidable. The walnut industry has developed a pellicle substitute, approved by the United States Food and Drug Administration, allegedly tasteless, harmless, colorless, and invisible, which does the work of the natural pellicle and acts as an active antioxidant; it is used commercially to protect the packaged nuts from rancidity and staleness.

The Franciscan fathers brought the walnut tree to the shores of California in the early 1700s either from Mexico or Spain. Through their efforts, walnut trees were planted in the courtyards of the California missions and flourished. Now the California walnut industry furnishes 95 percent of the walnut output in the United States. Some walnuts are still imported from France, China, and Italy, the best Italians being from Sorrento.

Walnuts are particularly delicious as a spiced appetizer and as a sugared sweetmeat after dinner. They are good right out of the shell for eating as a snack. They make great additions to vegetables and chicken dishes and behave like ground meat when finely chopped or ground and made into a loaf for a main course with the addition of cheese, grains, vegetables, or cereals. Walnuts are highly prized by Chinese and European cooks, and they are so beloved in Italy for cooking that they are used in a variety of sauces for pasta, particularly for fettucini. Americans are adding walnuts to various culinary creations.

To eliminate any tangy taste, cover the nuts with boiling water 10–15 minutes to blanch them (even though in general this is unnecessary); then rub them in a towel to remove the brown inner skin. Dry and toast the nuts in the oven to improve the quality of taste and texture and to eliminate the bite that can be a problem for those whose taste buds and mouths are sensitive to walnuts.

PURCHASE

Walnuts are available in the shell in most markets. They come in 3 sizes: large, medium, and "babies," and their flavor seems to have no relationship to their size. They are easy to shell and good to eat right out of the shell. After being shelled, they should be used or stored promptly.

Walnuts are also on hand in cans or plastic bags through which the buyer can actually see the size and ascertain the quality of the nuts. They are packaged in halves, large pieces, and finely chopped pieces. In the bags, the weight varies from 3–5 ounces, 10 ounces, and 1 pound and 2 pound amounts. Vacuum cans are 4 and 8 ounces.

---

*Early in 1976, the red-coloring #2 was labeled by the FDA as carcinogenic; and at the end of March 1976, red-coloring #40 was being questioned as to its safety.

 **PREPARATION**

To crack and chop. Place the walnut on its flat end, holding by the seam. Strike with a hammer on the pointed end. Or use any good nutcracker.

To use French knife method. Spread the walnut kernels on a chopping board. Hold the tip of a French knife with one hand, then move the knife handle up and down with the other hand.

To use other methods. Walnut choppers are available in most housewares sections of department stores. Or use the following items: the wooden bowl and metal chopper combination; food chopper, the next to the finest blade for ground walnuts; blender or food processor; or place walnut kernels inside a plastic bag, then roll lightly with a rolling pin.

To toast. Drop walnut kernels into rapidly boiling water; boil 3 minutes. Drain well. Next, spread kernels evenly in a shallow pan and bake at 350°, stirring often, 12–15 minutes or until the kernels are golden brown.

To measure. Measure walnuts after they are chopped. Ground or very finely chopped walnuts should be the consistency of coarse meal; finely chopped, the size of peppercorns; medium chopped, about the size of medium peas; coarsely chopped, approximately the size of cranberries or even larger when coarsely broken.

AMOUNTS

4 ounces shelled walnuts equals 1 cup shelled walnuts.
8 ounces shelled walnuts equals 2 cups shelled walnuts.
1 pound shelled walnuts equals 4 cups shelled walnuts.
2 pounds shelled walnuts equals 8 cups shelled walnuts.

STORAGE

In the shell, walnuts in not too warm a room will survive in a nut bowl for several months. Best insurance, of course, is the refrigerator. Since many of the shelled nuts have been treated with pellicle substitutes, the danger of their becoming rancid and stale is minimal. Yet storage in airtight containers in the refrigerator is recommended.

Freeze nuts to keep them any length of time. When you thaw them, be sure to let the collected moisture evaporate before they are to be used. Once thawed, it is best not to refreeze the nuts.

GINGERED BEEF PASTRIES

2 tablespoons butter
½ teaspoon curry powder
¾ cup lean ground beef
  (about ⅓ pound)
1 tablespoon finely
  chopped onion
½ teaspoon garlic salt
1 cup finely chopped
  toasted walnuts
1 tablespoon finely
  chopped preserved
  ginger
seasoned salt to taste
48 pastry rounds

1. Preheat oven to 450°.

2. In medium skillet, melt butter with curry powder; add beef, onion, and garlic salt. Cook until beef loses its pink color, stirring.

3. Remove skillet from heat. Mix in nuts and ginger. Cool slightly.

4. Meanwhile, prepare pastry rounds.

5. Generously pile beef mixture in center of 24 pastry rounds. Top each with second round. Lightly press edges to seal.

6. Prick tops with tines of a fork, and sprinkle each pastry with seasoned salt.

7. Bake 12–15 minutes until crisp and golden brown. Serve hot or cold.

Pastry Rounds

2 cups sifted flour
1 teaspoon seasoned salt
¾ cup vegetable
  shortening
4–5 tablespoons cold milk
  or cold water

1. Into medium bowl, sift flour with seasoned salt.

2. Cut in shortening until in fine pieces.

3. Add just enough cold milk to hold mixture together.

4. Roll dough to about ⅜-inch thickness. Using a fluted or plain-edged cutter about 2½ inches in diameter, cut dough in 48 rounds.

Makes 24

WALNUT CREAM CHEESE

1 package (8 ounce) cream
  cheese
1 package (4 ounce)
  Roquefort cheese
3 tablespoons chopped
  toasted walnuts
1 tablespoon chopped
  black olives
3 tablespoons sherry
5 tablespoons sour cream

1. Combine ingredients and mix well.

2. Serve in a bowl with crackers.

Makes 2 cups

CHEDDAR WHIZZERS

½ cup butter, softened
2 cups grated sharp
 cheddar cheese
1½ cups flour
1 teaspoon baking powder
1 teaspoon celery salt
½ teaspoon dried parsley
¼ teaspoon dried mustard
1 cup finely chopped
 walnuts
4 slices bacon, crisply
 cooked, crumbled
1 egg, beaten

1. Preheat oven to 350°.
2. In order given, combine all ingredients except ½ cup nuts, mixing with hands to blend thoroughly.
3. Form cheese mixture into 4-dozen small balls. Roll each in coating of remaining nuts. Or shape cheese mixture into 8-inch rolls and coat with remaining nuts; slice rolls about ¼ inch thick, reshaping slices with hands if necessary.
4. Place balls or slices on buttered baking sheet. Bake 15 minutes.

Makes 4 dozen

 ## ENGLISH PICKLED WALNUTS

green walnuts, immature
 shells, as many as
 available
1 pound salt
1 gallon water
1 teaspoon pickling spices
2 cups vinegar

1. Prick green walnuts with knitting needle.
2. Dissolve salt in water.
3. Soak nuts in this brine 1 week, then drain.
4. Place nuts on a tray or dish and leave in sun 2–3 days, turning occasionally. They will turn black.
5. Add pickling spices to vinegar. (The amount of spice can be adjusted to your taste.) Boil spiced vinegar the day before you plan to use it. Let it cool.
6. Pack nuts into preserving jars. When adding filling to the jars, boil spiced vinegar again just before using it and cover nuts in jars with liquid.
7. Cover with a "bladder," such as a sausage casing. The English claim the vinegar and spice will eat through a metal top.
8. Let rest at least 1 month, and then they will last indefinitely.

WALNUT-MUSHROOM BISQUE

1 cup half-and-half
1 cup chopped walnuts
4 tablespoons butter
6 fresh medium
   mushrooms, diced
1 green onion, with a little
   of the top, minced
1 garlic clove, pressed
2 tablespoons flour
1 can (10¾ ounce) chicken
   broth, undiluted
1 teaspoon seasoned salt
1 egg yolk, beaten with 2
   tablespoons cream or
   half-and-half
2–3 teaspoons fresh lemon
   juice

1. Scald half-and-half and add nuts. Let stand, covered, for flavor to permeate.

2. In small skillet with a lid, melt 2 tablespoons butter. Sauté mushrooms, green onion, and garlic in butter until just soft, covered.

3. Meanwhile, in small saucepan, melt remaining butter and blend in flour. Cook 2–3 minutes. Stir in ¼ cup chicken broth, stirring until mixture is smooth and thick. Add seasoned salt and egg yolk beaten with cream. Stir, but do not boil, until thickened further.

4. Combine all mixtures. Put through blender in 2 parts.

5. Pour soup from blender into top of a double boiler; heat thoroughly. Just before serving, mix in lemon juice.

6. Serve alone or with small browned croutons and chopped toasted walnuts. This is also delicious cold.

Serves 6

 ## ENDIVE SALAD

3 endives
1 bunch celery
2 apples
⅔ cup chopped toasted
   walnuts
½ cup chopped, drained
   canned beets
1 cup mayonnaise, colored
   with 1 teaspoon tomato
   paste
salt to taste
pepper to taste

1. Slice endives.

2. Cut celery and apples in cubes.

3. Combine endives with nuts, celery, apples, and beets.

4. Season salad with pink mayonnaise, salt, and pepper.

Serves 6–8

Hint: This is good as an hors d'oeuvre too.

Depending on rest of menu, summer savory is a nice addition to pink mayonnaise.

RHUBARB CONSERVE

3 pounds rhubarb, cut up
7 cups sugar
1 package (15 ounce)
  raisins
1 cup chopped walnuts

1. In large enamel pot, combine rhubarb with sugar and raisins. Cook until thick, uncovered, stirring constantly.

2. Add nuts to conserve.

3. Taste conserve and adjust seasoning if necessary—either with more sugar or a bit of lemon juice.

4. Pour into hot sterilized jars and seal.

Makes 6 pounds

 ## FLORENTINE SPINACH

1½ pounds fresh spinach
salt and pepper to taste
¼ teaspoon nutmeg
½ pound ricotta cheese
1 egg
1 cup ground walnuts
2 tablespoons flour
flour for dusting spinach
  balls
3 tablespoons butter
⅓ cup grated Romano
  cheese

1. Steam spinach until limp.

2. Mix together salt, pepper, nutmeg, and ricotta cheese. Stir egg into cheese mixture.

3. Combine egg mixture with spinach, nuts, and then 2 tablespoons flour.

4. With hands, form spinach mixture into balls. Roll balls in flour.

5. Drop balls into boiling salted water and cook 5–6 minutes, but do not allow water to boil again.

6. Remove spinach balls to serving platter with slotted spoon. Pour melted butter over them and sprinkle with Romano cheese.

Serves 6–8

 ## NUTTY RELISH

1 jar (10 ounce)
  watermelon pickles,
  with liquid
½ cup walnut halves or
  walnut pieces
½ cup pineapple chunks
ginger to taste

1. Combine ingredients, blending well.

2. Cover relish and refrigerate until completely chilled.

Makes generous 2 cups

Hint: This is a delicious accompaniment to poultry.

PEAS WITH BACON AND WALNUTS

¼ pound bacon cut in
   1-inch pieces
½ cup large walnut pieces
½ cup chopped onion
2 packages (10 ounce)
   frozen peas
1 teaspoon salt
⅛ teaspoon pepper
⅛ teaspoon thyme
¼ cup water

1. In large skillet with a lid, fry bacon until crisp; remove bacon from skillet; drain off all but 2 tablespoons bacon fat. Set aside bacon.

2. Sauté nuts in bacon fat 1 minute; with a slotted spoon, remove nuts.

3. Sauté onion in same skillet until transparent.

4. Add peas, salt, pepper, thyme, and water to skillet. Cover and cook about 10 minutes just until peas are tender, stirring once or twice.

5. Drain off any remaining cooking liquid. Add bacon pieces and nuts; toss lightly. Serve at once.

Serves 6–8

GOLDEN NUGGET DRESSING

1 package (3 ounce) cream
   cheese, softened
⅓ cup finely chopped
   toasted walnuts
⅓ cup mayonnaise
⅓ cup orange juice
1 tablespoon lemon juice
1 tablespoon sugar

1. Combine cream cheese with remaining ingredients. With rotary beater, beat dressing until well blended.

2. Store dressing in covered container in refrigerator.

3. This is delicious over any fruit or gelatin salad. For a green salad, it works best adding ¼ cup Roquefort cheese.

Makes 1½ cups

SPRING CASSEROLE

¼ cup butter
1 pound zucchini, sliced
1 cup diced green pepper
1 garlic clove or ⅛
   teaspoon garlic powder
½ pound mushrooms,
   sliced
⅛ teaspoon pepper
½ cup coarsely broken
   walnuts

1. In large skillet, melt butter. Sauté zucchini, green pepper, and garlic in butter until almost tender, stirring occasionally.

2. Add mushrooms and pepper. Sauté 10 minutes or until all vegetables are tender, tossing well.

3. Add nuts. Serve hot.

Serves 6

FESENJAN FROM IRAN

1 plump stewing chicken
3 cups boiling water
1 onion, chopped
1 garlic clove
1 carrot, diced
4 stalks celery with leaves,
   coarsely chopped
½ teaspoon salt
¼ teaspoon pepper

1. Cut chicken in quarters and place in heavy stew pot.
2. Pour boiling water and all remaining ingredients over chicken. Bring to a boil, reduce heat, cover, and cook slowly 1½–2 hours, testing for tenderness.
3. Meanwhile, prepare sauce.
4. Cool chicken in broth; and then skin it, bone it, and cut chicken meat in relatively large pieces.
5. Add chicken to sauce and cook 30 minutes more. Serve over white rice.

Sauce

2 medium onions
2 tablespoons vegetable oil
2 cups pulverized walnuts
2–3 tablespoons
   pomegranate paste,
   diluted in 2 cups boiling
   water (If unavailable,
   use pomegranate juice
   or syrup.)
salt to taste
2–3 tablespoons sugar
   (Taste should be on the
   sweet side.)

1. Cut onions in chunks and blend in blender until a pulp. In medium skillet, fry onion pulp in 1 tablespoon oil until golden; this is difficult because a great amount of onion juice must evaporate during frying process.
2. In large skillet, fry nuts in remaining oil, stirring carefully until they brown—they burn easily.
3. Add onions and diluted pomegranate paste to nuts. Stir in salt and sugar. Cook 1½–2 hours.

Serves 4

Hint: For added flavor, use broth chicken was cooked in to dilute the pomegranate paste.

BEEF ROLLS WITH RICE STUFFING

4 tablespoons butter
⅓ cup raw white rice or
　raw brown rice
½ cup thinly sliced celery
3 tablespoons finely
　chopped onion
1 cup beef broth
½ cup coarsely chopped
　walnuts
6 slices beef round steak,
　each about 7 x 5 x ¼
　inch
¼ teaspoon crumbled
　dried oregano
½ teaspoon salt
¼ cup water
¼ cup rosé wine

1. In medium saucepan with a lid, melt 2 tablespoons butter. Sauté rice, celery, and onion in butter until golden.
2. Pour in broth; cover; and simmer 20 minutes or until rice is tender.
3. Let mixture cool until it can be handled, and then stir in nuts. Spread on top of steaks.
4. Roll up steaks, tying each with string.
5. In large skillet with a lid, melt remaining butter. Brown meat rolls in butter, turning to brown all sides.
6. Sprinkle meat rolls with oregano and salt. Pour in water and stir to pick up pan drippings; add wine.
7. Simmer 20–30 minutes until meat is tender, covered.

Serves 6

BAKED HALIBUT WITH
WALNUTS AU GRATIN

1½ pounds halibut steaks,
　fresh or frozen
salt to taste
pepper to taste
3 tablespoons lemon juice
2 tablespoons dry white
　wine
1 cup finely chopped
　toasted walnuts
1 cup grated sharp
　cheddar cheese
¼ cup milk
½ cup dry bread crumbs
1 tablespoon butter

1. Preheat oven to 400°.
2. Place fish on well-buttered sheet of heavy-duty foil.
3. Sprinkle fish with salt, pepper, lemon juice, and wine.
4. Combine nuts, cheese, and milk; spread on top of fish.
5. Sprinkle fish with bread crumbs and dot with butter.
6. Wrap fish tightly with the foil, sealing ends and top with double folds. Bake on baking sheet 25–30 minutes until fish is tender and flaky.

Serves 6

BASIC CALIFORNIA WALNUT BREAD

3 cups sifted flour
1 cup sugar
4 teaspoons baking
   powder
2 teaspoons salt
1½ cups coarsely chopped
   toasted walnuts
1 egg, beaten
¼ cup butter, softened
1½ cups milk
1 teaspoon vanilla

1. Preheat oven to 350°.
2. Into large bowl, sift together flour, sugar, baking powder, and salt. Stir in 1¼ cups nuts.
3. Add egg, butter, milk, and vanilla, mixing only until ingredients are blended.
4. Pour batter into buttered, floured 9 x 5 x 3-inch loaf pan. Sprinkle remaining nuts over top.
5. Bake 60–70 minutes. Remove from oven and let loaf rest in pan at least 10 minutes. Turn out on a rack to cool.

Makes 1 loaf

STICKY BUNS

1 cake yeast
⅓ cup warm water
¾ cup milk
⅓ cup sugar
⅓ cup butter
1½ teaspoons salt
¼ teaspoon mace
⅛ teaspoon cardamom
1 egg, beaten
3⅓ cups sifted flour
1½ cups dark brown
   sugar, packed
7 tablespoons butter
¼ cup water
¾ cup walnut pieces
¼ teaspoon cinnamon
¾ cup walnut halves

1. In large bowl, dissolve yeast in warm water.
2. Scald milk mixed with sugar, ⅓ cup butter, salt, mace, and cardamom. Cool to lukewarm.
3. Combine scalded mixture and egg. Stir into yeast.
4. Beat about half of flour into yeast· mixture until smooth. Gradually blend in remaining flour to make a soft dough.
5. Turn dough out on floured board and knead lightly. Cover with tea towel and let rise in warm place about 1 hour until doubled.
6. Meanwhile, heat ¾ cup brown sugar with 4 tablespoons butter and water until sugar dissolves.
7. Butter 13 x 9 x 2-inch pan; pour in brown sugar syrup and sprinkle with nut pieces.
8. When dough has risen, turn out on floured board and roll into 15 x 12-inch rectangle.
9. Melt remaining butter and spread over dough.
10. Mix remaining brown sugar with cinnamon and sprinkle over dough.
11. Top dough with nut halves.
12. Roll up dough from long side to make a 15-inch roll. Cut in 1-inch slices. Place slices in syrup mixture in pan.
13. Let buns rise about 30 minutes until light.
14. Meanwhile, preheat oven to 365°. Bake 35 minutes or until nicely browned. Invert over serving tray at once. Allow pan to rest over rolls a minute to drain syrup. Serve warm.

Makes 15

TORTE WITH COFFEE FLAVOR

6 eggs, separated
1 cup sugar
¼ teaspoon salt
2 tablespoons raw coffee
2 cups ground English
  walnuts
3 tablespoons cake flour
1 teaspoon vanilla

1. Preheat oven to 375°.
2. In large bowl, beat egg yolks until thick and lemon colored.
3. Gradually beat sugar, salt, and raw coffee into egg yolks.
4. Vigorously stir nuts and flour into coffee mixture. Blend in vanilla.
5. Beat egg whites until stiff but not dry; fold into coffee mixture.
6. Bake torte in 2 buttered-and-floured 9-inch layer pans 25 minutes. Cool on a rack.
7. Prepare chocolate cream.
8. Put layers together with chocolate cream, and cover torte completely with chocolate cream.

Chocolate Cream

2 cups heavy cream
6 tablespoons cocoa
½ cup powdered sugar

1. Gently combine ingredients. Chill in refrigerator at least 2 hours.
2. Whip chocolate cream in electric mixer.

Serves 10

CHOCOLATE-WALNUT ROLL

¼ cup sifted cake flour

¼ cup unsweetened cocoa

1 teaspoon baking powder

½ teaspoon salt

¾ cup sugar

1 cup finely chopped
walnuts

4 eggs, separated

¼ teaspoon cream of tartar

2 tablespoons strong coffee

2 tablespoons fine dry
bread crumbs

2 tablespoons powdered
sugar

12 walnut halves

6 maraschino cherries

1. Preheat oven to 400°.

2. Sift flour with cocoa, baking powder, salt, and ¼ cup sugar. Mix thoroughly with finely chopped nuts.

3. In large bowl, beat egg whites with cream of tartar until stiff. Gradually beat in ½ cup sugar.

4. In separate large bowl with same beater, beat egg yolks well. Add coffee, then flour mixture, and mix well.

5. Pour batter over egg whites; carefully fold in until no streaks of white remain.

6. Turn batter into 15 x 10 x 1-inch pan lined with buttered waxed paper and sprinkled with bread crumbs. Smooth batter level in pan. Bake 10 minutes.

7. Turn cake out on tea towel sprinkled with powdered sugar. Carefully peel off paper from bottom of cake. Cover with pan and let cool.

8. Meanwhile, prepare walnut cream filling and chocolate glaze.

9. Spread cake with walnut cream filling, and roll up lengthwise.

10. Spread top and sides with chocolate glaze. Decorate with nut halves and cherries.

Walnut Cream Filling

1 cup heavy cream

2 tablespoons sugar

½ teaspoon vanilla or 1
tablespoon brandy

½ cup chopped walnuts

¼ cup chopped candied
cherries, half red, half
green

1. Whip heavy cream with sugar. Stir in vanilla.

2. Fold in nuts and cherries.

Chocolate Glaze

2 squares (1 ounce)
semisweet chocolate

2 teaspoons butter

2 teaspoons light corn
syrup

1. Over hot water, melt chocolate with butter.

2. Remove from heat and stir in corn syrup. Cool slightly before spreading.

Serves 8

POLISH WALNUT CAKE

1 cake yeast
1 tablespoon sugar
1 cup warm milk
½ cup sugar
1 cup butter, melted
1 teaspoon salt
3 eggs, well beaten
4 cups flour
1 egg yolk, beaten with 1
  tablespoon water

1. Preheat oven to 350°.

2. Crumble yeast with 1 tablespoon sugar. Gradually add to warm milk in large bowl, letting yeast dissolve about 5 minutes.

3. In order, stir in sugar, butter, salt, eggs, and flour; mix well. Knead dough on floured board.

4. Grease dough all over with additional melted butter or oil. Put buttered dough in a buttered bowl, and cover well with tea towel. Place in refrigerator to rise overnight.

5. The next day, divide dough in half and roll each section into rectangle about ¼ inch thick.

6. Prepare nut filling, then spread on each section and roll up jelly-roll fashion.

7. Brush top with egg yolk. Let both rolls rise in warm place until almost double in bulk. Bake 30 minutes. Cool on a rack.

Nut Filling

1 pound ground walnuts
1 cup sugar
1 tablespoon honey
1 teaspoon vanilla
cream or half-and-half to
  form a thick, spreadable
  paste

1. Combine ingredients.

Makes 2 rolls

 WALNUT SYRUP

1 cup light corn syrup
¼ cup water
¼ teaspoon maple
  flavoring
1¼ cups coarsely chopped
  walnuts

1. In heavy medium saucepan with a lid, combine corn syrup, water, and maple flavoring. Stir in nuts. Simmer over low heat 25 minutes, covered.

2. Let syrup cool. Turn into jars, cover tightly, and refrigerate until ready to use.

3. Serve cold or hot as a topping for desserts.

Makes 1¾ cups

Hint: This syrup is a dream over vanilla ice cream. To splurge, you can use half or all maple syrup instead of corn syrup and eliminate maple flavoring.

A HONEY OF A SAVARIN

1 package (13¾ ounce) hot
   roll mix
¼ cup warm water
⅓ cup milk
3 tablespoons butter
3 eggs
¼ cup sugar
1 teaspoon grated lemon
   rind
¾ cup coarsely chopped
   toasted walnuts
⅓ cup honey
½ cup apricot nectar
¼ cup brandy

1. Dissolve yeast packet from hot roll mix in warm water.

2. In small saucepan, heat milk to scalding. Melt butter in milk; cool to lukewarm.

3. In large bowl, beat eggs with sugar. Add yeast mixture, milk, and lemon rind.

4. Gradually blend hot roll mix into sugar mixture, beating well.

5. Stir nuts into batter.

6. Spoon batter into well-buttered 6-cup ring mold. Cover with tea towel and let rise in warm place about 1 hour until almost doubled in bulk.

7. Meanwhile, preheat oven to 350°.

8. Bake savarin about 40 minutes until baked through and nicely browned. Let stand 5 minutes, and then turn out on deep plate.

9. Combine honey, nectar, and brandy, and warm slightly. Prick savarin with long-tined fork or skewer. Slowly spoon honey mixture over savarin, adding more as absorbed.

Serves 8

WHAT CRUST FOR A PIE!

1½ cups ground walnuts
¼ cup butter
2 tablespoons sugar
2 tablespoons graham
   cracker crumbs or
   unseasoned bread
   crumbs (optional)

1. Preheat oven to 400°.

2. Combine nuts, butter, sugar, and crumbs until well blended.

3. Press nut mixture into bottom and sides of a well-buttered 9-inch pie plate, using fingers and back of a spoon. Bake 8–10 minutes.

4. Cool on a rack before filling.

Makes 1 pie shell

Hint: This crust is excellent for fruit pies in which fruit has already been cooked. It is likewise wonderful for Bavarian and cream pies which need only refrigeration.

The crumbs will bind the crust together.

WALNUT PIE

1 cup sugar
1 cup graham cracker
  crumbs
½ cup chopped walnuts
3 eggs, well beaten
1 cup heavy cream,
  whipped
12 walnut halves

1. Preheat oven to 350°.
2. Combine sugar, cracker crumbs, and chopped nuts. Beat in eggs well.
3. Pour mixture into buttered 9-inch pie plate. Bake 20-25 minutes.
4. Cool on a rack. Serve topped with whipped cream and decorated with nut halves.

Serves 8

 BRANDY CONES

½ cup butter
⅓ cup light corn syrup
½ cup sugar
2 tablespoons brandy
½ cup sifted flour
¼ teaspoon salt
½ cup finely chopped
  walnuts

1. Preheat oven to 350°.
2. In medium saucepan, combine butter, corn syrup, and sugar. Heat slowly until butter melts. Cool.
3. Beat brandy, flour, and salt into sugar mixture until smooth. Stir in nuts well.
4. Bake 2 cookies at a time. Drop 1 teaspoonful of batter on lightly buttered baking sheet for each cookie and space about 6 inches apart.
5. Bake 6–8 minutes until lightly browned and bubbly. Let cool about 1 minute.
6. Remove each cookie from baking sheet and quickly roll around a metal cone or handle of wooden spoon to shape.
7. Remove cookies from metal cones as soon as they are cool in about 4–5 minutes. Store cookie cones in tightly covered tin.

Makes 16–18

Hint: If cookies are too crisp to roll, set baking sheet back in oven about 1 minute to soften.

WALNUTS / DESSERTS AND SWEETS

VIENNESE WALNUT COOKIES

½ cup butter
⅓ cup sugar
¼ teaspoon salt
1 teaspoon vanilla
1¼ cups sifted flour
1⅓ cups finely chopped
    walnuts
walnut halves or large
    walnut pieces

1. Preheat oven to 350°.
2. In medium bowl, cream butter, sugar, salt, and vanilla together.
3. Blend flour and finely chopped nuts into butter mixture.
4. Using your hands, form dough into a ball. Chill 30 minutes.
5. Roll ball out on lightly floured board to a little less than ¼-inch thickness. With 2-inch cutter, cut dough in circles.
6. Bake cookies on unbuttered baking sheets 10–12 minutes until slightly browned. Cool on racks.
7. Prepare butter cream frosting.
8. Put cookies together in pairs with butter cream frosting. Top with a swirl of frosting and decorate with nut halves or large nut pieces.

Butter Cream Frosting

4 tablespoons butter,
    softened
2 cups powdered sugar
1 egg
1 tablespoon sherry

1. In small bowl, cream butter; gradually add powdered sugar, beating with electric mixer.
2. Stir in egg and sherry; continue beating until completely blended.

Makes 2 dozen

 ## LEBKUCHEN

4 eggs
1 package (1 pound) dark
    brown sugar
1¼ cups flour
1 teaspoon cinnamon
½ teaspoon nutmeg
1 teaspoon ground cloves
½ teaspoon allspice
2 tablespoons favorite
    liqueur or whiskey
1 cup chopped walnuts
1 cup golden seedless
    raisins (optional)

1. Preheat oven to 375°.
2. In large bowl with electric mixer, beat eggs. Gradually add brown sugar, continuing to beat well.
3. Mix flour with cinnamon, nutmeg, cloves, and allspice. Add to egg mixture, beating thoroughly.
4. Stir in liqueur, nuts, and raisins.
5. Spread on well-buttered 15 x 10-inch baking sheet. Bake 17 minutes. Remove from oven. Place baking sheet on a rack to cool. While warm, cut dessert in squares or bars.

Makes 36 squares

Hint: You can ice Lebkuchen with a lemon powdered sugar frosting, but purists prefer it plain.

BLACK
WALNUT

Juglans nigra

BLACK WALNUT

A NATIVE OF the United States and still found wild in the woods of the East and the cold Middle West too, this nut was once used by the Indians and colonial settlers. Despite hundreds of years of availability, however, its powerful and distinctive flavor may have limited its usage; most early and even current recipes use black walnuts exclusively in cakes, cookies, and candies. In this way, it is the most specialized nut in the book. Considered rich in taste, it dominates other flavors. But those who like the black walnut flavor become ardent fans and eagerly look for additional uses. I have provided a number, some quite radical in their combinations of foods.

While there is now increasing cultivation of the black walnut in Missouri and California, the nuts still grow wild in the Missouri woods. In their shell, they bear a slight resemblance in shape to the English walnuts to which they are distantly related, but their shell is all in one piece without the bisecting ridge. Although the California black walnut is of the *Juglans hindsii* strain, it and the native northern California black walnut, which is used as a root stock for commercial orchards, have much in common. The Californians are a little lighter in color with smoother shells; those from the cold climate are dark, almost black, in color and handsomely furrowed and grooved. Both are quite round in shape and hard to crack, the eastern being the more difficult. Because of the shelling problem, black walnuts are seldom available in the shell; commercially shelled, they are always found in pieces—it seems an impossible task to ferret them out in complete halves. Despite the color of the shells, the nut actually derives its name from the dark brown color of the tree.

A truly American nut, the black walnut played a very important part in the dietary life of the American Indians and colonial Americans. The nuts have a great deal of nutritional value and can be safety stored over the long winter months in cool dry places. Not only were they food for Indians and settlers, but they supplied fodder for herds of frontier swine. Particularly in what we now call Appalachia, the harvesting and shelling provided employment to many families. Throughout the years, more than 100 varieties of black walnuts have been found.

Marvelous in ice creams as well as candies and pastries, and used more and more in breads, the black walnut is growing in appeal for cooks and devotees of nuts. I foresee that it will be given much wider use for its distinctive flavor.

 PURCHASE

Black walnuts are seldom available in the shell. If you buy them that way, be prepared for problems in cracking; they are very hard, and when they are finally opened, the nutmeat must be dug out with a nutpick.

Shelled, they are available in vacuum tins (4½ ounces), which are the equivalent of 1 cup coarsely chopped nutmeats.

 PREPARATION

Just open the can.

 STORAGE

Keep shelled, opened nuts in an airtight container in refrigerator, and freeze in same container if you plan to keep them for any length of time.

GOLDEN CHEESE MOLD

1 package (3 ounce) lemon
   gelatin
1 cup boiling water
1 cup pineapple juice
½ package (3 ounce)
   cream cheese, chilled
⅔ cup chopped black
   walnuts
1 can (10½ ounce) crushed
   pineapple, drained
1 cup shredded carrot
lettuce leaves

1. In large bowl, dissolve gelatin in boiling water. Stir in pineapple juice.
2. Chill gelatin until partially set.
3. Cut cream cheese in 18 cubes.
4. Coat cream cheese with nuts and roll into balls.
5. Stir pineapple and carrot into gelatin.
6. Add coated cream cheese balls to gelatin. Gently pour into oiled mold.
7. Chill salad several hours or overnight until firm. Serve on lettuce leaves.

Serves 6

 ## BLACK WALNUT-TOPPED SQUASH

3 pounds yellow summer
   squash
1 large brown onion, finely
   minced
½ cup butter, melted
½ cup fine bread crumbs
2 eggs, lightly beaten
1½ tablespoons brown
   sugar
1 teaspoon salt
¾ teaspoon finely ground
   pepper
¾ cup chopped black
   walnuts

1. Pare, slice, and cook squash in lightly salted boiling water until barely tender. Drain squash well and mash.
2. Preheat oven to 350°.
3. Sauté onion in ¼ cup butter until onion is soft, but not brown.
4. Stir crumbs, eggs, sautéed onions with butter, brown sugar, salt, and pepper into mashed squash, mixing well.
5. Fold in ⅜ cup nuts.
6. Pour squash mixture into medium buttered casserole. Sprinkle remaining nuts on top, and carefully dribble remaining butter over all.
7. Bake 1 hour, checking toward the last 15 minutes to be sure the nuts do not burn.

Serves 6–8

Hint: This is delicious served with poultry or pork.

DARE-DEVIL HAMBURGER

1 pound ground round
   steak
½ cup ground black
   walnuts
1 teaspoon seasoned salt

1. Mix ingredients together.
2. Make 4–5 hamburger patties, handling mixture gently and as little as possible.
3. Fry patties in large buttered skillet or barbecue.

Serves 4–5

 BLACK WALNUT-MEAT LOAF

1 egg, beaten
⅓ cup milk
2 pounds ground beef
4 tablespoons minced
   onion
1½ teaspoons
   Worcestershire sauce
¼ teaspoon pepper
2 teaspoons salt
3 cups soft bread crumbs
1½ cups chopped celery
¼ teaspoon poultry
   seasoning
½ cup milk or water or
   stock
1 cup coarsely chopped
   black walnuts
½ cup tomato catsup
¼ cup water
6 orange slices
¼ cup chopped toasted
   black walnuts

1. Preheat oven to 375°.
2. Beat egg and milk together. Combine with beef, 2 tablespoons onion, Worcestershire sauce, ⅛ teaspoon pepper, and 1½ teaspoons salt. Flatten mixture out on waxed paper in ¾-inch-thick rectangle.
3. Prepare stuffing by combining bread crumbs, remaining onion, remaining salt, remaining pepper, celery, poultry seasoning, milk, and coarsely chopped nuts.
4. Shape stuffing into a roll on top of meat close to lengthwise side. Roll so that meat completely covers stuffing.
5. Remove waxed paper. Place meat roll in large shallow baking pan.
6. Mix catsup with water; pour over meat roll. Bake 1 hour.
7. Garnish with orange slices and chopped nuts.

Serves 6–8

ORANGE-BLACK WALNUT BREAD

1 cake yeast
¼ cup tepid water
3 tablespoons butter,
 melted
¾ cup orange juice
1 tablespoon sugar
2 tablespoons honey
1 teaspoon salt
1 egg
1 teaspoon grated orange
 rind
⅛ teaspoon cardamom
3 cups sifted flour
½ cup finely chopped
 · black walnuts

1. Soften and mix yeast in tepid water.
2. In large bowl, mix butter and orange juice; combine with sugar, honey, salt, egg, orange rind, and cardamom.
3. Vigorously mix in flour and nuts.
4. Knead dough well.
5. Let dough rise in bowl about 45–60 minutes. Punch down.
6. Place dough in 9 x 5 x 3-inch loaf pan and let rise again about 45 minutes.
7. Meanwhile, preheat oven to 375°.
8. Bake bread 10 minutes; reduce heat to 350° and bake 35 minutes more. During first 25 minutes of baking period, cover bread with pan that allows it room to rise but still protects it from browning oven heat; remove pan and finish baking. Cool on a rack.

Makes 1 loaf

 ## PUMPKIN BREAD

1⅔ cups flour
1½ cups sugar
1 teaspoon baking soda
¼ teaspoon baking
 powder
¾ teaspoon salt
1 teaspoon nutmeg
½ teaspoon ground cloves
½ teaspoon cinnamon
½ cup finely chopped
 black walnuts
2 eggs
1 cup canned pumpkin
½ cup water
½ cup butter, melted

1. Preheat oven to 325°.
2. In large bowl, mix together flour, sugar, baking soda, baking powder, salt, nutmeg, cloves, and cinnamon. Add nuts.
3. Beat eggs until fluffy. Stir eggs into pumpkin, water, and melted butter.
4. Beat egg mixture into dry ingredients well. Pour into well-buttered 9 x 5 x 3-inch loaf pan.
5. Bake 1 hour and 30 minutes. Cool on a rack.

Makes 1 loaf

BLACK WALNUT DESSERT

¾ cup ground black walnuts
3 cups flaked coconut
¼ cup raisins
¾ cup butter, melted
¾ cup dark brown sugar
5 apples, with skin, sliced
½ cup hot apple juice or hot water or hot cider
1 cup light cream or 1 pint ice cream

1. Preheat oven to 325°.
2. Mix nuts, coconut, raisins, butter, and brown sugar into a crumb mixture. Press about ⅓ mixture into bottom of small baking dish.
3. Layer alternately apples and crumb mixture, ending with crumb mixture on top.
4. Pour hot apple juice over this. Bake 25 minutes, covered.
5. Remove cover and bake 5 minutes more to brown top. Serve warm with cream.

Serves 6–8

BLACK WALNUT-DATE PUDDING

1 cup flour
1 cup sugar
¼ teaspoon salt
2 teaspoons baking powder
1 cup dates
½ cup raisins
½ cup chopped black walnuts
½ cup milk
1 teaspoon vanilla
1 teaspoon rum extract
¾ cup dark brown sugar
1½ cups boiling water
2 tablespoons butter
1 tablespoon vegetable oil
1 cup heavy cream, or 1 pint ice cream

1. Preheat oven to 300°.
2. In large bowl, combine flour, sugar, salt, and baking powder.
3. Stir dates, raisins, and nuts into dry ingredients.
4. Mix milk, vanilla, and rum extract into nut mixture.
5. Pour batter into buttered 8-inch square pan.
6. Combine brown sugar with boiling water, butter, and oil; pour on top of batter.
7. Bake pudding 1 hour. Serve pudding with whipped cream.

Serves 8

BLACK WALNUT JIFFY CAKE

2 cups sugar
1 cup butter, softened
2 cups sifted flour
¼ teaspoon salt
1 cup finely chopped black walnuts
1 teaspoon lemon extract
1 teaspoon vanilla
5 large eggs or 6 medium eggs

1. Preheat oven to 350°.
2. In above order, place all ingredients in electric-mixer bowl. Beat at high speed 5 minutes.
3. Prepare streusel mixture.
4. Pour half of batter into buttered and floured 10-inch bundt pan; sprinkle with half of streusel mixture, and carefully pour remaining batter on top.
5. Sprinkle remaining streusel on top.
6. Bake 1 hour and 15 minutes.
7. Cool cake on a rack before loosening and turning upside down on serving plate.

Streusel Mixture

⅓ cup sugar
1 teaspoon cinnamon
½ cup finely chopped black walnuts

1. Combine ingredients.

Serves 10–12

Hint: This is good plain or just dusted with powdered sugar. However, any favorite frosting adds glamour.

 ## BLACK WALNUT SHEET CAKE

2 cups flour
2 cups sugar
1 teaspoon baking soda
½ teaspoon salt
1 cup butter
4 tablespoons cocoa
1 cup water
½ cup buttermilk
2 eggs

1. Preheat oven to 350°.
2. Into large bowl, sift together flour, sugar, baking soda, and salt.
3. In small saucepan, melt butter. Mix in cocoa with water, and bring to rapid boil. Pour over sifted dry ingredients, stirring vigorously.
4. Mix in buttermilk and eggs.
5. Pour batter into well-buttered baking sheet with edge. Bake 15–20 minutes. Let stand to cool.
6. Prepare frosting.
7. Spread hot frosting on cake.

Frosting

½ cup butter
4 tablespoons cocoa
6 tablespoons buttermilk
1 package (1 pound) powdered sugar
1 cup chopped black walnuts

1. In medium saucepan, melt butter. Stir in cocoa and buttermilk, and bring to a boil.
2. Stir powdered sugar and nuts into cocoa mixture.

Serves 10–12

ELEGANT MERINGUE

3 egg whites
1 cup sugar
1 teaspoon baking powder
4 single saltines, rolled
 fine
1 cup chopped black
 walnuts
1 tablespoon sherry
1 teaspoon powderd sugar
1 cup heavy cream,
 whipped

1. Preheat oven to 275°.
2. In large bowl, beat egg whites until stiff but not dry. Combine sugar and baking powder and gradually beat into egg whites a little at a time, beating constantly.
3. Fold in saltine crumbs and nuts.
4. Spread meringue on buttered flat plate on which you plan to serve it. Bake 45–60 minutes. Cool.
5. Blend sherry and powdered sugar into whipped cream. Serve meringue topped with whipped cream.

Serves 6–8

Hint: Low oven temperature is safe for serving plates. If skeptical, bake meringue in 10-inch buttered pie plate or cake pan and transfer to serving plate.

FUDGE BARS

1 cup plus 2 tablespoons
 butter
2 cups light brown sugar
2 eggs
4 teaspoons vanilla
1½ cups sifted flour
1 teaspoon baking soda
½ teaspoon salt
3 cups quick-cooking
 rolled oats
1 package (12 ounce)
 semisweet chocolate bits
1 cup sweetened
 condensed milk
1 cup chopped black
 walnuts

1. Preheat oven to 350°.
2. In large bowl, cream 1 cup butter and brown sugar. Vigorously beat in eggs and 2 teaspoons vanilla.
3. Into large bowl, sift together flour, baking soda, and salt.
4. Add oats to flour. Stir dry ingredients into creamed mixture. Set aside while making filling.
5. In medium saucepan over boiling water, mix together chocolate bits, milk, and remaining butter, stirring until smooth. Stir in nuts and remaining vanilla.
6. Spread about ⅔ oatmeal mixture in bottom of a jelly-roll pan. Cover this layer with chocolate mixture.
7. Dot chocolate layer with remaining oatmeal mixture and swirl. Bake 25–30 minutes.

Serves 8

BLACK WALNUT COOKIES

1 cup butter, softened
2 cups dark brown sugar,
 firmly packed
2 eggs
3½ cups sifted flour
1 teaspoon baking soda
1½ teaspoons salt
1 teaspoon cinnamon
½ teaspoon nutmeg
½ teaspoon ginger
¼ teaspoon mace
⅓ cup milk
2 cups chopped black
 walnuts

1. Preheat oven to 400°.
2. In large bowl, cream butter thoroughly. Gradually add brown sugar, blending well. Beat in eggs until smooth and fluffy.
3. Sift together flour, baking soda, salt, cinnamon, nutmeg, ginger, and mace.
4. To batter, gradually add sifted dry ingredients alternately with milk, blending well. Add nuts with last addition of dry ingredients, mixing thoroughly.
5. Drop by teaspoonsful 2 inches apart on unbuttered baking sheet. Bake 10–12 minutes.

Makes about 8 dozen

 REFRIGERATOR COOKIES

1½ cups butter, melted
1 cup sugar
1 cup dark brown sugar
3 eggs, well beaten
1 cup finely chopped black
 walnuts
4½ cups flour
2 teaspoons baking soda
1 teaspoon salt
½ teaspoon nutmeg
½ teaspoon ground cloves
1 teaspoon cinnamon

1. In large bowl, cream butter and sugars.
2. Add eggs 1 at a time, mixing thoroughly. Stir in nuts.
3. Sift together remaining ingredients. Blend into mixture.
4. Shape dough into a roll 2 inches in diameter and refrigerate overnight.
5. Next morning, preheat oven to 425°.
6. Cut dough in ¼-inch-thick cookies and place on buttered baking sheet. Bake 8 minutes.

Makes about 6 dozen

 HONEY BARS

1 cup honey
3 eggs, well beaten
1⅓ cups flour
1 teaspoon baking powder
1 cup chopped black
 walnuts
1 pound pitted dates
1 teaspoon vanilla
powdered sugar to coat

1. Preheat oven to 350°.
2. In large bowl, mix honey with eggs.
3. Sift flour with baking powder; blend into honey mixture.
4. Chop dates. Stir in dates, nuts, and vanilla.
5. Pour batter into buttered 12 x 9-inch baking pan. Bake 16 minutes.
6. While still hot, cut in bars. Cool on a rack.
7. Before serving, roll each bar in powdered sugar.

Makes 40

APPLE SAUCE COOKIES

½ cup butter
1 cup dark brown sugar
1 egg, beaten
1 cup apple sauce
2 cups flour
1 teaspoon baking soda
½ teaspoon ground cloves
½ teaspoon cinnamon
½ teaspoon salt
½ teaspoon nutmeg
1 cup raisins
1 cup chopped black
   walnuts

1. Preheat oven to 350°.
2. In large bowl, cream butter and brown sugar.
3. Stir in egg and apple sauce.
4. Into large bowl, sift together flour, baking soda, cloves, cinnamon, salt, and nutmeg. Stir raisins and nuts into sifted dry ingredients.
5. Gradually add nut mixture to apple sauce mixture, stirring vigorously until well blended.
6. Drop batter by teaspoonsful on buttered baking sheet. Bake 12–18 minutes.

Makes 4 dozen

 ## BLACK WALNUT CRUNCH

1 cup sugar
⅔ cup coarsely chopped
   black walnuts
4 squares (1 ounce)
   semisweet chocolate
⅔ cup finely chopped
   black walnuts

1. In small saucepan over high heat, melt sugar.
2. Stir coarsely chopped nuts into sugar.
3. Quickly pour candy onto buttered baking sheet. Cool.
4. Melt chocolate; spread on cooled brittle. Sprinkle finely chopped nuts over chocolate. Cool candy and break in pieces.

Makes 1 pound

 ## BLACK WALNUT DIVINITY FUDGE

3 cups sugar
1 cup cold water
2 teaspoons white vinegar
⅛ teaspoon salt
2 egg whites
1 teaspoon vanilla
½ cup chopped black
   walnuts

1. In large saucepan, slowly heat sugar, cold water, vinegar, and salt, stirring constantly until sugar melts. Cook rapidly to soft-ball stage at 234°–240° without stirring. When syrup reaches about 230°, start beating egg whites in large bowl until stiff but not dry.
2. When syrup reaches 234°–240°, pour syrup over egg whites in a thin stream, beating constantly.
3. Beat mixture until it is creamy and holds its shape, adding vanilla and nuts.
4. Drop candy from tip of teaspoon on waxed paper. Let stand several hours until set.

Makes 1⅔ pounds

NIBBLE NUTS

NIBBLE NUTS

NUTS, FRUIT, and wine have appeared through the ages as a happy trio. By themselves, nuts are enjoyed for their delicious tastes, pop-in-the-mouth handiness, and crunch. They constitute a nourishing concentrated food. Raw, roasted, salted, or unsalted, they are excellent for a midafternoon snack and even for a morning coffee break, providing quick delicious protein with real staying power.

Even in prebiblical days, nuts were endowed with two properties: simultaneously, they were excellent for preventing drunkenness and inducing thirst.

For nibbling, they are appropriate as a natural accompaniment to relaxation and good conversation before or after dinner. Highly seasoned nuts add zest and nourishment at the drinking hour; and after dinner, sugared nuts are interesting instead of conventional candy.

CURRIED ALMONDS

⅓ cup butter
1 teaspoon curry powder
1 teaspoon salt
4 cups whole almonds

1. Preheat oven to 300°.
2. In large skillet, melt butter.
3. Add curry powder and salt, mixing well until dissolved. Stir in nuts, coating them thoroughly.
4. Turn out mixture on buttered baking sheet. Bake about 25 minutes, stirring at least once.
5. Put baking sheet on a rack to cool nuts without them becoming soggy. Store cooled nuts in airtight container.

Makes 1 quart

Hint: According to your preference, use blanched or natural almonds.

 ## MINTED ALMONDS

½ cup water
1 tablespoon light corn
 syrup
1 cup sugar
½ teaspoon salt
8 marshmallows
½ teaspoon peppermint
 extract
3 cups whole almonds,
 blanched

1. In small saucepan, cook water, syrup, sugar, and salt to soft-ball stage at 236°.
2. Stir in marshmallows and peppermint extract.
3. Put nuts in heat-resistant bowl, and pour syrup mixture over them. Stir thoroughly.
4. Cool. Separate pieces with 2 forks.

Makes 3½ cups

 ## CHILI FILBERTS

⅓ cup butter
1½ teaspoons chili powder
dash of salt
4 cups whole filberts

1. Preheat oven to 275°.
2. In large saucepan, melt butter.
3. Add chili powder, salt, and nuts, coating nuts well.
4. Turn out nut mixture on baking sheet. Bake 20 minutes, stirring at least once.
5. Put baking sheet on a rack to cool nuts without them becoming soggy. Store in airtight container.

Makes 1 quart

SUGARED BRAZIL NUTS

1 cup brown sugar
¼ cup evaporated milk
1 tablespoon butter
1 teaspoon cinnamon
pinch of salt
1 teaspoon vanilla
2 cups whole Brazil nuts or
    Brazil nuts cut in half

1. In medium saucepan, mix brown sugar, milk, butter, cinnamon, and salt. Cook to soft-ball stage at 236°.
2. Remove pan from heat. Stir in vanilla and nuts until mixture is thick and nuts are coated.
3. Spoon mixture onto waxed paper, and separate nuts with 2 forks. Let harden.

Makes 2½ cups

 ## CINNAMON CASHEWS

1 cup sugar
1 teaspoon cinnamon
⅛ teaspoon cream of tartar
¼ cup hot water
1½ cups cashews
½ teaspoon vanilla

1. In small saucepan, mix sugar, cinnamon, cream of tartar, and hot water. Boil mixture to firm-ball stage at 242°.
2. Add nuts and vanilla, stirring until mixture sugars.
3. Place mixture on baking sheet, and separate nuts.

Makes 2 cups

 ## BRAZIL NUT CHIPS

1½ cups whole Brazil nuts
2 tablespoons butter
1 teaspoon salt or celery
    salt or onion salt or
    garlic salt or seasoned
    salt

1. Preheat oven to 350°.
2. Cover nuts with cold water. Slowly bring to a boil; simmer 2–3 minutes.
3. Drain nuts. Cut lengthwise in ⅛-inch-thick slices.
4. Spread nuts in shallow baking pan. Dot with butter and sprinkle with salt.
5. Bake 15–20 minutes, stirring occasionally.
6. While still warm, serve chips in a bowl on a tray with 1 or 2 favorite spreads. To store, cool before putting chips in tightly covered container; serve as needed.

Makes 2 cups

COCONUT CHIPS

1 fresh coconut
salt to taste

1. Preheat oven to 300°.
2. Using a vegetable peeler, shave shelled coconut meat that still has brown skin into thin strips.
3. Spread coconut strips in thin single layer in shallow baking pan. Bake until golden, stirring often to color coconut evenly.
4. Sprinkle chips with salt.
5. Store in airtight container.

Hint: Serve as snack with drinks.

 ## COFFEE FILBERTS

1 cup brown sugar
½ cup sugar
½ cup sour cream
1 tablespoon instant coffee
  powder
1 teaspoon vanilla
2½ cups whole roasted
  filberts

1. In large saucepan, combine sugars, sour cream, and coffee powder. Cook mixture to soft-ball stage at 236°, stirring.
2. Remove from heat and add vanilla and nuts. Gently stir until each nut is coated.
3. Pour mixture onto buttered baking sheet, and separate nuts with 2 forks.
4. Cool until coating sets. Store in airtight metal container.

Makes 3½ cups

 ## GINGER MACADAMIAS

1 cup sugar
¼ cup water
¼ teaspoon salt
½ teaspoon ginger
1 teaspoon cinnamon
3 cups whole macadamia
  nuts

1. In small saucepan, mix together sugar, water, salt, ginger, and cinnamon. Boil slowly 10 minutes.
2. In large bowl, pour mixture over nuts; stir until cool.
3. Spread out mixture on waxed paper, and separate nuts with 2 forks. Store cooled nuts in airtight tin.

Makes 3½ cups

SPICED MACADAMIAS

1 cup sugar
½ teaspoon salt
2 teaspoons cinnamon
½ teaspoon nutmeg
½ teaspoon ground cloves
½ cup water
2 cups whole macadamia
  nuts

1. In medium saucepan, boil sugar, salt, cinnamon, nutmeg, cloves, and water to soft-ball stage at 236°.
2. Remove from heat and add nuts. Stir until creamy. Turn out mixture on waxed paper, and separate nuts with 2 forks.

Makes 2½ cups

 ## GLAZED PEANUTS

1 cup sugar
½ cup water
2 cups whole peanuts,
  raw, shelled, with red
  skins on

1. In large heavy skillet over medium heat, dissolve sugar in water.
2. Add nuts. Cook over medium-high heat until nuts appear shiny, glazed, and rosy, stirring constantly.
3. Spread nuts on foil to cool. Break apart while still slightly warm. After cooling, store in airtight container.

Makes 2½ cups

 ## PARMESAN PEANUTS

2 tablespoons peanut oil
3⅓ cups dry roasted salted
  peanuts
2 tablespoons Parmesan
  cheese
1 teaspoon garlic salt

1. Preheat oven to 350°.
2. In oven, heat peanut oil in shallow baking pan 5 minutes.
3. Remove pan from oven and add nuts, stirring until coated with hot oil.
4. Return to oven 5 minutes.
5. Remove pan from oven. Sprinkle nuts with cheese and garlic salt; stir to coat nuts well.
6. Cool and serve.

Makes 3½ cups

220

 ## HONEY CANDIED PECANS

1½ cups sugar
¼ teaspoon salt
¼ cup honey
½ cup water
½ teaspoon vanilla
3 cups pecan halves

1. In large saucepan, boil sugar, salt, honey, and water together to firm soft-ball stage at 242°, stirring often.
2. Remove mixture from heat and add vanilla and nuts. Stir until creamy.
3. Turn out mixture on waxed paper, and separate nuts with 2 forks.

Makes 3½ cups

 ## ORANGE PECANS

2 cups sugar
¾ cup evaporated milk
¼ cup water
1½ tablespoons grated orange rind
4 tablespoons orange juice
1½ cups large pecan halves

1. In large saucepan, combine sugar, milk, water, and orange rind.
2. Stir mixture over low heat until sugar dissolves. Cook to soft-ball stage at 236°, stirring occasionally to prevent sticking.
3. Add orange juice. Remove from heat and cool to lukewarm. Beat until creamy.
4. Stir in nuts until well coated.
5. Pour mixture onto large buttered baking sheet, and separate each nut with 2 forks.

Makes 2¼ cups

 ## PECANS PIQUANT

2 tablespoons butter
⅓ cup Worcestershire sauce
2 dashes of Tabasco sauce
2 cups raw pecan halves
salt to taste

1. Preheat oven to 300°.
2. In medium saucepan, melt butter. Mix in Worcestershire and Tabasco sauces well. Remove from heat.
3. Mix nuts in well 4–5 minutes.
4. Line baking sheet with foil, and spread seasoned nuts evenly on top.
5. Crisp nuts in oven 15–20 minutes. Watch carefully and stir twice to prevent burning.
6. Salt nuts. Cool and store in airtight container.

Makes 2 cups

A PINE NUT SNACK

2 tablespoons butter
2 cups shelled pine nuts
salt to taste
pepper to taste

This has long been a favorite of American Indians.

1. In large heavy pan, melt butter.
2. Add nuts, frying slowly and stirring until they are coated with butter and become a light gold.
3. Sprinkle salt and pepper on nuts, and mix well.
4. Pour seasoned nuts onto double thickness of paper towels to absorb extra butter.
5. Serve hot as a snack.

Makes 2 cups

Hint: This simple snack is fabulous enough to serve on special occasions.

 ## WALNUT BITES

1 package (8 ounces) cream
    cheese
½ pound bleu cheese
1 teaspoon seasoned salt
¼ teaspoon
    Worcestershire sauce
86 walnut halves

1. Early in day, mix cream cheese with bleu cheese, seasoned salt, and Worcestershire sauce. Refrigerate until firm and easy to handle.
2. Form cheese mixture into 43 balls, sandwiching each between 2 nut halves.
3. Refrigerate until ready to serve.

Makes 43

 ## BARBECUED WALNUTS

2 tablespoons butter
¼ cup Worcestershire
    sauce
1 tablespoon catsup
2 dashes of Tabasco sauce
4 cups walnut halves
salt to taste

1. Preheat oven to 400°.
2. In large saucepan, melt butter.
3. Mix in Worcestershire sauce, catsup, and Tabasco sauce.
4. Stir in nuts.
5. Spread nut mixture in 1 layer in glass baking dish. Toast in oven about 20 minutes, stirring frequently.
6. Turn out nuts on paper towels and sprinkle with salt. Serve warm or cold.

Makes 1 quart

SPICED WALNUTS

¾ cups powdered sugar
½ teaspoon ground cloves
2 tablespoons cinnamon
½ teaspoon nutmeg
1 teaspoon salt
2½ tablespoons vegetable oil
2 cups walnut halves

1. Blend together sugar, cloves, cinnamon, and nutmeg.
2. In large skillet, combine 3 tablespoons of sugar mixture and salt with oil. Cook gently 5–10 minutes.
3. When blended and hot, add nuts. Cook 5–10 minutes more, stirring constantly.
4. Drain nuts and mix with remaining sugar mixture, tossing with 2 forks.

Makes 2¼ cups

Hint: Step 2 is optional but adds to flavor; you may immediately add and toast nuts.

 ## SUGARED WALNUTS

2 cups sugar
¾ cup milk
1 tablespoon butter
2 tablespoons orange marmalade or 1 teaspoon cinnamon
3½ cups walnut halves

1. In large saucepan, boil sugar and milk to soft-ball stage at 236°.
2. Add butter and marmalade. Remove from heat and beat until creamy.
3. Add nuts and stir only until coating starts to sugar.
4. Turn out mixture on brown paper, and separate nuts with 2 forks.

Makes 4½ cups

 ## CHOCOLATE-COVERED NUTS

1 package (6 ounce) semisweet chocolate bits
¾ cup sweetened condensed milk
2 cups whole, halves, or large pieces nuts

1. In top of double boiler, melt chocolate.
2. Gradually stir in milk.
3. Remove chocolate mixture from hot water and cool 3-5 minutes.
4. Stir in nuts, mixing so they are well covered.
5. Drop by teaspoonsful on lightly buttered baking sheet. If using whole nuts or perfect halves, separate by piece.
6. Wrap in waxed paper if desired.

Makes 2½ cups

NUTTY MEAT
ALTERNATIVES

NUTTY MEAT ALTERNATIVES

IN PREVIOUS CHAPTERS, I have used nuts
not only as a highly concentrated food but as an addition to
many foods because of their taste, crunch, texture, and appearance. This chapter features the total substitution of nuts for
meats in conjunction with cheeses, grains, legumes, and other
vegetarian foods, providing dishes that serve as entrees as well
as accompaniments and desserts. The inclusion of nuts in vegetarian dishes adds marvelous texture and substance and
greatly increases their nutritional value. In terms of the concentrated proteins, vitamins, and minerals nuts provide, their cost
is relatively low. While they do provide necessary fat, the actual
saturated fat content in most nuts is relatively low. Nuts do not
have cholesterol, and many nuts are high in polyunsaturated
fats. Their total dietary value is outstanding, except in the cases
of chestnuts and coconuts, which rate high in carbohydrates but
quite low in other food values.

Nuts are readily available and can always be kept on hand
with careful storage.

For use in cooking, nuts have additional virtues. They give
body and substance to dishes. Coupled with other foods, such
as rice, pastas, and cereals, they help produce marvelous-
tasting and elegant dishes offering the lasting satisfaction of the
conventional meat-and-potatoes meal. For the organic food
enthusiasts who philosophically believe in vegetarianism,
these dishes can be described not only as alternatives but also as
nutty retreats from meat!

ARTICHOKE LOAF

3 artichokes
1 onion, chopped
½ cup butter, melted
3 egg yolks
½ cup chopped parsley
salt to taste
pepper to taste
5 crackers, crumbled
½ cup grated sharp cheese
1 cup milk
½ cup ground Brazil nuts

1. Cook artichokes. Scrape tender part off each leaf into small bowl; remove and discard choke; and mash heart in same bowl.
2. Preheat oven to 350°.
3. In small saucepan, sauté onion in ¼ cup butter.
4. In large bowl, beat egg yolks.
5. Add onions and parsley, stirring well; season with salt and pepper.
6. Mix in cracker crumbs and cheese alternately with milk.
7. Beat in nuts until well blended. Stir in remaining butter.
8. Bake in buttered 9 x 5 x 3-inch loaf pan 30 minutes or until firm.
9. Prepare cream sauce. Serve cream sauce in separate bowl.

Cream Sauce

3 tablespoons butter
2 tablespoons flour
1 cup milk
garlic salt to taste
onion salt to taste
1 tablespoon sherry

1. In small saucepan, melt butter.
2. Stir in flour. Cook 2–3 minutes.
3. Gradually add milk, stirring until mixture is thick and smooth.
4. Add garlic salt, onion salt, and sherry. Serve warm.

Serves 4

BEAN-AND-CHEESE LOAF

1 cup whole-grain bread
  crumbs
1 cup pineapple juice
1 cup cooked garbanzo
  beans
¼ cup minced parsley
1 teaspoon salt
1 cup chopped onion
½ cup diced celery
3 tablespoons vegetable oil
1½ cups chopped peanuts
1 egg
2 teaspoons soy sauce
⅛ teaspoon cayenne
1 cup grated cheddar
  cheese

1. Preheat oven to 350°.
2. In large bowl, soak bread crumbs in pineapple juice.
3. Coarsely grind beans.
4. Mix beans into soaked crumbs. Combine with remaining ingredients.
5. Place mixture in buttered 9 x 5 x 3-inch loaf pan. Bake 40 minutes or until edges are browned.

Serves 6

CARROT-AND-PEA LOAF

1 cup drained cooked
  tomato pieces
1 cup cooked peas
1 cup diced cooked carrots
¾ cup chopped walnuts
1 teaspoon salt
3 tablespoons minced
  onion
1 cup soft bread crumbs
½ cup milk
2 eggs, beaten
1 tablespoon butter,
  melted
⅛ teaspoon pepper

1. Preheat oven to 350°.
2. Combine ingredients thoroughly.
3. Turn mixture into buttered 8 x 4 x 2-inch loaf pan. If desired, top with additional nuts. Bake 60 minutes.

Serves 8

CASHEW NOODLES

8 ounces egg noodles
2 tablespoons butter
1 garlic clove, sliced
¼ cup chopped green
  onions
1 teaspoon soy sauce
⅛ teaspoon cayenne
1½ cups cottage cheese
1 cup sour cream
½ cup sliced cashews
2 tablespoons Madeira
½ cup chopped
  mushrooms
½ cup grated Romano
  cheese

1. Preheat oven to 350°.
2. Cook noodles and drain. Place in large bowl and add butter.
3. Mix together garlic, green onions, soy sauce, cayenne, cottage cheese, sour cream, nuts, Madeira, and mushrooms. Stir into noodles.
4. Place mixture in medium buttered casserole. Sprinkle with Romano cheese.
5. Bake 25 minutes or until hot and bubbly.

Serves 4–6

CURRIED VEGETABLE CASSEROLE

1 tablespoon vegetable oil
1 tablespoon butter
2 teaspoons curry powder
1 teaspoon salt
⅛ teaspoon pepper
¼ teaspoon mace
2 tablespoons flour
1 cup milk
1 cup sour cream
2 cups steamed green
  beans
2 cups steamed Brussels
  sprouts
2 cups steamed cauliflower
½ cup chopped toasted
  almonds

1. Preheat oven to 400°.
2. In small saucepan, blend oil, butter, curry powder, salt, pepper, and mace. Add flour, stirring 2 minutes.
3. Add milk, stirring until thick.
4. Lower heat and blend in sour cream.
5. In large buttered casserole, place beans, sprouts, and cauliflower. Top with sauce.
6. Bake 12 minutes or until hot. Sprinkle with nuts.

Serves 6–8

FETTUCCINE IN NUT SAUCE

½ teaspoon salt
1½ pounds fettuccine or
  favorite pasta
1 cup butter, melted
2 cups ground walnuts
½ cup toasted pine nuts
  (optional)
1 garlic clove, pressed
1 tablespoon marjoram
2 tablespoons chopped
  fresh parsley, preferably
  Italian
½ cup ricotta cheese or
  small-curd cottage
  cheese
1 tablespoon red wine
6 tablespoons olive oil
½ cup grated Parmesan
  cheese (optional)

1. In large quantity of boiling salted water, cook fettuccine noodles until al dente (firmly tender). Drain noodles and toss with melted butter.
2. Make sauce by using either a mortar and pestle or, more conveniently, your blender or food processor. Pound or blend nuts, garlic, marjoram, and parsley into a paste, adding ricotta cheese and wine.
3. Gradually drop olive oil into paste, beating to blend as it is added.
4. In a double boiler, warm sauce.
5. Add sauce to buttered fettuccine and toss. Sprinkle with Parmesan cheese, and serve immediately.

Serves 4–6

Hint: This is a delicious meal served with an Italian green salad of lettuce, watercress, slivered mushrooms, and marinated artichokes, dressed with oil and vinegar. Hot Italian bread and strong coffee complete this unusual Italian treat.

NUT-COVERED EGG CURRY

12 eggs, hard-boiled,
   quartered
½ cup bread crumbs
½ cup chopped
   macadamia nuts
2 tablespoons butter,
   clarified
3 tablespoons butter
3 teaspoons curry powder
2 tablespoons flour
salt to taste
pepper to taste
2 cups milk

1. Preheat oven to 350°.
2. Arrange eggs in large buttered casserole.
3. Brown crumbs and nuts in clarified butter.
4. In small saucepan, melt 3 tablespoons butter. Blend in curry powder, flour, salt, and pepper. Stir in milk. Cook slowly until thick, stirring constantly.
5. Pour curry sauce over eggs and top with nut mixture.
6. Bake 12 minutes.

Serves 6

 ## FILBERT RICE SUPREME

1 large onion, chopped
2 cups chopped celery
3 tablespoons vegetable oil
1 cup finely chopped
   roasted filberts
3 cups cooked rice
1 pound cottage cheese
1 cup diced cooked carrots
¼ cup filbert butter
¼ cup chopped green
   pepper
2 tablespoons parsley
4 eggs, beaten
1 teaspoon salt

1. Preheat oven to 375°.
2. In large saucepan, sauté onion and celery in oil.
3. Add remaining ingredients. Stir until mixture is smooth and well blended.
4. Line 9 x 7 x 3-inch loaf pan with foil; butter well. Pack mixture into pan.
5. Bake 1 hour and 15 minutes.
6. Unmold loaf onto heated platter and carefully strip off foil. This is especially good with a white or mushroom sauce.

Serves 6–8

GARLIC-SAUCED PASTA

½ cup olive oil
4 garlic cloves, thinly
   sliced
½ cup water
1 tablespoon chopped
   parsley
4 tablespoons chopped
   walnuts
⅛ teaspoon pepper
1 pound spaghetti
½ teaspoon salt
½ cup Parmesan cheese

1. In small skillet, heat olive oil. Add garlic, carefully cooking until brown, but not at all burned.
2. Slowly stir in water; add parsley, nuts, and pepper.
3. Simmer sauce 10 minutes, uncovered, carefully stirring.
4. Meanwhile, cook spaghetti in boiling salted water until al dente. Drain in colander.
5. Toss spaghetti with sauce and sprinkle half of cheese on it. Serve remaining cheese in separate dish.

Serves 4

 ## MACARONI AND CHEESE WITH PEANUTS

1 package (8 ounce)
   macaroni or spaghetti
3 tablespoons butter
2 tablespoons flour
1 teaspoon salt
1 teaspoon cayenne
1½ cups milk
¾ cup chopped salted
   peanuts
⅔ cup grated Romano
   cheese
¼ cup fine bread crumbs,
   mixed with 1 tablespoon
   melted butter

1. Preheat oven to 375°.
2. Cook macaroni in boiling salted water until tender. Drain.
3. In small saucepan, melt butter; blend in flour, salt, and cayenne. Add milk. Cook slowly until thickened, stirring constantly.
4. Arrange alternate layers of nuts, macaroni, and cheese in buttered 12 x 6 x 2-inch baking dish, saving some nuts and cheese for top.
5. Cover with white sauce and sprinkle with bread crumbs, nuts, and cheese.
6. Bake 20 minutes or until hot and browned.

Serves 6

WALNUT LOAF

⅓ cup butter
1 cup chopped
  mushrooms
2 large onions, finely
  chopped
¼ cup chopped green
  pepper
3 cups grated carrots
1½ cups chopped celery
½ cup sunflower seeds
¾ cup coarsely chopped
  walnuts
5 eggs, beaten
3 cups soft, whole wheat
  bread crumbs
dash of basil
dash of oregano
dash of salt
dash of pepper

1. Preheat oven to 325°.
2. In large skillet, melt butter. Sauté mushrooms, onions, and green pepper in butter until tender, but not brown.
3. In large bowl, combine mushroom mixture with carrots, celery, sunflower seeds, nuts, eggs, and bread crumbs.
4. Mix combination well with remaining ingredients.
5. Butter 9 x 5 x 3-inch loaf pan and line it with waxed paper.
6. Turn mixture into prepared loaf pan. Bake 1 hour.

Serves 6–8

PEANUT PATTIES

4 tablespoons butter
1 small onion, minced
2 medium tomatoes,
  skinned, seeded,
  chopped
1 tart apple, cored, pared,
  chopped
½ cup soft bread crumbs,
  preferably whole wheat
  or oatmeal
1 teaspoon seasoned salt
1 cup finely chopped
  peanuts
1 small egg, beaten
2–4 tablespoons milk or
  broth to moisten
¼ cup fine bread crumbs
¼ cup ground peanuts
1 egg, beaten with 1
  tablespoon water or
  milk, for dipping

1. In medium skillet, melt 2 tablespoons butter. Sauté onion, tomatoes, and apple in butter until tender and blended.
2. Mix soft bread crumbs, seasoned salt, and chopped nuts into onion mixture.
3. Remove skillet from heat; cool. Mix in egg and milk to moisten. After mixing well, shape into patties.
4. Mix fine bread crumbs with ground nuts. Dip each pattie into egg mixture and then into fine bread crumb mixture. Let coated patties lie on waxed paper at least 30 minutes for coating to adhere.
5. In large skillet, fry patties in remaining butter 15 minutes, turning to brown evenly. Serve alone or with tomato or cream gravy. Highly seasoned coleslaw and marinated cucumbers are good accompaniments.

Serves 4

CHILEAN CORN SOUFFLÉ

1 can (12 ounce) whole
   kernel corn, drained
½ cup milk
¼ cup cold milk
¼ cup powdered milk
1½ tablespoons whole
   wheat flour
½ teaspoon salt
dash of pepper
2 eggs, separated
½ cup shredded mild
   cheddar cheese
½ cup chopped walnuts
3 tablespoons butter
½ medium onion,
   chopped
½ cup fresh mushrooms
⅛ teaspoon ground red
   pepper
⅛ teaspoon cumin
¼ teaspoon oregano
¼ teaspoon cinnamon
dash of nutmeg
1 teaspoon chopped fresh
   parsley
½ cup black olives, pitted

1. Preheat oven to 350°.
2. In large saucepan, simmer corn in ½ cup milk.
3. Blend ¼ cup cold milk with powdered milk, flour, salt, and pepper. Add to corn and milk. Simmer 5 minutes, stirring constantly.
4. Cool corn mixture and fold in beaten egg yolks, cheese, and nuts.
5. In small saucepan, melt butter. Sauté onion and mushrooms in butter with red pepper, cumin, oregano, cinnamon, nutmeg, and parsley until limp.
6. Stir sautéed mixture and olives into corn mixture, blending thoroughly.
7. Beat egg whites until stiff but not dry, and fold them into corn mixture.
8. Pour corn mixture into medium well-buttered casserole. Bake 45–60 minutes. If not serving immediately, turn off heat, open oven to cool a minute, and then let soufflé remain in closed oven until serving time.

Serves 6

 ANY-NUT-WILL-DO NUTCORN

2 quarts popped corn
1 can (4 ounce) favorite
   salted nuts
2 cups dark brown sugar,
   firmly packed
2 tablespoons corn syrup
2 tablespoons butter
⅔ cup water
1 teaspoon vanilla

1. In large bowl, lightly toss popped corn and nuts together.
2. In heavy saucepan, combine brown sugar, syrup, butter, and water. Bring to a boil, uncovered, and cook to hard-ball stage at 250°. Stir in vanilla.
3. Slowly pour hot candy syrup over popped corn and nuts, tossing lightly and carefully with a spoon and fork to distribute syrup throughout mixture.
4. Shape caramel corn into balls, or let cool slightly and then break apart into clusters. Spread balls or clusters on waxed paper to cool completely.

Makes 24–30

ANY-NUT-WILL-DO SOUFFLÉ

3 tablespoons butter
3 tablespoons flour
1 cup light cream
½ cup sugar
4 egg yolks
heaping ¾ cup ground
   nuts, 1 kind or any
   mixture
3 tablespoons sherry
6 egg whites
pinch of salt
⅛ teaspoon cream of tartar
1 cup heavy cream,
   whipped
2 tablespoons powdered
   sugar

1. In large saucepan, melt butter. Blend in flour, cooking at least 5 minutes to eliminate raw-flour taste.

2. Warm cream and gradually add to flour blend, whisking while adding. Stir until smooth and thick.

3. Dissolve sugar in cream mixture, and then remove from heat. Preheat oven to 400°.

4. Prepare 1-quart soufflé dish by buttering it well and tying a 4-inch-wide, buttered, waxed-paper collar around it.

5. To cream mixture, add egg yolks 1 at a time; continue to beat. Add nuts and 1 tablespoon sherry.

6. Beat egg whites until frothy; add salt and cream of tartar and continue beating until stiff but not dry.

7. Fold egg whites into nut mixture and blend

8. Pour into prepared soufflé dish. Place dish in center of oven. Close oven door, and immediately reduce heat to 375°.

9. Bake 40 minutes. When you remove soufflé from oven, place dish on a tray. Gently remove collar and serve soufflé immediately with whipped cream that has been sweetened with powdered sugar and flavored with 2 tablespoons sherry.

Serves 6

Index

242